UNDERSTANDING THE MIXED ECONOMY OF WELFARE

Other titles in the series

Understanding the finance of welfare
What welfare costs and how to pay for it
Howard Glennerster, Department of Social Administration, London School of Economics and Political Science

"... a brilliant and lively textbook that students will enjoy."
Ian Shaw, School of Sociology and Social Policy, University of Nottingham
PB £17.99 (US$26.95) ISBN-10 1 86134 405 8 ISBN-13 978 1 86134 405 2
HB £50.00 (US$59.95) ISBN-10 1 86134 406 6 ISBN-13 978 1 86134 406 9
240 x 172mm 256 pages May 2003

Understanding social security
Issues for policy and practice
Jane Millar, Department of Social and Policy Sciences, University of Bath

"This first-class text provides students with the most up-to-date review and analysis of social security issues. It will fast become the definitive guide to the subject." **Jonathan Bradshaw, Department of Social Policy and Social Work, University of York**
PB £17.99 (US$26.95) ISBN-10 1 86134 419 8 ISBN-13 978 1 86134 419 9
HB £50.00 (US$59.95) ISBN-10 1 86134 420 1 ISBN-13 978 1 86134 421 2
240 x 172mm 360 pages May 2003

Understanding social citizenship
Themes and perspectives for policy and practice
Peter Dwyer, Department of Sociology and Social Policy, University of Leeds

"An excellent introduction to current debates about citizenship and the only general social policy text on the subject. Highly recommended. Students will certainly benefit from reading this book."
Nick Ellison, Department of Sociology and Social Policy, University of Durham
PB £17.99 (US$28.95) ISBN-10 1 86134 415 5 ISBN-13 978 1 86134 415 1
HB £50.00 (US$75.00) ISBN-10 1 86134 416 3 ISBN-13 978 1 86134 416 8
240 x 172mm 240 pages May 2004

Understanding the policy process
Analysing welfare policy and practice
John Hudson and **Stuart Lowe**, Department of Social Policy and Social Work, University of York

"Hudson and Lowe's book provides an excellent review of the issues about the policy process in a changing society and a changing world." **Michael Hill, Visiting Professor in the Health and Social Policy Research Centre, University of Brighton**
PB £17.99 (US$28.95) ISBN-10 1 86134 540 2 ISBN-13 978 1 86134 540 0
HB £50.00 (US$75.00) ISBN-10 1 86134 539 9 ISBN-13 978 1 86134 539 4
240 x 172mm 304 pages June 2004

Forthcoming

Understanding health policy
Rob Baggott
PB £18.99 (US$34.95) ISBN 978 1 86134 630 8
HB £60.00 (US$80.00) ISBN 978 1 86134 631 5
240 x 172mm 256 pages tbc June 2007 tbc

Understanding health and social care
Jon Glasby
PB £18.99 (US$34.95) ISBN 978 1 86134 910 1
HB £60.00 (US$80.00) ISBN 978 1 86134 911 8
240 x 172mm 224 pages tbc June 2007 tbc

If you are interested in submitting a proposal for the series, please contact
The Policy Press
e-mail tpp-info@bristol.ac.uk
tel +44 (0)117 331 4054
fax +44 (0)117 331 4093

INSPECTION COPIES AND ORDERS AVAILABLE FROM

Marston Book Services
PO Box 269 • Abingdon • Oxon OX14 4YN UK
INSPECTION COPIES
Tel: +44 (0) 1235 465500
Fax: +44 (0) 1235 465556
Email: inspections@marston.co.uk
ORDERS
Tel: +44 (0) 1235 465500
Fax: +44 (0) 1235 465556
Email: direct.orders@marston.co.u

www.policypress.org.uk

UNDERSTANDING THE MIXED ECONOMY OF WELFARE

Edited by Martin Powell

First published in Great Britain in 2007 by

The Policy Press
University of Bristol
Fourth Floor, Beacon House
Queen's Road
Bristol BS8 1QU
UK

Tel +44 (0)117 331 4054
Fax +44 (0)117 331 4093
e-mail tpp-info@bristol.ac.uk
www.policypress.org.uk

British Library Cataloguing in Publication Data
A catalogue record for this book is available from the British Library

Library of Congress Cataloging-in-Publication Data
A catalog record for this book has been requested

ISBN 978 1 86134 759 6 paperback
ISBN 978 1 86134 760 2 hardcover

Martin Powell is Professor of Health and Social Policy at the Health Services Management Centre, School of Public Policy, University of Birmingham, UK.

Cover design by Qube Design Associates, Bristol.
Front cover: photograph kindly supplied by Getty Images.
Printed and bound in Great Britain by MPG Books, Bodmin.

To the memory of Hazel and Megan

Contents

Detailed contents   viii
List of boxes, figures and tables   xiii
Notes on contributors   xv

one   The mixed economy of welfare and the social   1
          division of welfare
          Martin Powell

two   The mixed economy of welfare in historical context   23
          John Stewart

three   State welfare   41
          Brian Lund

four   Private welfare   61
          Mark Drakeford

five   Voluntary and community sector welfare   83
          Pete Alcock and Duncan Scott

six   Informal welfare   107
          Hilary Arksey and Caroline Glendinning

seven   Tax welfare   129
          Adrian Sinfield

eight   Occupational welfare   149
          Edward Brunsdon and Margaret May

nine   The mixed economy of welfare: a comparative   177
          perspective
          Michael Hill

ten   The global and supra-national dimensions of the   199
          welfare mix
          Nicola Yeates

eleven   Conclusion: analyses in the mixed economy of   221
          welfare and the social division of welfare
          Martin Powell

Index   241

Detailed contents

one   **The mixed economy of welfare and the social**   **1**
          division of welfare
Overview   1
Introduction   2
Social policy and the welfare mix   4
The social division of welfare   7
Components of the mixed economy of welfare   8
Dimensions of the mixed economy of welfare   9
Conclusion   15
Summary   15
Questions for discussion   16
Further reading   16
Electronic resources   16
References   16

two   **The mixed economy of welfare in historical**   **23**
          context
Overview   23
Introduction   24
Thinking historically about the state and welfare   26
Thinking historically about the family and welfare   28
Thinking historically about the market and welfare   31
Thinking historically about the voluntary/charitable sector 33
   and welfare
The historically changing relationship between the   36
   components of the 'mixed economy of welfare'
Conclusion   37
Summary   37
Questions for discussion   38
Further reading   38
Electronic resources   38
References   39

three **State welfare**   **41**
Overview   41
Introduction   42
State finance/state provision: central government   42
State finance/state provision: local government   45
State finance/voluntary provision   48

State finance/informal 'neighbourhood' provision — 49
Market finance/state provision 50
The state and the redistribution of income 51
New Labour/New State? 51
Social inclusion 52
Conclusion 53
Summary 56
Questions for discussion 56
Further reading 57
References 57

four **Private welfare** **61**
Overview 61
Introduction 62
The idea of privatisation 63
Privatisation and social welfare 64
New Labour's first term 66
Blair's second term 68
Going private: hospital treatment 70
Going private: residential care 72
Conclusion 77
Summary 78
Questions for discussion 79
Further reading 79
Electronic resources 79
References 79

five **Voluntary and community sector welfare** **83**
Overview 83
Introduction 84
Development 88
Policy context 90
Description 95
Future prospects 99
Conclusion 100
Summary 101
Further reading 102
Electronic resources 102
References 103

six	**Informal welfare**	**107**
	Overview	107
	Introduction	108
	Carers – who are they?	110
	New Labour's policy response to carers	112
	Financial support for carers	115
	What difference have New Labour policies made for carers?	116
	Barriers to providing effective support to carers	118
	Conclusion	120
	Summary	122
	Questions for discussion	122
	Further reading	123
	Electronic resources	123
	References	124
seven	**Tax welfare**	**129**
	Overview	129
	Introduction	130
	The move to tax credits	133
	Tax welfare for retirement	136
	Tax welfare and the welfare state	140
	Conclusion	142
	Summary	143
	Questions for discussion	143
	Further reading	144
	Electronic resources	144
	Acknowledgement	145
	References	145
eight	**Occupational welfare**	**149**
	Overview	149
	Introduction	150
	What is occupational welfare?	151
	Current forms of occupational welfare	153
	Case studies in current occupational welfare	161
	Conclusion	170
	Notes	171
	Summary	171
	Questions for discussion	172
	Further reading	172
	Electronic resources	172
	References	173

nine   **The mixed economy of welfare:**   177
         a comparative perspective
Overview   177
Introduction   178
Comparative theory and the mixed economy   178
Social security   181
Healthcare   183
Education   187
Social care   189
Purchase and provision   193
Conclusion   194
Summary   195
Questions for discussion   195
Further reading   195
References   196

ten   **The global and supra-national dimensions of** 199
         the welfare mix
Overview   199
Introduction   200
The scale and scope of IOs' involvement in social policy 201
Understanding the influence of IOs on social policy   203
IGOs' social policy prescriptions and impacts   209
Conclusion   214
Notes   215
Summary   216
Questions for discussion   216
Further reading   216
Electronic resources   217
References   217

eleven **Conclusion: analyses in the mixed economy**   221
         of welfare and the social division of welfare
Overview   221
Introduction   222
MEW and SDW over time and space   222
MEW and SDW under New Labour   225
The three-dimensional MEW   229
Analysing MEW   231
'The ghost at the feast': MEW's links to other debates   232
The impact of MEW and SDW   234
Conclusion   235
Summary   236

Questions for discussion   236
Further reading   236
Electronic resources   237
References   237

List of boxes, figures and tables

Boxes

2.1	An historical illustration	25
3.1	New Labour's social protection strategy	43
3.2	Exit, Voice and Loyalty	45
3.3	Examples of New Labour's performance indicators	46
3.4	New Labour: examples of attaching to obligations to rights	53
4.1	John and private welfare	67
4.2	Privatisation: the example of Hospital Trusts	70
4.3	Jill and public welfare	76
5.1	Key terms	84
5.2	The voluntary and community sector	86
5.3	ICNPO classification	87
5.4	Cross Cutting Review	92
5.5	Tumble Tots – informal/VCS	96
5.6	Small Potatoes – private/VCS	97
5.7	Family Friends – public/VCS	98
6.1	Care giving in England and Wales in April 2001	110
6.2	Policy landmarks for carers	112
6.3	Summary of key points in the National Strategy for Carers	113
6.4	Case example of changes over time in carer support	115
7.1	Key terms	130
7.2	Tax allowances and tax credits	131
7.3	Child Tax Credit	134
7.4	Working Tax Credit	134
7.5	The new tax regime for non-state pensions, April 2006	138
8.1	Titmuss' inventory of occupational welfare	151
8.2	Main types of occupational pension	163
8.3	The main wellness services offered by UK employers	167
10.1	The OECD and national policy reform	206
11.1	Sidney Webb's account of the importance of the state	223

11.2	Alternative account of the importance of non-state welfare	223
11.3	The modern MEW	228
11.4	Debates not linked to MEW	232

Figures

1.1	One-dimensional MEW (provision)	10
1.2	Three-dimensional MEW (provision, finance and regulation)	13
5.1	Inter-sectoral landscapes	85
11.1	Recent moves in MEW	229

Tables

7.1	Major tax and other reliefs related to social policy, United Kingdom, 1994-95, 2004-05 and 2005-06 (estimates in millions)	132
8.1	Mandatory and voluntary forms of occupational welfare	154
9.1	Social security funding through social insurance contributions	182
9.2	Private pension investment, 2003, as share of GDP	184
9.3	Public sector health spend as a percentage of total health spend, 2002	185
9.4	Bambra's healthcare 'regime' typology	186
9.5	Public sector spend as a percentage of total spend on education, 2000	187
9.6	A typology of systems highlighting alternative approaches to care	189
9.7	Logical alternative care patterns	189
9.8	Contrasting care patterns within Europe	190
10.1	Examples of global and regional IGOs and INGOs	202
10.2	Examples of IGO involvement in provision, finance and regulation	203
10.3	Surveillance and enforcement mechanisms of selected IGOs	208
10.4	Global social policy discourse	210
10.5	World Bank and ILO approaches to pension reform	212

Notes on contributors

Pete Alcock is Professor of Social Policy and Administration and Head of the School of Social Sciences at the University of Birmingham. He is the author of *Understanding Poverty* (3rd edn) (Palgrave, 2006), *Social Policy in Britain* (2nd edn) (Palgrave, 2003) and co-editor of *The Blackwell Companion to Social Policy*, (2nd edn) (Blackwell, 2003), *The Blackwell Dictionary of Social Policy* (Blackwell, 2002) and *International Social Policy* (Palgrave, 2001). He has also written widely on poverty, social inclusion and the voluntary sector in the UK. He is a former chair of the Social Policy Association and of the Editorial Board of the *Journal of Social Policy*.

Hilary Arksey is a Senior Research Fellow in the Social Policy Research Unit at the University of York. Her research interests are in the areas of informal care, employment and disability, and qualitative research methods. She has recently completed studies focusing on carers' aspirations and decision making around work, retirement and pensions, and carers as asset managers for older people.

Edward Brunsdon is a Principal Lecturer in HRM in the Department of Management and Professional Development at London Metropolitan University, where he teaches on a wide range of HRM courses. His main research interests are occupational welfare and performance management, and he has published widely in these areas.

Mark Drakeford is Professor of Social Policy and Applied Social Sciences at the University of Cardiff. He currently works as the Cabinet health and social policy adviser, and special adviser to the First Minister at the Welsh Assembly Government.

Caroline Glendinning is Professor of Social Policy and Assistant Director in the Social Policy Research Unit (SPRU) at the University of York. She manages the SPRU's Department of Health-funded research programme and the national evaluation of the Individual Budgets Pilots, which is also based at SPRU. She is co-editor (with Professor Peter Kemp) of *Cash and Care: Policy Challenges for the Welfare State* (The Policy Press, 2006).

Michael Hill is Visiting Professor in the Health and Social Policy Research Centre, University of Brighton, and at Queen Mary, University of London, and is Emeritus Professor of Social Policy at University of Newcastle upon Tyne. Publications include *Understanding Social Policy* (Blackwell, 1980, 7th edn 2003), *The Public Policy Process* (Pearson Education, 2004), *Social Policy in the Modern World* (Blackwell, 2006) and *Implementing Public Policy* (with Peter Hupe, Sage Publications, 2002).

Brian Lund is Principal Lecturer in Social Policy at the Manchester Metropolitan University. He is the author of *Understanding State Welfare* (Sage Publications, 2002) and *Understanding Housing Policy* (The Policy Press, 2006). He served as an elected local councillor for many years.

Margaret May is Principal Lecturer in HRM in the Department of Management and Professional Development at London Metropolitan University, where she teaches on a wide variety of HRM and employee relations courses. Her main research interests are occupational welfare, employee relations and comparative social policy. She has published widely in these areas and is also co-editor of the *Student's Companion to Social Policy* (2nd edn) (Blackwell, 2003).

Martin Powell is Professor of Health and Social Policy at the Health Services Management Centre, University of Birmingham. He has research interests in health policy, the history of the welfare state, and New Labour's social policy. He is the co-author (with Martin Hewitt) of *Welfare State and Welfare Change* (Open University Press, 2002) and is the editor of *New Labour, New Welfare State?* (The Policy Press, 1999).

Duncan Scott is a research fellow in the Department of Sociology at the University of Manchester. Previously, he was a senior lecturer in Social Policy and Head of the Department of Social Policy and Social Work at the University of Manchester. He is the co-author of *Moving Pictures: Realities of Voluntary Action* (The Policy Press, 2000), *Social Enterprise in the Balance: Challenges for the Voluntary Sector* (Charities Aid Foundation, 2004) and *Researching Voluntary and Community Action* (Joseph Rowntree Foundation, 2005). He has also researched and written about a wide range of policy and practice issues in the voluntary and community sectors. He is a founder member and trustee of the Voluntary Sector Studies Network, and a co-founder of his local community association.

Adrian Sinfield is Professor Emeritus of Social Policy at the University of Edinburgh, where he has worked since 1979. He has written mainly on social security, poverty, unemployment and the social division of welfare. He has been both chair and president of the Social Policy Association; a co-founder of the Unemployment Unit, which he chaired for its first 10 years; and Vice-Chair of the Child Poverty Action Group. Publications include *The Long-term Unemployed* (OECD, 1968), *What Unemployment Means* (Martin Robertson, 1981), *The Workless State* (co-edited, Martin Robertson, 1981) and *Comparing*

Tax Routes to Welfare in Denmark and the United Kingdom (co-authored, Danish National Institute for Social Research, 1996).

John Stewart is Professor of History of Medicine and Social Policy at Oxford Brookes University. His publications, which focus on the history of social care and healthcare, include *Taking Stock: Scottish Social Welfare after Devolution* (The Policy Press, 2004) and articles in journals such as *Medical History, Twentieth Century British History*, and *Bulletin of the History of Medicine*. He is currently working on a history of child guidance in Britain.

Nicola Yeates is Senior Lecturer in Social Policy in the Faculty of Social Sciences at the Open University. She has researched and published extensively on various aspects of the social policy dimensions of 'globalisation'. Publications include *Globalisation and Social Policy* (Sage Publications, 2001), and contributions to *New Risks, New Welfare* (edited by N. Manning and I. Shaw, Blackwell, 2000) and to the journal *Global Social Policy*. She is researching the development of international health and social care markets and the role of migrant workers therein. She is co-editor of the journal *Global Social Policy*.

one

The mixed economy of welfare and the social division of welfare

Martin Powell

Overview

This chapter introduces the concepts of mixed economy of welfare (MEW) and social division of welfare (SDW). It points out that these have varied over time and space. It outlines the components of MEW – state, market, voluntary and informal welfare – and of SDW – statutory, occupational and fiscal welfare. While most writers examine the new MEW from a one-dimensional view, it is vital to move to a three-dimensional view that also considers finance and regulation.

Key concepts

Mixed economy of welfare • welfare pluralism • social division of welfare • provision • finance • regulation

Introduction

The mixed economy of welfare (MEW) or welfare pluralism (WP) is a vital, but relatively neglected, part of social policy. Johnson (1999, p 22) writes that the two terms have identical meanings and can therefore be used interchangeably. He claims that WP first came into general use in Britain following the Wolfenden Report (Wolfenden, 1978) on the future of voluntary organisations, while MEW is of slightly more recent origin. Despite a good deal of exploration of MEW within the UK (Hadley and Hatch, 1981; Hatch and Mocroft, 1983; Beresford and Croft, 1984; Johnson, 1987; Pinker, 1992; Lund, 1993) and in a comparative context (for example, Evers and Wintersberger, 1990; Hantrais et al, 1992; Evers and Svetlik, 1993), the concept remains problematic. This text takes a broader view, examining not only the traditional sectors of MEW – state, market, voluntary and informal – but also the social division of welfare (SDW) and its statutory, occupational and fiscal components.

Knapp (1989, pp 225-6) writes that to the vast majority of the British population the term welfare is synonymous with state provision. Mention healthcare and most people think immediately of the national health service (NHS); social care and social service departments are seen as one and the same; education is the local comprehensive school. However, these popular views are over-simplistic, as in reality there is a fascinating variety of organisational and economic arrangements for the delivery, funding and regulation of welfare, and it is necessary to examine the 'forgotten dimensions' of social policy in order to reach a full rather than a partial picture.

More surprisingly, some of these dimensions have also been largely forgotten in many social policy texts. The terms MEW, WP and SDW do not appear in the indexes of some introductory texts (for example, Alcock et al, 2000; Alcock, 2003) and have only brief mentions in others (for example, Page and Silburn, 1999; Alcock et al, 2003; Baldock et al, 2003; Blakemore, 2003; Ellison and Pierson, 2003; but see Alcock et al, 2002; Spicker, 1988, 1995). In the first edition of their book, Lavalette and Pratt (1997) include a chapter on quasi-markets and the mixed economy of welfare, but this was omitted in the second (2001) edition. Some of these texts mentioned above have extensive discussions of the components of MEW. For example, Alcock (2003) and Alcock et al (2003) have chapters on state, market, voluntary and informal welfare. Page and Silburn (1999) contains chapters on voluntary and informal, and commercial and occupational welfare. Turning to the social policy theory texts, although there are discussions of components such as the voluntary sector, there are no index entries for MEW, SDW or WP in Forder (1974), Jones et al (1983), Forder et al (1984), Fitzpatrick (2001) and Malin et al (2002). In Hill and Bramley (1986), MEW and SDW each have a mere single-page entry, although there is reference to subjects such as privatisation.

Some texts chart MEW over time (Finlayson, 1994; Gladstone, 1995; Page and Silburn, 1999). Others examine variations over space (Johnson, 1999; Ascoli and Ranci, 2002; Gough et al, 2004). There are texts that deal with individual components of MEW, such as the voluntary sector (Brenton, 1985; Kendall and Knapp (1996), the market sector (Papadakis and Taylor-Gooby, 1987; Johnson, 1995; Drakeford, 2000) and the community/informal sectors (for example, Deakin, 2001; Taylor, 2003; see, for example, Land, 1978; Rose, 1981; Ungerson, 1987 on gender implications). There are fewer texts that deal with SDW and the occupational and fiscal sectors (Mann, 1989, 1992). One of the few texts that focuses on MEW is the pioneering work of Johnson (1987; see also Mayo, 1994; Rao, 1996; Johnson, 1999). Nevertheless, most accounts tend to examine the components of welfare in isolation (for example, in separate discussions or chapters) and tend not to analyse the relationships between them. They tend to focus on provision, rather than on the additional dimensions of finance and regulation. In other words, the focus has been on individual trees rather than on the whole wood. Put another way, while the individual pieces of the jigsaw have been described, there has been little attempt to piece them together in order to see the full picture. This means that, as concepts, MEW, and particularly SDW, have been neglected, and it is hardly surprising that this translates into student essays on the mixed economy and social divisions rather than on MEW and SDW respectively.

This text examines MEW (state, market, voluntary and informal welfare) and the SDW (statutory, fiscal and occupational welfare). While much of the book focuses on the elements of the welfare mix, it also aims to stress two major points. First, the mix of the elements in the contemporary British welfare state is not the only or the best way of organising welfare, and the mix has varied over time and space. It has long been recognised that social policy extends far beyond the welfare state, and that MEW varies significantly over different times, services and spaces. The 'classic welfare state' (from roughly the 1940s to the 1970s: see Powell and Hewitt, 2002) tends to be associated with *étatiste* perspectives, but, at certain times and places, commercial, voluntary and informal sectors may be more important. Before 1945, sectors other than the state were dominant, and their importance may be increasing again in recent years. While state provision in services such as health and education has been the norm since 1945, housing has been more in the realm of the market. In some ways, the UK experience of the dominance of the state in welfare is unusual compared with other countries where voluntary and commercial agencies assume much greater importance. For example, at its peak, 'council housing' in the UK accounted for about a third of all houses, but 'welfare housing' in the US has always been a much more residual service, accounting for about 2% of houses. In the comparative field, the 'welfare mix' is an integral but largely unexplored component in welfare regimes (Esping-Andersen, 1990, 1999; but see Powell and Barrientos, 2004).

Second, while it is important to examine the welfare mix in terms of provision, it is necessary to move beyond this 'one-dimensional' account and to examine the other dimensions of finance and regulation. State ownership or provision is not the only, or necessarily the best, method of state intervention. The state can finance or subsidise non-state providers to ensure that users have access to goods or services at zero or reduced price. The costs of private residential care may be fully or partially met by the state. Many charities providing services for groups such as homeless people are funded by local or central government. Finally, the state can intervene without ownership or finance by using its legal authority to regulate prices or standards. For example, private residential homes are subject to inspection. For many years, the government, through rent control, set maximum rents for private landlords letting out property. A full picture of MEW can, therefore, only be achieved through a 'three-dimensional' consideration involving provision, finance and regulation.

Social policy and the welfare mix

Some discussions differentiate between the descriptive and prescriptive uses of the terms MEW and WP (Beresford and Croft, 1984). In the descriptive or neutral sense, it is pointed out that there are four components of MEW. The prescriptive sense suggests a change to the mix such as 'rolling back the state'. This distinction hangs on whether the different parts of the mix are viewed as equal. On the one hand, Rose and Shiratori (1986) argue that 'total welfare' is the sum of state, market, voluntary and informal sources. They continue that the welfare mix varies between countries, which means that an *étatiste* definition of welfare, which assumed that the only welfare in society was that produced by the state, is misleading. On the other hand, Mishra (1990, pp 110-14) claims that a focus on 'total welfare' is not simply the 'sum of the parts'. The mix in the 'mixed economy of welfare' cannot be ignored; the components "cannot simply be regarded as functionally equivalents" (p 110) as they are based on different principles and they differ in scope. It is important to distinguish between means and ends. For example, a transfer from state to informal (read: female) care leads to increasing gender inequality, and ignores entitlement (citizenship), as there are no 'rights' to informal care. In short, it is more than a "mere rearranging of furniture in the drawing room" (p 112). Similarly, Esping-Andersen (1999, p 36) writes that the claim that welfare pillars are functional equivalents and therefore mutually substitutable is a hazardous assumption.

The prescriptive use of the term MEW shows that different welfare ideologies favour different welfare mixes. Very broadly, the political left has tended to favour a large role for the state in welfare, while there is little or no place for the market (eg Titmuss, 1963, 1968; Beresford and Croft, 1984). The main reason relates to equity. Only the state can ensure that welfare benefits and services are fairly distributed to all citizens. A large role for the commercial, voluntary and informal sectors is associated with inequality. Similarly, the left tends to favour statutory rather than occupational or fiscal welfare, as the latter are generally assumed to be regressive. On the other hand, the political right has tended to favour commercial, voluntary and informal over state solutions, advocating a welfare society rather than a welfare state (for example, Marsland, 1996). Seldon (1996) argues that welfare should be re-privatised after the 'lost century' of state control. This is due to reasons of economic efficiency and morality. It is claimed that the state is an inefficient producer and that extensive state responsibility leads to welfare dependency. The right tends to be more relaxed about occupational and fiscal welfare, although some supporters of the market argue against fiscal measures such as mortgage tax relief as these distort the market.

In a descriptive sense, some British historians and social policy analysts point out the importance of non-state welfare (see Chapter Two of this volume). According to Harris (1992), legislation after the Second World War created in Britain one of the most uniform, centralised, bureaucratic and 'public' welfare systems in Europe, and indeed in the modern world. Yet a social analyst of a hundred years ago would have observed and predicted the exact opposite: that the provision of social welfare in Britain was and would continue to be highly localised, amateur, voluntaristic and intimate in scale by comparison with the more coercive and *étatiste* schemes of her continental neighbours (in particular, imperial Germany). According to Lewis (1995, p 3), it may be necessary to rethink the nature of the 'welfare state'; rather than seeing the story of the modern welfare state as a simple increase in state intervention, it is more accurate to see Britain as always having had a mixed economy of welfare, in which the voluntary sector, the family and the market have played different parts at different times. The place of welfare pluralism in the 'classic welfare state' remains unclear (for example, Brenton, 1985; Pinker, 1992; Finlayson, 1994; Hewitt and Powell, 1998; Powell and Hewitt, 1998).

There has been a reaction to the 'whig account of welfare' history where greater state intervention is seen as inevitable (for example, Finlayson, 1994; Green, 1996). Thane (1996, p 277) has protested that "although this was once the ruling paradigm of welfare state histories in the optimistic 1950s and 1960s ...in the mid-1990s it is difficult to think of a serious historian who has written in this mode for at least twenty years". She is correct to point out that since the Conservative government of 1979, greater state intervention is no longer seen as *inevitable*. However, many writers – implicitly or explicitly – regard it as *desirable*. Similarly, Finlayson (1994) clearly distinguishes between the arguments that welfare agencies outside the state 'could not cope' and 'should not cope' with the delivery of welfare services. In other words, the debate about the appropriate role of the state is a normative one, with traditional disagreements between the political right and left.

At one level, the comparative literature reflects the descriptive sense, pointing out that analytically simply focusing on state provision misses much of the picture. Esping-Andersen (1999, pp 33-4) argues that social policy, welfare states and welfare regimes are not the same (cf Powell and Hewitt, 2002). Social policy can exist without welfare states, but not the other way around. Social policy predates welfare states. Studying just the welfare state leaves a huge 'welfare residual' unaccounted for. Gilbert and Gilbert (1989) write that the 'direct public expenditure model' is an important part of the picture, but conveys a somewhat distorted view of welfare benefits and beneficiaries, within a narrow frame of reference. Klein (1985) asks us to consider a mythical country whose government decides to keep public expenditure below 25% of gross national product. Instead of introducing a social security scheme or a national health service, it makes it mandatory for every firm to insure its employees and their families. Instead of building motorways, it offers generous tax concessions to turnpike trusts. Instead of subsidising jobs to prevent unemployment, it offers legislation forbidding companies to dismiss anyone. Instead of spending money on pollution control, it compels private companies to clean up the polluted air and rivers they have created. This country has virtually no welfare spending as measured by conventional public expenditure statistics. Klein goes on to say that the country is mythical, but the instances are actual, reflecting Japan, France, Italy and Sweden, respectively.

Other parts of the comparative literature tend to be more (if not always explicitly) prescriptive. Different models or regimes of welfare have been presented by Wilensky and Lebeaux (1965), Titmuss (1974) and Esping-Andersen (1990, 1999). Wilensky and Lebeaux (1965) differentiated between residual and institutional models of welfare, describing the US as an under-developed or reluctant welfare state. Titmuss (1974) set out three models of social policy: the residual, industrial-achievement and institutional models. The residual model is based on the premise that there are two 'natural' channels through which an individual's needs are properly met: the private market and the family. Only when these break down should social welfare institutions come into play and then only temporarily.

Esping-Andersen (1990) drew on Titmuss to develop his 'three worlds of welfare capitalism', the liberal, conservative and social democratic regimes (see Chapter Nine of this volume). One of the major features of these regimes was the extent to which the welfare states offer social rights that entail a decommodification of the status of individuals *vis-à-vis* the market. Decommodification occurs when a person can maintain a livelihood without reliance on the market. Responding to criticism of this work, Esping-Andersen (1999, p 12) claims that his earlier work defined welfare regimes in terms of the mix of public and market provision. He notes that the 'second generation' of welfare state research examined the interplay of public and private provision during the 1980s. Welfare regimes can be defined as the combined, interdependent way in which welfare is produced and allocated between state, market and family, which represent three radically different principles of risk management. (In a footnote, he writes that to this triad should be added the 'third sector' of voluntary, non-profit welfare delivery. Put another way, the triad should be a diamond (Esping-Andersen, pp 33-5).) The three liberal, social democratic and conservative regimes have the market, state and family dominant respectively (Esping-Andersen, p 85).

The social division of welfare

The social division of welfare was developed by Richard Titmuss in a lecture in 1956, and has been seen as "one of the influential works, possibly the most influential, in the field of social administration" (Spicker, 1983, p 182) and a 'watershed' in the development of social policy as a subject (Spicker, 1995, p 121). It was written as a response to those who were arguing that the welfare state was associated with excessive taxation of the rich and the indiscriminate and excessive delivery of benefits to the poor. Titmuss (1963) pointed out that welfare was delivered by fiscal and occupational mechanisms in addition to the more familiar 'social services'. Fiscal welfare (FW) refers to benefits delivered through the taxation system such as tax relief on mortgages, and later on private pensions and health insurance. Occupational welfare (OW) refers to the 'fringe benefits' of employment, such as subsidised pensions, health insurance, mortgages and company cars. Titmuss argued that fiscal and occupational welfare were clearly regressive in nature in that they gave most to those with higher incomes. In other words, critics of excessive redistribution focused on the 'narrow' welfare state of social welfare, and ignored the wider picture that also included fiscal and occupational welfare. SDW has not featured heavily in analyses of social policy (but see Sinfield, 1978; Spicker, 1983, 1988, 1995; Mann, 1992; Walker, 1997). According to Spicker (1995, p 121), it is "remarkable how little the original essay has itself been discussed". Similarly, Mann (1992, p 13) writes that, with the exception of Sinfield (1978), there has been a peculiar reluctance to treat Titmuss's theoretical, as opposed to his descriptive framework, seriously (a comment that also seems appropriate to MEW). As state/statutory, occupational and fiscal welfare are the subjects of Chapters Three, Seven and Eight, they are only briefly mentioned here.

Statutory welfare

Statutory welfare refers to publicly provided goods and services. It may be better, following Sinfield (1978), to refer to social welfare as public welfare. This is the visible part of the welfare state as opposed to the 'hidden welfare state'.

Occupational welfare

Johnson (1999, p 134) writes that in spite of the fact that Titmuss identified OW in 1956, surprisingly limited attention has been paid to it since (but see Mann, 1989; Shalev, 1996). Occupational welfare is related to people's occupations, and may also be termed fringe benefits or corporate welfare. One of the best-known examples is occupational pensions.

Fiscal welfare

Similarly, relatively little has been written about taxation and social policy (Sandford et al, 1980). FW refers to costs or benefits delivered through the taxation system. The state can encourage citizens to consume more of a commodity through lowering its price through tax relief (in the case of private medical insurance, pensions and mortgages, for example, or measures such as no capital gains tax (CGT) on owner-occupation). On the other hand, the state might try to reduce consumption of 'bads', such as cigarettes, alcohol and private transport, through increasing taxes.

Components of the mixed economy of welfare

The components of the MEW will be discussed further in Chapters Three to Six, and will only be briefly outlined here.

State welfare

Of all the elements of the MEW, it is obviously the 'state' element that is most clearly associated with the 'welfare state'. Many on the left argue that 'public service' should be 'public', pointing to 'market failure' and providing arguments favouring the state (for example, Johnson, 1987, 1999; Whitfield, 1992). However, some of these accounts fail to give sufficient detail as to whether the state should be national or local, or to differentiate between arguments for state production, finance or regulation (to be discussed later; see also Chapter Eleven).

Market welfare

Conversely, advocates of a greater role for the market (for example, Marsland, 1996; Seldon, 1996) point to 'state failure'. They argue that the 'market' is more efficient than the state, but this hides a range of possible policies, from contracting out through quasi-markets and vouchers to privatising major parts of the welfare state.

Voluntary welfare

Although the voluntary sector tends to be the dominant term within the MEW literature, it is sometimes termed the independent, non–profit, non-governmental organisation (NGO), *'économie sociale'*, 'shadow state' or simply the 'third sector' (Johnson, 1999; Deakin, 2001). It is seen as a 'loose and baggy monster', but is normally divided into philanthropic and mutual elements (Beveridge, 1948). The former tends to be associated with hierarchical, rich-to-poor charity, while the latter refers to horizontal, self-help activities. There has been also a revival of interest in mutual or civil society solutions (Deakin, 2001; Taylor, 2003). From a broadly left perspective, Hirst (1994) suggests associative democracy, Giddens (1998) argues for an expansion of welfare rooted in civil society and Field (2000) puts forward stakeholder pensions operated through approved welfare suppliers. From the right, Green (1996) proposes reinventing the old mutual organisations that were destroyed by the state.

Informal welfare

While supporters of mutual solutions encompass both left and right, in general those favouring informal welfare – support from family, friends and neighbours – are largely located on the political right. Such views have been criticised by feminists, who claim that this view of the 'traditional' family and 'male-breadwinner model' reinforces the 'sexual division of welfare'. Mixing personal experience and rich qualitative interviews, Ungerson (1987) clearly demonstrates that "policy is personal". She points out that Titmuss (1968) in a powerful essay on community care did not mention informal carers or women. She discusses the growing feminist literature, such as Land (1978), but claims that the watershed came with Finch and Groves (1980, p 494), who produced the 'double equation' that "in practice community care equals care by the family, and in practice care by the family equals care by women" (pp 9-10).

Dimensions of the mixed economy of welfare

While accounts tend to discuss – albeit briefly – the components of MEW, and to a lesser extent SDW, it is argued here that the debate is limited. It tends to be one-dimensional (to be discussed later) in that it refers to the changed MEW or changed mix without specifying roles or dimensions. For example, Beresford and Croft (1984) stress 'sources' of welfare, and tend to neglect the dimensions of finance and regulation. Johnson (1999, pp 22-5) writes that welfare states have always been mixed and the same four sectors have always been present. The crucial consideration is not the existence of these four sectors, but the balance between them along the following dimensions: between countries; over time; between services; and between components of services.

However, a one-dimensional move 'from state to market' does not differentiate between the dimensions of production, finance and regulation. A move from state to market fails to distinguish between very different strategies, such as charging, contracting out, quasi-markets, vouchers, and so on (cf Knapp, 1989). In other words, debates on MEW tend to be conceptually limited, and insular in that they are rarely linked to other debates (see Chapter Eleven).

A one-dimensional account focuses on the single issue of provision. For example, Walker (1984, pp 20, 23) writes of a continuum from the public sector, through private and voluntary services to the informal sector (but later recognises regulation). From this perspective, nationalisation and privatisation may be seen as the key features of MEW. For example, when the hospitals were nationalised in 1948 to become part of the NHS, this represented a large transfer from voluntary to public provision. Conversely, the sale of council houses to their tenants under the Conservatives' Right to Buy scheme introduced under the 1980 Housing Act involved privatisation. The assumption here appears to be that ownership matters: a place in a private residential home is different to a place in a public residential home (whoever finances it).

A two-dimensional account examines provision and finance. This means that a state-to-market movement can take place through different routes. First, it can involve private finance, charging or 'commodification'. For example, a free service can become a 'fee' (or paid) service. Second, it can enforce market competition on state producers through quasi or internal markets (Le Grand and Bartlett, 1993; Walsh, 1995). Third, it can transfer state provision to commercial producers in an external market (Powell, 2003), but with state finance so that users still have free access to services. Fourth, it can change production and finance, suggesting that citizens who used to have free services from the state now become market consumers who consume a purchased service from a choice of private providers. Useful two-dimensional diagrams appear in Judge (1982), Spicker (1988), Knapp (1989) and Glennerster (2003).

Judge (1982) has provided a crude but useful 'classificatory framework of the mixed economy of welfare' that differentiates the mode of finance (public, private-collective, private-personal or 'no exchange') from the mode of production (public, private, voluntary or informal).

Knapp (1989; see also Wistow et al, 1994) differentiates between four basic production or supply sectors: public, voluntary, private and informal. The funding or demand dimension has six categories: coerced-collective demand, uncoerced or voluntary collective demand, corporate demand, uncompensated individual consumption, compensated individual consumption, and individual

Figure 1.1: *One-dimensional MEW (provision)*

State	Market	Voluntary	Informal

donation. He puts these two dimensions together to form a matrix with 24 cells. For example, NHS hospital stays are placed in the public supply/coerced-collective demand cell.

Spicker (1988, p 84; 1995, p 116) provides a two-dimensional framework, with axes of production (public, private, voluntary and informal) and finance (public, private corporate, private-cooperative, charges to consumers, voluntary), giving 20 cells.

Glennerster (2003, p 7) draws a sharp distinction between who pays for a service and who provides it. The provision dimension consists of public sector bodies (central government, public trusts and local government), private organisations (for-profit and non-profit) and private-informal. The finance dimension differentiates between public and private finance. For example, Her Majesty's prisons occupy the top left-hand box. They are an unusual case, one of the last examples of a service wholly run and financed by central government (Glennerster, 2003, pp 8-9), although some private prisons exist).

The Institute for Public Policy Research Commission on Public Private Partnerships (IPPR, 2001) reasserts the case for publicly funded, universal services, but distinguishes clearly between the funding and provision of public services. It differentiates means and ends: the case for public services needs to be made in terms of values and outcomes rather than particular forms of delivery. The founding principles of the NHS were that it should be free, universal and comprehensive, not that it should be provided through a particular structure, process, or set of employees. It rejects the blind alleys of the 'privatisers' – private good, public bad – and the 'monopolists'– public good, private bad. It sets out four models of public management: command and control; networks and trust; purchase and provide; privatise and regulate.

In relation to healthcare, Salter (2004) suggests two dimensions of provision and finance, with respect to state and private, resulting in a four cell matrix – public provision/public finance; public provision/private finance; private provision/public finance and private provision/private finance; and public and private provision and funding (cf Keen et al, 2001, p 26).

One of the main problems with two-dimensional accounts is that boundaries are permeable and ambiguous (Hill and Bramley, 1983, p 136). Knapp's (1989, p 228) definitions of sectors are not without controversy and the margins between them are blurred. According to Walker (1984, pp 27-8), the importation of market principles into the public social services – 'privatism' – has a long history and some elements of a free market of welfare were built into the original framework of services. For example, public–private boundaries in healthcare are both blurred and shifting (Keen et al, 2001, p 77). GPs, sometimes seen as a clear part of the state NHS, are 'independent contractors', and classified in the National Accounts as 'unincorporated businesses' (Keen et al, 2001, p 89; cf IPPR, 2001; Salter, 2004).

However, other commentators argue that this has become more problematic over time. Spicker (1988, p 86) writes that the provision of finance by the state is used to such an extent that it becomes difficult to separate state and private sector activity in any meaningful sense. According to Miller (2004, p 62), the distinctions between the four traditional sectors – state, market, voluntary and informal – no longer adequately describe what is a much more complex and graded set of arrangements.

There are two different versions of three-dimensional accounts, with the third dimension being decision or regulation. A three-dimensional framework of provision, finance and decision is presented by Burchardt (1997), Burchardt et al (1999) and Hills (2004). The third element here is 'decision': can individuals choose for themselves the provider used or the amount of service, or are these decided for them by the state? This typology generates eight possible combinations, which are shown diagramatically in the form of concentric circles. The polar types are the 'pure public sector', with public finance, provision and decision such as child benefit, and the 'pure private' sector, with private finance, provision and control such as unassisted places at private schools.

While decision or choice is important in other social policy debates, it does not seem to be as directly relevant to the MEW debate as regulation, and so this text focuses on the dominant framework of provision, finance and regulation (Johnson, 1999). Regulation is not new, with price controls and controls over production for social purposes able to be traced back at least to Roman times (Moran 2003, p 38). Unlike other disciplines (for example, Hood et al, 1999; Moran, 2003), the social policy literature has tended to ignore regulation (but see Bolderson, 1986; Powell and Hewitt, 2002). This is despite the long history of inspection and regulation in sectors such as health, education and housing. Moran (2003, pp 41-2 and 49-50) points to the Victorian regulatory state, which included Factory Inspectors, Poor Law Commissioners, the Prison Inspectorate, the Lunacy Commission, the General Board of Health and the Charity Commission, as well as professional regulation such as the Medical Act of 1858 that set up the General Medical Council. Rent control predates the welfare state, and its partial repeal in the 1957 Rent Act was one of the bitterest debates in the history of the welfare state. The Keynesian welfare state was based more on regulating employment than on direct employment in nationalised industries. One of the main points of Crosland's revisionist *The Future of Socialism* (Crosland, 1964) was that Labour governments did not need the 'clause four'-style nationalisation in the Labour Party's constitution in order to control the economy. The Labour Secretary of State for Social Services, Richard Crossman, set up the Hospitals Advisory Service as an inspectorate after a series of scandals at long-stay hospitals. The recent rise in importance of regulation/inspection has made a two-dimensional view untenable, with commentators claiming that we live in an 'audit society' (Power, 1997) and a 'regulatory state' (Hood et al, 1999; Majone, 1996; Moran, 2003). Hood and colleagues (1999, p 3) write that regulation is a "much used word rarely defined with precision". However, one basic distinction is between government regulating business, especially the privatised utilities, and regulating itself. As Hood and colleagues (1999, p 4) put it, just as a business firm is exposed to a different set of regulators – auditors, inspectors, licensing bodies, competition and fair-trading authorities – so a typical public organisation faces a collection of waste watchers, quality police, sleaze busters, and other 'regulators'.

Figure 1.2 is derived from a simplified version of two-dimensional accounts such as Knapp (1989) and Glennerster (2003). While it may be more accurate to have more categories of the finance axis (cf Knapp, 1989), for heuristic purposes, the finance axis of **Figure 1.2** follows the provision axis, giving 16 cells. This simple figure is limited in a number of respects. First, it is sometimes difficult to place phenomena into categories as boundaries may be blurred (cf Knapp, 1989). For example, some commentators argue that Foundation Hospitals are still part of the state, meaning that treatment in a Foundation Hospital would be placed in cell 1, while others claim that they are mutual organisations with some independence from the state, in which case treatment would be placed in cell 3. Second, the figure does not deal with choice or decision (cf Burchardt, 1997). For example, cell 1 – public provision/public finance – does not discriminate between the traditional NHS and quasi-markets based on the purchaser–provider split. If NHS Trusts are classified as 'state' or public agencies (Glennerster, 2003), they remain in cell 1, despite the very different hierarchical 'command and control' versus competitive mechanisms. Similarly, cell 1 includes both third-party and individual decisions about hospital treatment. An individual choice of public hospital using public money is

Figure 1.2: Three-dimensional MEW (provision, finance and regulation)

Finance		Provision			
		State	Market	Voluntary	Informal
State		1a (high regulation)	2a	3a	4a
		1b (low regulation)	2b	3b	4b
Market		5a	6a	7a	8a
		5b	6b	7b	8b
Voluntary		9a	10a	11a	12a
		9b	10b	11b	12b
Informal		13a	14a	15a	16a
		13b	14b	15b	16b

equivalent to the decision being made on individual's behalf by paternalistic NHS managers. Third, the regulation dimension is more problematic than provision or finance. Provision can be measured in rough and ready terms by ownership of resources. For example, the state might own 90% of all school places but only 50% of all places in residential homes. Similarly, finance can be measured by monetary terms: how much of the income of a residential home comes from state sources. However, measuring 'regulation' is more difficult. Regulation is associated with some level of control or power in the form of shaping behaviour in desired ways. Bozeman (1987) claims that some organisations are governmental, but that all organisations are public. He suggests a measure of 'publicness', which is defined as the degree to which an organisation is affected by political authority. He argues that some governmental organisations are more public than others; some business organisations are more public than others; and that some business organisations are more public in some respects than some government organisations. However, his empirical measure of 'publicness' is the proportion of funding from government sources. This is clearly an unsatisfactory measure, as control cannot be equated to resource inputs. In simple terms, our three dimensions relate to different types of control. Ownership is associated with hierarchical command and control structures. Finance is related to financial control. Regulation is associated with political authority. It is not clear whether any one type of control is stronger than the others in all contexts. It has been claimed that despite financing a high proportion of the budgets of some voluntary organisations, governments may not control them (for example, Deakin, 2001; Ascoli and Ranci, 2002). In the area of rent control, governments have been better able to control rent levels in the private sector than in the public sector. Fourth, it is far from clear whether the same categories should be used for the regulation axis. It is difficult to envisage regulation by actors in the market, voluntary or informal sectors. As regulation is aligned with legal authority, governments are the most obvious source of regulation. There are examples of government regulation (rent control). However, much regulation is carried out by agencies that have some degree of independence from government, such as Ofsted (the Office for Standards in Education) and the Commission for Healthcare Audit and Inspection. There is an unresolved debate about the degree to which these organisations are governmental/public (for example, Hood et al, 1999), whether control and accountability is direct or indirect, and the strength of regulation. Moreover, there is a further phenomenon of professional self-regulation. This is related to professional power (for example, Wilding, 1982) and is most obvious in services such as healthcare (for example, Salter, 2004). For example, the General Medical Council and the Royal Colleges have considerable power over many issues in healthcare, and the Secretary of State for Health cannot remove a doctor from the professional register. Although there have been moves to restrict professional self-regulation as a result of the activities at medical institutions such as the Bristol Royal Infirmary and the Alder Hey Hospital, and of individual practitioners such as the GP Harold Shipman, the professions still have considerable power (for example, Salter, 2004).

Instead of a three-dimensional cube with 64 cells, the figure is based on a simple and crude division of the 16 cells into high and low regulation, with 'a' denoting high regulation and 'b' low regulation. While, to paraphrase Bozeman (1987), all organisations are regulated, to paraphrase George Orwell, some organisations are regulated more than others. For example, while much complementary and alternative medicine would be placed in cell 6b, rent control would be placed in cell 6a. This figure will be examined again in a dynamic context, analysing moves from origin to destination cells, in Chapter Eleven.

Conclusion

The components of MEW – state, market, voluntary and informal welfare – and SDW – statutory, fiscal and occupational welfare – will be examined in greater detail in the following chapters, as will discussions of how MEW and SDW vary over time and space. The main aim of this chapter has been to provide a broad macro-level survey of the territory. It has set out two broad arguments. First, MEW and SDW are important but neglected parts of social policy. In short, there is more to social policy than the welfare state (especially if the role of the state is seen in narrow, direct-provider sense). Second, a one-dimensional view of provision alone is inadequate, and it is necessary to also examine the dimensions of finance and regulation.

Summary

- The mixed economy of welfare (MEW) and the social division of welfare (SDW) are important, but relatively neglected, parts of social policy.
- Social policy goes beyond a focus on 'the welfare state' and it is necessary to examine the other elements of MEW (private, voluntary and informal) and SDW (occupational and fiscal).
- MEW and SDW vary over time and space.
- It is necessary to go beyond a 'one-dimensional account' of provision to a 'three-dimensional account' that examines provision, finance and regulation.

Questions for discussion

- Why are MEW and SDW the forgotten and invisible dimensions in social policy?
- Think of the different elements of welfare from MEW and SDW that affect your family.
- Should the state provide all welfare goods and services to its citizens?

Further reading

The most comprehensive account of MEW, although it is now dated, remains **Johnson (1987)**. **Finlayson (1994)** examines the welfare mix over time, while **Ascoli and Ranci (2002)** examine it over space. Individual components are discussed in **Ungerson (1987)**, **Kendall and Knapp (1996)**, **Drakeford (2000)** and **Deakin (2001)**.

SDW was introduced in **Titmuss (1963)**, and discussed in **Sinfield (1978)** and **Spicker (1983)**.

Electronic resources

Paul Spicker's website at Robert Gordon University presents material on MEW and SDW, respectively:

www2.rgu.ac.uk/publicpolicy/introduction/socadmin.htm
www2.rgu.ac.uk/publicpolicy/introduction/equality.htm

A brief guide to MEW and SDW is given by Mike Reddin:
www.lse.u-net.com/Mixed%20Econ%20of%20Welfare.htm

References

Alcock, C., Payne, S. and Sullivan, M. (eds) (2000) *Introducing Social Policy*, Harlow: Prentice Hall.

Alcock, P. (2003) *Social Policy in Britain* (2nd edn), Basingstoke: Palgrave Macmillan.

Alcock, P., Erskine, A. and May, M. (eds) (2002) *The Blackwell Dictionary of Social Policy*, Oxford: Blackwell.

Alcock, P., Erskine, A. and May, M. (eds) (2003) *The Student's Companion to Social Policy* (2nd edn), Oxford: Blackwell.

Ascoli, U. and Ranci, C. (2002) *Dilemmas of the Welfare Mix. The New Structure of Welfare in an Era of Privatization*, New York, NY: Kluwer.

Baldock, J., Manning, N. and Vickerstaff, S. (eds) (2003) *Social Policy* (2nd edn), Oxford: Oxford University Press.

Beresford, P. and Croft, S. (1984) 'Welfare pluralism: the new face of Fabianism', *Critical Social Policy*, vol 9, pp 19-39.

Beveridge, Sir W. (1948) *Voluntary Action*, London: Allen and Unwin.

Blakemore, K. (2003) *Social Policy* (2nd edn), Buckingham: Open University Press.

Bolderson, H. (1986) 'The state at one remove: examples of agency arrangements and regulatory powers in social policy', *Policy and Politics*, vol 13, no 1, pp 17-36.

Bozeman, B. (1987) *All Organizations are Public*, San Francisco, CA: Jossey-Bass.

Brenton, M. (1985) *The Voluntary Sector in British Social Services*, Harlow: Longman.

Burchardt, T. (1997) *Boundaries between Public and Private Welfare*, CASEpaper 2, London: London School of Economics.

Burchardt. T., Hills, J. and Propper, C. (1999) *Private Welfare and Public Policy*, York: Joseph Rowntree Foundation.

Crosland, C.A.R. ([1956] 1964) *The Future of Socialism*, London: Jonathan Cape.

Deakin, N. (2001) *In Search of Civil Society*, Basingstoke: Palgrave.

Drakeford, M. (2000) *Privatisation and Social Policy*, Harlow: Pearson.

Ellison, N. and Pierson, C. (eds) (2003) *Developments in British Social Policy 2*, Basingstoke: Palgrave Macmillan.

Esping-Andersen, G. (1990) *The Three Worlds of Welfare Capitalism*, Cambridge: Polity Press.

Esping-Andersen, G. (1999) *Social Foundations of Postindustrial Economies*, Oxford: Oxford University Press.

Evers, A. and Svetlik, I. (eds) (1993) *Balancing Pluralism. New Welfare Mixes in the Care of the Elderly*, Aldershot: Avebury.

Evers, A. and Wintersberger, H. (eds) (1990) *Shifts in the Welfare Mix*, Boulder, CO: Westview Press.

Field, F. (2000) *The State of Dependency*, London: Social Market Foundation.

Finch, J. and Groves, D. (1980) 'Community care and the family', *Journal of Social Policy*, vol 9, no 4, pp 487-511.

Finlayson, G. (1994) *Citizen, State and Social Welfare in Britain 1830-1990*, Oxford: Clarendon Press.

Fitzpatrick, T. (2001) *Welfare Theory: An Introduction*, Basingstoke: Palgrave.

Forder, A. (1974) *Concepts in Social Administration*, London: Routledge and Kegan Paul.

Forder, A., Caslin, T., Ponton, G. and Walklate, S. (eds) (1984) *Theories of Welfare*, London: Routledge and Kegan Paul.

Giddens, A, (1998) *The Third Way*, Cambridge: Polity Press.

Gilbert, N. and Gilbert, B. (1989) *The Enabling State*, New York, NY: Oxford University Press.

Gladstone, D. (ed) (1995) *British Social Welfare*, London: UCL Press.

Glennerster, H. (2003) *Understanding the Finance of Welfare*, Bristol: The Policy Press.

Gough, I. and Wood, G. with Barrentos, A., Bevan, P., Davis, P. and Room, G. (2004) *Insecurity and Welfare Regimes in Asia, Africa and Latin America*, Cambridge: Cambridge University Press.

Green, D. (1996) *Communities without Politics*, London: Institute of Economic Affairs.

Hadley, R. and Hatch, S. (1981) *Social Welfare and the Failure of the State*, London: Allen and Unwin.

Hantrais, L., O'Brien, M. and Mangen, S. (eds) (1992) *The Mixed Economy of Welfare*, Loughborough: Loughborough University.

Harris, J. (1992) 'War and social history', *Contemporary European History*, vol 1, no 1, pp 17-35.

Hatch, S. and Mocroft, I. (1983) *Components of Welfare*, London: Bedford Square Press.

Hewitt, M. and Powell, M. (1998) 'A different "Back to Beveridge"? Welfare pluralism and the Beveridge welfare state', in E. Brunsdon, H. Dean and R. Woods (eds) *Social Policy Review 10*, London: Social Policy Association, pp 85-104.

Hill, M. and Bramley, G. (1986) *Analysing Social Policy*, Oxford: Blackwell.

Hills, J. (2004) *Inequality and the State*, Oxford: Oxford University Press.

Hirst, P. (1994) *Associative Democracy*, Cambridge: Polity Press.

Hood, C., Scott, C., James, O., Jones, G. and Travers, T. (1999) *Regulation Inside Government. Waste-watchers, Quality Police and Sleaze-busters*, Oxford: Oxford University Press.

IPPR (Institute for Public Policy Research) (2001) *Building Better Partnerships: Report of the IPPR Commission on Public Private Partnerships*, London: IPPR.

Johnson, N. (1987) *The Welfare State in Transition. The Theory and Practice of Welfare Pluralism*, Hemel Hempstead: Harvester Wheatsheaf.

Johnson, N. (ed) (1995) *Private Markets in Health and Welfare*, Oxford: Berg.

Johnson, N. (1999) *Mixed Economies of Welfare*, Hemel Hempstead: Prentice Hall.

Jones, K., Brown, J. and Bradshaw, J. (1983) *Issues in Social Policy* (2nd edn), London: Routledge and Kegan Paul.

Judge, K. (1982) 'Is there a crisis in the welfare state?', *International Journal of Sociology and Social Policy*, vol 2, no 1, pp 1-21.

Keen, J., Light, D. and Mays, N. (2001) *Public–Private Relations in Health Care*, King's Fund: London.

Kendall, J. and Knapp, M. (1996) *The Voluntary Sector in the United Kingdom*, Manchester: Manchester University Press.

Klein, R. (1985) 'Public expenditure in an inflationary world', in L. Lindberg and C. Maier (eds) *The Politics of Inflation and Economic Stagnation*, Washington DC, WA: Brookings Institute, pp 196-223.

Knapp, M. (1989) 'Private and voluntary welfare', in M. McCarthy (ed) *The New Politics of Welfare*, Basingstoke: Macmillan, pp 225-52.

Land, H. (1978) 'Who cares for the family?', *Journal of Social Policy*, vol 7, no 3, pp 257-84.

Lavalette, M. and Pratt, A. (eds) (1997) *Social Policy. A Conceptual and Theoretical Introduction*, London: Sage Publications.

Lavalette, M. and Pratt, A. (eds) (2001) *Social Policy. A Conceptual and Theoretical Introduction* (2nd edn), London: Sage Publications.

Le Grand, J. and Bartlett, W. (1993) *Quasi-markets and Social Policy*, Basingstoke: Macmillan.

Lewis, J. (1995) *The Voluntary Sector, the State and Social Work*, Aldershot: Edward Elgar.

Lund, B. (1993) 'An agenda for welfare pluralism in housing', *Social Policy and Administration*, vol 27, no 4, pp 309-22.

Majone, G. (1996) *Regulating Europe*, London: Routledge.

Malin, N., Wilmot, S. and Manthorpe, J. (2002) *Key Concepts in Health and Social Policy*, Buckingham: Open University Press.

Mann, K. (1989) *Growing Fringes*, Leeds: Armley.

Marsland, D. (1996) *Welfare or Welfare State?*, Basingstoke: Macmillan.

Mayo, M. (1994) *Communities and Caring. The Mixed Economy of Welfare*, Basingstoke: Macmillan.

Miller, C. (2004) *Producing Welfare*, Basingstoke: Palgrave Macmillan.

Mishra, R. (1990) *The Welfare State in Capitalist Society*, Hemel Hempstead: Harvester Wheatsheaf.

Moran, M. (2003) *The British Regulatory State*, Oxford: Oxford University Press.

Page, R. and Silburn, B. (eds) (1999) *British Social Welfare in the Twentieth Century*, Basingstoke: Macmillan.

Papadakis, E. and Taylor-Gooby, P. (1987) *The Private Provision of Public Welfare*, Brighton: Wheatsheaf.

Pinker, R. (1992) 'Making sense of the mixed economy of welfare', *Social Policy and Administration*, vol 26, no 4, pp 273-84.

Powell, M. (2003) 'Quasi-markets in British health policy: a *longue dureé* perspective', *Social Policy and Administration*, vol 37, no 7, pp 725-41.

Powell, M. and Barrientos, A. (2004) 'Welfare regimes and the welfare mix', *European Journal of Political Research*, vol 43, no 1, pp 83-105.

Powell, M. and Hewitt, M. (1998) 'The end of the welfare state?', *Social Policy and Administration*, vol 32, no 1, pp 1-13.

Powell, M. and Hewitt, M. (2002) *Welfare State and Welfare Change*, Buckingham: Open University Press.

Power, M. (1997) *The Audit Society*, Oxford: Clarendon Press.

Rao, N. (1996) *Towards Welfare Pluralism*, Aldershot: Dartmouth.

Rose, H. (1981) 'Rereading Titmuss: the sexual division of welfare', *Journal of Social Policy*, vol 10, no 4, pp 477-502.

Rose, R. and Shiratori, R. (1986) 'Introduction', in R. Rose and R. Shiratori (eds) *The Welfare State East and West*, Oxford: Oxford University Press.

Salter, B. (2004) *The New Politics of Medicine*, Basingstoke: Palgrave Macmillan.

Sandford, C., Pond, C. and Walker, R. (eds) (1980) *Taxation and Social Policy*, London: Heinemann.

Seldon, A. (ed) (1996) *Re-privatising Welfare*, London: Institute of Economic Affairs.

Shalev, M. (ed) (1996) *The Privatization of Social Policy? Occupational Welfare and the Welfare State in America, Scandinavia and Japan*, Basingstoke: Macmillan.

Sinfield, A. (1978) 'Analyses in the social division of welfare', *Journal of Social Policy*, vol 7, no 2, pp 129-56.

Spicker, P. (1983) 'Titmuss's "Social division of welfare": a reappraisal', in C. Jones and J. Stevenson (eds) *Yearbook of Social Policy*, London: Routledge and Kegan Paul, pp 182-93.

Spicker, P. (1988) *Principles of Social Welfare*, London: Routledge.

Spicker, P. (1995) *Social Policy*, Harlow: Prentice Hall.

Taylor, M. (2003) *Public Policy in the Community*, Basingstoke: Palgrave.

Thane, P. (1996) *Foundations of the Welfare State* (2nd edn), Harlow: Longman.

Titmuss, R. (1963) *Essays on the 'Welfare State'* (2nd edn), London: Allen and Unwin.

Titmuss, R. (1968) *Commitment to Welfare*, London: Allen and Unwin.

Titmuss, R. (1974) *Social Policy*, London: Allen and Unwin.

Ungerson, C. (1987) *Policy is Personal*, London: Tavistock

Walker, A. (1984) 'The political economy of privatisation', in J. Le Grand and R. Robinson (eds) *Privatisation and the Welfare State*, London: Allen and Unwin, pp 19-44.

Walker, A. (1997) 'The social division of welfare revisited', in A. Robertson (ed) *Unemployment, Social Security and the Social Division of Welfare*, Edinburgh: University of Edinburgh.

Walsh, K. (1995) *Public Services and Market Mechanisms*, Basingstoke: Macmillan.

Wilding, P. (1982) *Professional Power and Social Welfare*, London: Routledge and Kegan Paul.

Whitfield, D. (1992) *The Welfare State*, London: Pluto.

Wilensky, H. and Lebeaux, C. (1965) *Industrial Society and Social Welfare*, New York, NY: The Free Press.

Wistow, G., Knapp, M., Hardy, B. and Allen, C. (1994) *Social Care in a Mixed Economy*, Buckingham: Open University Press.

Wolfenden, Lord (1978) *The Future of Voluntary Organisations. The Report of the Wolfenden Committee*, London: Croom Helm.

two

The mixed economy of welfare in historical context

John Stewart

Overview

Until recently, historians had a view of welfare provision, particularly in the 20th century, that we now recognise over-emphasised the role of the state. While state-provided welfare services are, and have been, important, we need to look beyond them to see the bigger picture. The family has always been one of the key providers of welfare and will continue to be so. The role of the market has been especially stressed over the past quarter of a century, but it, too, has always had a part to play in welfare provision. It would appear that governments are looking increasingly to the voluntary/charitable sector to supplement state provision. But it is important to recognise that the voluntary/charitable sector comprises a wide range of bodies; and that its relationship to the state has altered significantly over the past hundred years.

Key concepts
Changing institutions • changing relationships • 'the moving frontier' • citizenship • civic society

Introduction

Until relatively recently, historical accounts of welfare provision tended to focus on the role of the state, and especially the growing role of the central state. In particular, works published during the 'golden age' of the 'classic' welfare state – that is, from the mid-1940s through to the mid-1970s – argued that purportedly comprehensive and universal welfare services were the outcome of an increasing recognition of the need for social 'rights'; and that the appropriate agency to deliver these was the state (see, for example, Marshall, 1950). Historical change was, by such accounts, unilinear and 'progressive' and resulted in a citizenship of entitlement – 'social' citizenship. Various metaphors, such as the 'welfare state escalator', were used to explain how this happy state of affairs had come about (Finlayson, 1994, p 3). Such versions of welfare history are important historical documents in their own right, evidence of the optimism surrounding the post-war settlement.

With the socioeconomic and political instability of the 1970s, however, historical writing changed in at least two ways. First, it was acknowledged that the development of modern welfare services was not a simple story of ceaseless improvement. Second, it was recognised that 'welfare' has always been delivered by a range agencies and institutions – there is, and always has been, a mixed economy of welfare. Attention is now paid not only to the state, but also to the market, families (the 'informal' sector), and voluntary/charitable bodies (the 'third' sector). As Lewis pointedly remarks, all this might have been "more obvious earlier had British historians and social policy analysts engaged in more European comparative research" (Lewis, 1999b, p 249). This reminds us that the mixed economy is characteristic of both the British and other welfare regimes (see Chapters Nine and Ten).

This chapter examines historical dimensions of welfare delivery. The aim is to alert readers to the necessity of seeing the mixed economy of welfare in historical terms. Two central points arise: first, that the agencies and institutions that deliver welfare are not of themselves fixed entities. Rather, they have changed, and will continue to change, over time. Second, the relationship between these institutions is likewise, and consequently, subject to change. In a much-used expression, there is a 'moving frontier' (Finlayson, 1990) between the various sectors of welfare provider. The boundaries between each sector, furthermore, are porous and overlapping, not rigid. In discussing the mixed economy of welfare, we are thus dealing with a complex phenomenon whose form and content changes according to historical circumstances.

The remainder of this chapter is organised as follows. First, we use a fictional historical example to show the mixed economy of welfare in action (**Box 2.1**). Second, we look at the state, the family, the market, and the voluntary/ charitable sectors in their historic relationship to welfare. Third, we examine the shifting relationship between these components of the mixed economy of welfare. Fourth, we make some concluding remarks about the historical dimensions of the 'mixed economy of welfare'.

Box 2.1: An historical illustration

Susan is a child living with her father and mother in inter-war Britain. Her father is in employment, and so Susan's mother stays at home to take care of her daughter and the household. Susan and her parents live in housing rented, at below the market rate, from the local authority. Susan is educated at the school run by the local education authority. Here, because her family's household income is relatively low, she receives subsidised school meals, a form of welfare provision that thus overlaps with that provided within the family. Although not officially part of the labour market, Susan nonetheless baby-sits for her neighbour, thus enabling her to contribute to her family's income as well as providing her with small luxuries. Susan's father contributes, voluntarily, to a mutual-aid hospital insurance scheme. So when Susan falls ill and has to be hospitalised, she is able to go to the local voluntary institution. Susan is thus receiving 'welfare' from a mixture of the family; the state (in the form of the local education authority); the market (through her paid baby-sitting and her father's participation in the labour market); and the voluntary sector (through her father's hospital insurance scheme).

Fifty years later Susan's granddaughter, Linda, also receives a free school education, although by now one of longer duration, and free school meals. When she falls sick, though, diagnosis and treatment are carried out by the National Health Service (NHS). Her parents, as a result of post-war affluence, were able to buy their own home but have now divorced. This came about despite the efforts of the Marriage Guidance Council, a voluntary agency set up after the Second World War. So Linda lives with her mother, who, to make ends meet, goes out to work. Economic assistance is, though, provided by the state in the form of child benefit, something that had not available to Susan's mother when Susan was growing up. Like her grandmother, Linda contributes to the family income by baby-sitting for a neighbour – she participates, in other words, in the labour market. Linda has thus experienced, as did her grandmother, the mixed economy of welfare. But the balance has changed. So, for instance, while Susan received hospital care from a voluntary agency, all of Linda's healthcare needs are met by the NHS. And although both undoubtedly received welfare in the family – in particular parental care – what constitutes 'the family' has changed. Susan and Linda are fictitious, but such experiences were common in reality and illustrate the existence of the mixed economy of welfare and its shifting composition over time.

Thinking historically about the state and welfare

In mid-19th-century Britain, the role of government was, as Thane puts it, "to provide a firmly established and clearly understood framework within which society could very largely run itself" (Thane, 1990, p 1). This was the cornerstone of classic Victorian liberalism, with the central state in an 'enabling' rather than directing role. A further dimension of this world-view was the idea of local autonomy. Local bodies, official or otherwise, were to act as a bulwark against any encroachments by an overbearing central state such as was thought to characterise governance in other parts of Europe. Indeed, the powers of local government actually increased in the mid-19th century. Consequently, publicly funded welfare services – for instance, poor relief and public health – were delivered by, in these particular cases, poor law boards of guardians and municipal authorities. Such services were overwhelmingly funded by local, rather than national, taxation. Local autonomy and local rights were fiercely guarded.

However, by the end of the 19th century, attitudes were changing. Concerns were raised about the condition of the mass of the population in an era of heightened economic and military competition. Doubts also began to be expressed about the ability of local bodies to deliver welfare services in an adequate and/or equitable manner. Alongside this, a more positive view of the central state and what it could achieve was being articulated. As a result, social issues became concerns of 'high politics' in a way that had not previously been the case. One outcome was, as Harris puts it, a more dramatic change from the beginning of the 20th century in the state's powers and functions "than in any comparable span of years in earlier history" (Harris, 1990a, p 64).

The 19th-century emphasis on localism began to be eroded by the controversial Liberal welfare reforms of the Edwardian era. These included old age pensions financed out of general taxation and mildly redistributive fiscal policy (Hay, 1983). The Liberal welfare reforms also, though, alert us to an important issue in any discussion of the relationship between the state and welfare. While certain social services were funded and directly administered by the state, in other areas the relationship was more indirect. One crucial part of Edwardian child welfare policy, for instance, was the enhanced powers given to a voluntary body – the National Society for the Prevention of Cruelty to Children (NSPCC) – to act on the state's behalf (Stewart, 1995). In all historical (and contemporary) discussions of the state and welfare, it is therefore important to ascertain whether the state is acting as a direct provider, is providing financial support to other agencies, or is allowing other agencies to act on its behalf. To return to the Liberal welfare reforms, their passing was a clear indicator of the arrival of social reform in the realm of national politics.

But it was the era after 1945 when the central state came to the fore as one of the principal providers of social welfare. It did so through such measures as the creation of the NHS. The classic age of the welfare state was thus associated with the central state, not least in the historical writing noted at the outset. Even here, though, the picture was rather more complicated, for three reasons.

First, Harris notes that in welfare terms the Second World War resulted in local authorities ceasing to be, for the first time in centuries, "the main intermediaries between the citizen and the state". But she also points out that after the war local authorities saw their welfare responsibilities increase. This was especially notable in housing, in secondary education and in the personal social services (Harris, 1990a, pp 90, 98). The volume of local authority housing has shrunk dramatically over the past quarter of a century, but in education and social services local bodies continue to play a major role.

Second, even allowing for a significant shift towards centralisation in the course of the 20th century, the United Kingdom has never been a 'unitary state'. Scotland, Wales, and (from the 1920s) Northern Ireland all retained varying degrees of 'welfare autonomy'. This was further highlighted by political devolution after 1997 (Chaney and Drakeford, 2004; Stewart, 2004; McLaughlin, 2005). The mixed economy of welfare, and the relationship of its components, thus varies not only over time but also within the UK. To take a recent example, there have been policy differences between Scotland and England as to whether state-funded care for the elderly should be universal or selective. The Scottish Executive opted for the former, while in England the clear implication is that families and the private sector are to play the leading roles (Stewart, 2004, ch 5).

Third, and as we shall see, the central state never supplanted, or indeed sought to supplant, other forms of welfare provision. The family, the market, and the voluntary/charitable sector did not disappear under a tidal wave of collectivism.

Nonetheless, in the 'classic' age of the welfare state, it was the central state that was primarily associated with the delivery of welfare services, the culmination of a decisive shift in the course of the 20th century. Although the idea has been much disputed, it is often claimed that the classic welfare state was underpinned by the 'post-war consensus'. Consensus involved recognition by the main political parties of the need for a comprehensive welfare state, publicly funded and delivered by public agencies to all citizens as a matter of social right. This was to be complemented by Keynesian economic management, one of whose principal aims was the maintenance of full employment, a highly significant policy goal given the costs – human, social, and political – of unemployment in the era preceding the Second World War.

The NHS was the most popular institution of the welfare state, and in many ways its exemplar. The largest employer in Europe, with a centralised administrative structure, it had embraced virtually all aspects of healthcare, for instance through 'nationalising' both voluntary and municipal hospitals. The service's underlying principles were universal and comprehensive healthcare, provided free at the point of delivery and financed out of general taxation.

The last point is important. Funding through general taxation reinforced the idea that healthcare was a charge on the nation as a whole. The state was thus putting itself forward as the provider of all of the health needs of all of the people, who in turn received such services as a matter of social citizenship.

The post-war consensus began to break down in the 1970s. One factor here was a re-examination of the state's role in the funding and delivery of welfare. Famously, supporters of the 'New Right' sought to 'roll back the frontiers of the state'. Whether this was achieved, at least in economic terms, is another matter. But there was undoubtedly an attitudinal shift that saw much greater emphasis being placed by the Conservative administrations of 1979-97 on the welfare roles of the market, the family and the voluntary/charitable sector. When Margaret Thatcher described herself as a supporter of 'Victorian values', she was not just talking about her support for 'free market' economics. She was also commending, in broad terms, the notion of an 'enabling' state, which we encountered at the beginning of this section. New Labour's position on the central state's role is rather more ambiguous, not least because of its marked propensity to impose centrally determined 'targets' on the public sector. But there can be no doubt that it, too, seeks to bolster other parts of the 'mixed economy of welfare'. Equally, it is apparent that New Labour seeks to shift service delivery, if not necessarily funding, to other agencies. New Labour's critique of the 'command-and-control' version of the welfare state, and its stated desire to 'devolve' services to localities and communities, acquire particular resonance when we look at the historical context in which they should be placed.

The key point, then, is that the role of the state in the provision of welfare has changed over time. This in turn results from changes in attitude towards the state, and especially the central state. There have also been changes in the ways in which the state provides welfare. At certain historic points, this is through direct provision. At others, funding and/or support has been provided for non-state agencies. Put crudely, we might start with the individualism and localism of the 19th century. The 20th century then sees a rise in 'collectivism', culminating in the post-1945 welfare state, with central state being seen as both funder and direct provider of key welfare services. In the last quarter of the 20th century, there is a shift away from support for directly state-provided services, back to emphasis on the family, the market, and the voluntary/charitable sectors.

Thinking historically about the family and welfare

The family might seem a rather more immutable social institution, and certainly historians have shown conclusively that the nuclear family, as a form, is long established in British society. Although at various points the state and voluntary sector have sought to intervene in cases of perceived 'family failure', it is also now acknowledged that this key social institution has been, willingly or otherwise, the principal provider of welfare throughout history. In turn, family welfare provision has underpinned, and will no doubt continue to underpin, crucial aspects of welfare policy. The 19th-century poor law, for example, sought to impose a welfare regime wherein applicants for relief would only be accepted by showing both their own destitution and that their family's resources were inadequate to support them. But over the past 300 years there have been fundamental changes to population structure as well as in cultural and social attitudes towards the family. It is important to have some idea of these in order to understand the family's role in welfare provision.

Britain in the 18th and for much of the 19th centuries experienced – relatively speaking – high rates of marriage and of fertility and low life expectancy. In general terms, people lived in family groups in family-dominated households and, certainly compared with our own times, this was a 'young' society. All this started to change from around the middle of the 19th century. Life expectancy began to rise, and one important component of this was that women began to live longer than men. From around the same time, family size started to decline. One effect of the last of these was the greater premium placed on raising healthy and well-educated children, particularly when the impact of economic competition and restructuring came to be felt. 'Investing' in children was 'investing' in the future of the race and Empire, or, as we might more prosaically put it today, 'human capital'. In turn, this raised questions about the relative responsibilities of the family and the state for the welfare of the young. In the early 20th century, for instance, proponents of publicly supported school meals had to strike a balance between ensuring the ongoing integrity of the family and the need to support it at particular points in its life history (Stewart, 1993).

The family's historic role in welfare provision should not be romanticised, nor should it be seen as always being able to fulfil what was expected of it. There has been a common, but misplaced, idea that in the past there was a 'golden age of kin-based welfare provision'. But for a range of reasons, the family might not always operate as the 'locus of care' (Horden and Smith, 1998, p 2). So, for instance, one of the largest groups in late 19th-century poor law workhouses was old women. As noted, women now tended to live longer than men, so they might find themselves pre-deceased by their husbands and, if unfortunate, their children. The poor law was often their only means of support in old age (Thane, 1978).

Shifts in population structure continued into the 20th century, raising other issues about the family as welfare provider. So, for example, at the point at which the post-war welfare state was being created, concerns were already being raised about an ageing population. As Thane suggests, this was presented as a "social and economic problem, and took for granted a negative view of older people, their economic capability and social contributions" (Thane, 2000, p 347). In addition, recent decades have seen a rise in the number of people living on their own, whether through choice or otherwise. This derives from a combination of rising affluence and social and cultural changes. People are now able, and expect to be able, to form single households. Such a situation was much more uncommon a hundred, or even 50, years ago. One particularly contentious issue has been the rise in single-parent – in effect, single-female-parent – households because of the purported role that welfare benefits such as social housing have played in this phenomenon and the associated 'breakdown' in family life.

Such demographic and cultural changes raise a range of questions about the family and welfare provision. If we take an example with considerable contemporary purchase, how is the increasing number of old people to be cared for? If by the state, then how is this to be funded? If, on the other hand, the elderly are to be cared for by the market or by the voluntary/charitable sector, how are market failure and/or inequity of provision to be avoided? And if the elderly are to be cared for in the family, what implications does this have for, for instance, female labour market participation (given that most informal carers are female) and family income? Should the state pay 'carers' to opt out of the labour market to look after their own relatives? We have already seen that divisions within the UK have recently emerged over care for the elderly and it is worth emphasising that in part this derives from changes in population structure.

Similar questions can be posed of the family in respect of children. For a long period, much British social policy was predicated on the 'male-breadwinner model', whereby it was assumed that within the family the man would be responsible for gaining the family income while the woman would look after the children. Illustrating the value of comparative historical analysis, Pedersen shows how this led to different policy outcomes in Britain and France in the first half of the 20th century. France, a country long concerned with population decline, subsidised families in a way that did not initially happen in Britain (Pedersen, 1993, passim). Once again, though, a combination of socioeconomic and cultural change partially eroded this idea, leading to the introduction of family allowances in the mid-1940s (Macnicol, 1980). The ongoing proportionate decrease in the number of young people in the population has further implications. The emphasis on children and young people as 'investments' for the future is not, as we have seen, a new phenomenon. Nonetheless, much of New Labour's policies towards children are predicated on notions of enhancing 'human capital' while encouraging broader labour market participation. One outcome of this has been the emphasis on pre-school nursery and education provision, which again raises the long-standing issue of how to balance familial and societal responsibilities.

Qualifications notwithstanding, the family has undoubtedly been, and been seen as, a key welfare provider. In recent decades, a further dimension has been added by way of the New Right and its re-emphasis on the family as a social institution. Lewis points out that many New Right theorists "argued strongly in favour of parental responsibility" and saw "the intervention of the state employed professionals as the main reason for its decline". The family operated best, by this argument, when left alone (Lewis, 1995, p 12). This is essentially a moral and ideological position that seeks to re-emphasise, as in the 19th century, the responsibility of individuals and families for their own welfare. The central point is, therefore, that 'the family' is a socially and historically constructed institution that has clustered around it a huge range of shifting assumptions to do with, inter alia, care, gender roles, and intra-family relationships. As with other components of the mixed economy of welfare, the family cannot therefore be seen as a static, unchanging entity.

Thinking historically about the market and welfare

In the 19th century, Victorian liberalism claimed that the market could provide for most welfare needs for most people at most times. This belief did not deny the existence of poverty. On the contrary, poverty was a fact of economic life whose impact could be softened by economic prudence, family support, or, as a last resort, charity aimed at the 'respectable' poor. But what could be avoided was the degraded condition of pauperism, brought about by moral failure. Pauperism involved dependence on others – and specifically the ratepayers who funded the poor law – in an era when 'independence' was a key moral virtue. It was thus a fundamental principle of the New Poor Law that any welfare given should be on the basis of 'less eligibility' – that is, at a level lower than that of the worst-off labourer in employment. By the same token, those who did receive relief were to be re-moralised and so equipped for participation in the free market. It is worth considering the extent to which these 'principles of 1834' persisted into the post-war welfare state.

By the end of the 19th century, though, it was increasingly recognised that the market did not always operate as proponents of classical economic theory claimed. Social problems such as unemployment were not necessarily the fault of the individuals who experienced them. Rather, there could be a whole range of imperfections and failures in the market resulting in, for example, loss of employment. It is significant in this context that the word 'unemployment' itself acquired its modern meaning at this historical juncture (Harris, 1972). In actual welfare provision, even some of the staunchest advocates of classical political economy recognised the need for state-funded education such as was instituted from the 1870s.

Such market 'failure' was recognised in the early 20th century through mechanisms such as social insurance and labour exchanges, further components of the Liberal welfare reforms (Hay, 1983). In the immediate aftermath of the First World War, local authorities, backed by the central state, provided a growing volume of social housing. This was prompted in part by fears of social unrest and the accurate perception that the market was not delivering an acceptable range and quality of accommodation (Harris, 2004, ch 16). The vogue for 'planning' in the crisis-ridden 1930s, especially in areas such as health, was based on the perceived need for state action in areas where the market was again not fulfilling social needs (Marwick, 1964). In economic theory, meanwhile, Keynes was formulating his tools of economic management. All of this was designed not to supplant free market capitalism, but rather to curb what were seen as its (self-) destructive tendencies. We return to the persistence of the market below. Nonetheless, scepticism about the market's ability to provide welfare and security fed into post-war reconstruction, and, in the work of social thinkers such as Titmuss, we find outright hostility to the idea of market solutions to welfare problems (Titmuss, 1967).

Reaction against such views came, in the last quarter of the 20th century, from the New Right. Its proponents sought to uncouple welfare from the state. Public monopolies, such as state-provided welfare, were inherently inefficient as well as affecting the proper operations of the free market. Welfare 'dependency' – a further outcome of universal state-provided services – corroded individual, familial and social responsibility. If allowed to operate as it should, the free market would generate enough wealth and welfare to satisfy most social needs, with residual state welfare providing a 'safety net'. As Finlayson puts it, this argument stressed that 'the market rather than the state was the enabler to a better life'; and that the social rights of citizenship were of themselves a hindrance to it (Finlayson, 1994, pp 408, 420). One influential exponent of this idea was the historian Correlli Barnett, who argued that what had been created in the 1940s was not the 'new Jerusalem' but rather welfare dependency and obstacles to British competitiveness (see Harris, 1990b).

This is not to say that things did not go wrong in individual or family life. But once again, for the New Right the market could offer solutions by way of, for example, private health insurance and this was encouraged by the Conservative administrations of the 1980s and 1990s (Le Grand and Vizard, pp 96-8). As we have already seen, the New Right also saw the family as a key provider of welfare and we shall presently note its approach to the voluntary sector. For the moment, though, what needs to be stressed is that the market had reasserted itself.

This does, though, need to be put in its broader historical context. Even when the efficacy or justice of the market has been under attack, the labour market has always been seen as the best provider of welfare through paid employment. Similarly, the ability, indeed the right, to purchase welfare in the market has never been seriously challenged. Individuals with the necessary resources have always been able to buy education, healthcare, housing, pension, and other forms of social security. All this held true for the Liberal welfare reformers of the early 20th century, the advocates of planning in the 1930s and indeed the Labour governments of 1945-51. Nonetheless, the centrality of the market has been re-emphasised over the past three decades. In a range of welfare fields, market mechanisms have been introduced in an attempt to improve efficiency. This was most obviously the case in the NHS in the 1980s and 1990s. New Labour has stressed expanded labour market participation and has sought to implement policies whereby the state has continued to fund welfare services while turning their delivery over to private companies. Equally, New Labour shows no signs of abolishing private education or private healthcare and has a pensions strategy that, at least in part, rests on property ownership rather than entitlement through social insurance and/or social citizenship. While this should not be overstated, we are here some way from the collectivist, and public service ethos, aspirations of the welfare state in its 'classic' phase.

Thinking historically about the voluntary/ charitable sector and welfare

We noted earlier that in the 19th century the state's role was perceived as providing a framework wherein society could more or less run itself. Alongside this, it was also believed that, left to its own devices, the market could provide for most people most of the time. Equally, though, it was recognised that, through circumstances not always of their own choosing, individuals could find themselves in difficulty. In an era when the social casualties of industrialisation and urbanisation were highly visible, and prompted by factors such as Christian evangelicalism and fear of social disturbance, the latter half of the 19th century saw the 'triumph' of philanthropy (Prochaska, 1988, p 41). A huge range of voluntary/charitable bodies existed raising and disbursing significant volumes of money. Famously, the Charity Organisation Society set about coordinating charitable relief. The aim here was that the recipients of such relief would be the 'deserving' poor, 'respectable' members of society fallen on hard times. The 'undeserving' – 'unrespectable' on account of their moral laxity – were to be consigned to the rigours of the poor law. Charitable giving and charitable relief were an integral part of the Victorian world-view. Giving money or time was a key component of 'citizenship'. This version of citizenship, with its notions of duty, is thus rather different from the 'social' citizenship already encountered. As Finlayson puts it, this was a "citizenship of contribution" (Finlayson, 1994, p 4 and passim). Against this background, five further points arise.

First, charitable relief undoubtedly helped many people. It also afforded the opportunity for women, such as the poor law reformer Louisa Twining, to gain a foothold in social politics (Deane, 1998). Nonetheless, by the late 19th century, problems were evident. Charitable relief was often viewed by its recipients as patronising and imbued with particular class and social attitudes. By its very nature, furthermore, such effort was not geographically evenly spread. The cluster of voluntary hospitals in or around the City of London, for example, reflected both philanthropy and population in the Middle Ages, not the needs of Londoners in the modern era. Many workers for voluntary or charitable bodies were untrained and unpaid and so could be seen as acting in an amateurish way, however well intentioned. All of this fed into arguments for state-provided services staffed by trained professionals in order to ensure equity and a disinterested approach.

Second, this sector has always been highly heterogeneous. It has included direct providers of welfare; single-issue campaigning groups; mutual aid organisations; and agencies, often working alongside or on behalf of the state, in fields such as child protection. The sector has thus historically embraced such diverse institutions and bodies as the voluntary hospitals; organisations such as the Child Poverty Action Group that emerged in the 1960s; hospital contributory schemes that gave (and still give) their members access to hospital care; and the NSPCC. It is therefore important, when looking at this sector historically and in the present, to distinguish between, in particular, self-help ('mutual') bodies, wherein individuals come together to provide for their own welfare through collective endeavour, and philanthropic organisations, which 'give' charitable relief to particular groups of recipients. Nonetheless, what binds all participants in the voluntary sector is their formal autonomy from the state.

Third, the composition of the voluntary/charitable sector has changed significantly over time, with one notable feature being its capacity to adapt to new, often unforeseen, circumstances. Voluntary hospitals, for instance, were done away with under the NHS and in any event had in some areas been suffering from loss of revenue and competition from the municipal sector. However, bodies such as the King's Fund – initially set up to defend London's voluntary hospitals – successfully adapted to new circumstances by, in this particular case, working alongside the NHS in the fields of training and research (Prochaska, 1992). In the inter-war period, there emerged the 'new philanthropy', among the features of which were, first, the growth of professionalism in the sector, in part a response to the sector's perceived amateurism. Second, voluntary bodies began to cooperate more closely both with each other and, crucially, with the state. The latter was in marked contrast to the previous prevailing attitude, which was to fiercely assert autonomy and, in many cases, to oppose state-sponsored welfare (Harris, 2004, pp 186-90). From a rather different perspective, the campaigning bodies that emerged in the 1960s and thereafter were in large part concerned with the failures or inadequacies of the post-war welfare state. Shelter, for instance, sought to deal with problems of homelessness. And, as Lowe points out, some voluntary organisations have been set up to deal with issues thought inappropriate for state action – for example, the Marriage Guidance Council, founded in1947 (Lowe, 2005, pp 247, 287).

Fourth, the voluntary sector is self-evidently not immune from what occurs in other parts of the mixed economy of welfare. The increase in state welfare provision had a particularly profound impact. However, it should not be assumed that the voluntary sector ever 'went away', even during the period of the 'classic' welfare state. We have already seen that the welfare state of itself engendered new forms of voluntary/charitable activity. Certain pre-existing bodies also carried on, albeit on smaller scale. Gorsky and his colleagues, for example, demonstrate the persistence of hospital contributory schemes based on mutualism. In the early days of the NHS, there were still some three million members of such schemes, many of which were deeply embedded in particular workplaces or localities. Contributors, in return for their subscriptions, received a range of health-related benefits. These took on particular significance as various types of health service charge were introduced, for example, for eye and dental care (Gorsky et al, 2005).

Finally, the last quarter of a century has seen another crucial shift in the relationship between the voluntary sector and, in particular, the state. In part, this was due to the introduction of market principles and 'consumer choice' into welfare provision. As Lewis remarks, governments in the 1980s and 1990s "consciously sought to promote the role of the voluntary sector as an alternative to state provision". As she also points out, this was explicitly not a return to the circumstances of the 19th century when the voluntary sector exercised a high level of autonomy. Rather, it involved a "completely new relationship" between voluntarism and the state, with central government setting fiscal conditions that "limited the room for manoeuvre on the part of the voluntary organisations" (Lewis, 1999a, pp 260-1). Thus, in the last decade of the 20th century, as Glennerster observes, charitable giving actually declined. But the role of voluntary organisations 'grew substantially' as they were "used more by the state as the means of delivering social welfare services". So while between 1991 and 2001 charities' total income grew by one third, "income from government received by charities grew by 40%" (Glennerster, 2003, p 14). As for New Labour, it has argued for a culture of partnership with the voluntary sector, purportedly in contrast to the 'instrumental' approach adopted by preceding Conservative administrations. This has so far proved more problematical than was presumably intended, and Lowe sees the government as '(d)efying the logic of its rhetoric' by its domineering approach (Lewis, 2005; Lowe, 2005, pp 412-13).

The historically changing relationship between the components of the 'mixed economy of welfare'

Given the issues raised in the preceding sections, our next point comes as no surprise and can be stated briefly. There has not been a fixed relationship between the state, families, the market, and voluntary/charitable bodies in terms of welfare provision. Lewis sees, for example, three distinct eras in the relationship between the state and the voluntary sector: 'separate spheres' (1900-14); 'complementary or supplementary' (1918-80); and 'alternative providers' (post-1980s) (Lewis, 1999c). Finlayson, likewise discussing the state and voluntarism in the 20th century, talks of a 'moving frontier', but this is a useful analogy for the relationship between all of the sectors we are concerned with here (Finlayson, 1990, passim). Boundaries thus shift over time as well as being porous and overlapping, rather than rigidly fixed and delineated.

Nor should it be assumed that these various components of the mixed economy of welfare are mutually exclusive or somehow 'competing' with each other. As we have seen, for instance, it is more useful to see the voluntary/ charitable sector as working in tandem with state-led activities as the 20th century evolved, albeit that the actual meaning of this relationship is also subject to change over time. To put it crudely in order to illustrate the point: when we talk of the relationship between the voluntary sector and the state a hundred years ago and the same relationship today, we are not in all respects comparing like with like. The relationship has changed, as has the content of what we understand by 'the state' and 'the voluntary sector'.

We should also be aware that the internal dynamics of the mixed economy will, at any given historical point, both reflect and shape notions of 'civic society' and 'citizenship'; and have a significant part to play in the formation of human and social capital. It can be argued, therefore, that societies that emphasise collective action or charitable activity as a 'duty' have a rather different view of social capital than societies that stress market individualism.

The 'unintended consequences' effect in history is also worth noting, as action in one part of the 'mixed economy' can have unforeseen consequences on another. To take an obvious, but highly pertinent, example, measures designed to re-engage certain groups with the labour market – thereby diminishing their 'welfare dependency' – can have the consequence of requiring state intervention in other spheres, most notably the provision of pre-school childcare.

These are obviously complex ideas, but one way of thinking about them is through the person of William Beveridge. As Harris's biography shows, Beveridge's views on welfare changed over the course of his long and active life, of itself an indicator of shifting attitudes and policy stances (Harris, 1997). If we focus on Beveridge in the 1940s, we might first note his 1942 report, usually seen as the 'blueprint' of the collectivist post-war welfare state. A few years later, though, he published a work extolling the virtues of voluntary action. This embodied his belief in voluntary welfare activity and in an active citizenry with duties as well as rights. It was through this multi-dimensional approach that the 'good society' would be achieved. Beveridge was likewise sceptical about some aspects of free market capitalism. But he was no socialist – indeed, he was briefly a Liberal MP – and predicated much of his state welfare proposals on full employment achieved through economic management rather than direct state control. He also had fairly conventional views about the family and its role in society and in welfare (Harris, 1997, pp 480-90 and passim). In the life of Beveridge, one of the 'founders' of the post-war welfare state, we therefore find a range of ideas about the welfare 'mix'.

Conclusion

The central points made in this chapter are thus as follows. First, there has always been a 'mixed economy of welfare'. Second, the components of this are, for present purposes, the state, the family, the market and the voluntary/charitable sector. Third, that while these are useful categories, we must be aware that the content of each has changed over time. What constitutes the voluntary/charitable sector in the early 21st century, for instance, is rather different from what constituted it a hundred years ago. The state poses particular problems here. Its role is not homogeneous: rather, it can be that of direct provider, or funder, or enabler of welfare. Which of these is to the fore will vary according to particular historical circumstances. Finally, and unsurprisingly given the previous point, the relationship between each component of the mixed economy of welfare also changes over time and according to particular circumstances. As we saw with the fictional case of 'Susan' and 'Linda' (**Box 2.1**), the mixed economy of welfare has always been with us, but has nonetheless operated in different ways at different times.

Summary

- There has always been a 'mixed economy of welfare', involving the state, the family, the market and the voluntary/charitable sector.
- The role and extent of each of these in delivering 'welfare' has changed over time.
- Consequently, the relationship between each of these sectors has changed over time.
- The 'mixed economy of welfare' is thus a dynamic and changing phenomenon, whose contours will depend on the particular historical circumstances prevailing at any particular time.

Questions for discussion

- How has the mixed economy of welfare changed over your lifetime, and those of your parents and grandparents?
- How would the stories of 'Susan' and 'Linda' (**Box 2.1**) vary for people of different social classes, genders or ethnic groups?
- What might William Beveridge make of today's mixed economy of welfare?

Further reading

Finlayson (1994) gives an insightful historical account of the shifting relationship between the components of the 'mixed economy of welfare' from before the New Poor Law to near the end of Thatcherism.

A good sense of the changing relationship between the voluntary sector and the state can be gained by reading, in chronological sequence, **Lewis, 1999a**, **1999b** and **2005**.

Lowe (2005) gives a stimulating account of the development of the post-war 'welfare state' from its inception to the present, with numerous examples of the kind of issues discussed in this chapter.

Electronic resources

The website of the Centre for the Analysis of Social Exculsion (CASE) – http://sticerd.lse.ac.uk/case/ – at the London School of Economics and Political Science has a useful online publications page, which includes much of interest for students of the 'mixed economy of welfare': see, for example, CASEpaper 93, 'Public and private welfare activity in the United Kingdom, 1979 to 1999', by Rachel Smithies.

The *History and Policy* website – www.historyandpolicy.org/ – contains articles that seek to show how historical understanding can positively inform current policy debate. Of particular interest in the context of this chapter is Martin Gorsky's 'Hospital governance and community involvement in Britain: evidence from before the National Health Service'.

References

Chaney, P. and Drakeford, M. (2004) 'The primacy of ideology: social policy and the first term of the National Assembly for Wales', in N. Ellison, L. Bauld and M. Powell (eds) *Social Policy Review 16: Analysis and Debate in Social Policy 2004*, Bristol: The Policy Press, pp.121-42.

Deane, T. (1998) 'Late nineteenth-century philanthropy: the case of Louisa Twining', in A. Digby and J. Stewart (eds) *Gender, Health and Welfare*, London: Routledge.

Finlayson, G. (1990) 'A moving frontier: voluntarism and the state in British social welfare, 1911-1949', *Twentieth Century British History*, vol 1, no 2, pp 183-206.

Finlayson, G. (1994) *Citizen, State, and Social Welfare in Britain, 1830-1990*, Oxford: Oxford University Press.

Glennerster, H. (2003) *Understanding the Finance of Welfare*, Bristol: The Policy Press.

Gorsky, M., Mohan, J. and Willis, T. (2005) 'From hospital contributory schemes to health cash plans: the mutual ideal in British health care after 1948', *Journal of Social Policy*, vol 34, no 3, pp 447-67.

Harris, B. (2004) *The Origins of the British Welfare State: Social Welfare in England and Wales, 1800-1945*, Basingstoke: Palgrave Macmillan.

Harris, J. (1972) *Unemployment and Politics: A Study in English Social Policy*, Oxford: Oxford University Press.

Harris, J. (1990a) 'Society and the state in twentieth-century Britain', in F.M.L. Thompson (ed) *The Cambridge Social History of Britain: Volume III Social Agencies and Institutions*, Cambridge: Cambridge University Press, pp 63-117.

Harris, J. (1990b) 'Enterprise and welfare states', *Transactions of the Royal Historical Society*, 40, pp 175-95.

Harris, J. (1997) *William Beveridge: A Biography* (2nd edn), Oxford: Oxford University Press.

Hay, J.R. (1983) *The Origins of the Liberal Welfare Reforms* (2nd edn), London: Macmillan.

Horden, P. and Smith, R. (1998) 'Introduction', in P. Horden and R. Smith (eds) *The Locus of Care: Families, Communities, Institutions, and the Provision of Welfare since Antiquity*, London: Routledge, pp 1-18.

Le Grand, J. and Vizard, P. (1998) 'The National Health Service: crisis, change, or continuity?', in H. Glennerster and J. Hills (eds) *The State of Welfare: The Economics of Social Spending* (2nd edn), Oxford: Oxford University Press, pp 75-121.

Lewis, J. (1995) 'Family provision of health and welfare in the mixed economy of care in the late nineteenth and twentieth centuries', *Social History of Medicine*, vol 8, no 1, pp 1-16.

Lewis, J. (1999a) 'Reviewing the relationship between the voluntary sector and the state in Britain in the 1990s', *Voluntas*, vol 10, no 3, pp 255-70.

Lewis, J. (1999b) 'Voluntary and informal welfare', in R. Page and R. Silburn (eds) *British Social Welfare in the Twentieth Century*, London: Macmillan, pp 249-70.

Lewis, J. (1999c) 'The voluntary sector and the state in twentieth century Britain', in H. Fawcett and R. Lowe (eds) *Welfare Policy in Britain: The Road from 1945*, London: Macmillan, pp 52-68.

Lewis, J. (2005) 'New Labour's approach to the voluntary sector: independence and the meaning of partnership', *Social Policy and Society*, vol 4, no 2, pp 121-31.

Lowe, R. (2005) *The Welfare State in Britain since 1945* (3rd edn), Basingstoke: Palgrave Macmillan.

Macnicol, J. (1980) *The Movement for Family Allowances*, London: Heinemann.

McLaughlin, E. (2005) 'Governance and social policy in Northern Ireland (1999-2004): the devolution years and prospect', in M. Powell, L. Bauld and K. Clarke (eds) *Social Policy Review 17: Analysis and Debate in Social Policy, 2005*, Bristol: The Policy Press, pp 107-24.

Marshall, T.H. (1950) *Citizenship and Social Class*, Cambridge: Cambridge University Press.

Marwick, A. (1964) 'Middle opinion in the Thirties: planning, progress and political agreement', *English Historical Review*, LXXIX, pp 285-98.

Pedersen, S. (1993) *Family, Dependence, and the Origins of the Welfare State: Britain and France 1914-1945*, Cambridge: Cambridge University Press.

Prochaska, F. (1988) *The Voluntary Impulse: Philanthropy in Modern Britain*, London: Faber and Faber.

Prochaska, F. (1992) *Philanthropy and the Hospitals of London: The King's Fund 1897-1990*, Oxford: Oxford University Press.

Stewart, J. (1993) 'Ramsay MacDonald, the Labour Party, and child welfare, 1900-1914', *Twentieth Century British History*, vol 4, no 2, pp 105-25.

Stewart, J. (1995) 'Children, parents and the state: The Children Act 1908', *Children and Society*, vol 9, no 1, pp 90-9.

Stewart, J. (2004) *Taking Stock: Scottish Social Welfare after Devolution*, Bristol: The Policy Press.

Thane, P. (1978) 'Women and the Poor Law in Victorian and Edwardian Britain', *History Workshop Journal*, 6, pp 29-51.

Thane, P. (1990) 'Government and society in England and Wales, 1750-1914', in F.M.L. Thompson (ed) *The Cambridge Social History of Britain: Volume III Social Agencies and Institutions*, Cambridge: Cambridge University Press, pp 1-61.

Thane, P. (2000) *Old Age in English History: Past Experiences, Present Issues*, Oxford: Oxford University Press.

Titmuss, R. (1967) *Choice and 'The Welfare State'*, London: Fabian Society.

three

State welfare

Brian Lund

Overview

The role of the state in supplying welfare services is contested, with disputes relating to different views about the state's nature. The 'classic' welfare state, said to have existed between 1948 and 1976, was based on the notion that the state embodied 'the common good' and that the 'common good' was best achieved by direct welfare provision by central and local government. This idea was challenged in the late 1970s by a representation of the welfare state as a threat to liberty and a barrier to market efficiency. Local government lost many of its direct provider functions and 'quasi-markets' were created to deliver welfare services. New Labour's strategy has been to continue to promote supply diversity but to steer the varied range of social welfare suppliers towards achieving 'the public interest' via direct financial support, social investment, regulation, linking rights to obligations, targets, performance indicators and tax concessions.

Key concepts

State; common good • quasi-market • social investment • neighbourhood • social inclusion • catallaxy • communitarianism • public interest • governance

Introduction

In essence, the state is the organisation that successfully upholds the claim to the monopoly of the legitimate use of physical force in the enforcement of its order (Weber, 1979). Authority for monopolising the use of force – the basis of the taxation necessary to finance welfare provision – is usually located in a democratic process through which the state is seen as representing its citizens' 'collective will'. However, the scope of the state's legitimate power is contested, with some theorists arguing that the state should be confined to upholding law and order, enforcing contracts, providing defence and supplying a very basic minimum income (Hayek, 1960, 1976) and others supporting a more extensive state directly involved in enhancing citizen well-being and redistributing income (Rawls, 1971; Titmuss, 1971). Disputes about the state's function reflect varied interpretations of the state's nature. 'Minimum state' advocates regard the state as a vehicle for promoting individual freedom. They make a sharp distinction between 'private' and 'public' spheres. In contrast, supporters of a more extensive state view the state as the embodiment of the 'common good', wherein citizens find their sense of purpose (Offer, 2006). They see no clear difference between the 'private' and the 'public'.

New Labour has extended the state's role - state expenditure absorbed 43.6% of gross domestic product (GDP) in 2004 compared with 41.4% in 1997 (OECD, 2005) – but, rather than try to attain its goals through direct central or local government provision, it has attempted to steer individuals and organisations towards achieving government objectives. The 16 cells of **Figure 1.2** (see Chapter One) illustrate some of the possible interactions between the central state and the other agencies involved in welfare delivery. In this chapter, selected cells will be used to highlight how these relationships are changing.

State finance/state provision: central government

Although state finance is often associated with direct central state provision, even in the 'classic' welfare state, said to have existed between 1948 and 1976, only social security and healthcare fitted well into the central state finance/ direct central state provision category.

Social security

Rather than rely on direct state income transfers to promote social security, as was the case in the 'classic welfare state', New Labour's social protection strategy has a number of components (see **Box 3.1**). New Labour's objective is to reduce the direct role of the state in providing social security: pensions policy, for example, has been aimed at ensuring that state spending per pensioner in relation to the GDP is reduced by 10% by 2025 and 42% by 2050 (Secretary of State for Social Security and Minister for Welfare Reform, 1998). However, these diverse pathways to ensuring social protection have been accompanied by policy objectives set by the 'core executive' – the Treasury, the Cabinet Office and the Prime Minister's Office – in the form of targets. The Treasury's 2004 Spending Review included the following target for the Department for Work and Pensions:

> Halve the number of children in relative low-income households between 1998-99 and 2010-11, on the way to eradicating child poverty by 2020, joint with HM Treasury. (HM Treasury, 2004, p 1)

This target provides a benchmark for evaluating New Labour's strategy. When measured in relative terms – less than 60% of median income after housing costs, allowing for differences in household composition – the percentage of children in poverty declined from 33% in 1996/97 to 27% in 2004/05 (DWP, 2006, p 53), with a fall in the number of children in workless households making a significant contribution to this reduction (Babb et al, 2005). However, reducing child poverty is the only poverty target set by New Labour and, whereas pensioner poverty has declined – from 28% in 1996/97 to 17% in 2004/05 (DWP, 2006, p 92) – the poverty rate for working age adults without children has increased (Brewer et al, 2006).

Box 3.1: New Labour's social protection strategy

- Means-tested direct cash benefits to supplement established 'universal' benefits, for example, the pensioner tax credit to enhance the basic state pension.
- Supplementing earned income (for example, with the working tax credit), thereby providing incentives to find a job.
- Regulation of commercial pension schemes. For example, stakeholder pensions, provided by for-profit financial services companies, are subject to a management charge cap and must be run in the interests of their members.
- Wage regulation. For example, under the 1998 Minimum Wage Act, it is a criminal offence for employers not to pay a centrally determined minimum wage.
- The imposition of work obligations: New Labour's welfare-to-work programme explicitly imposes responsibilities on people without work to seek employment.
- The supply of information. As part of a programme of 'activation, education and information' (DWP, 2004, p v), pension forecasts are provided in the expectation that individual citizens will act in accordance with the forecast.

> • Redefining state responsibility. For example, an Inland Revenue/HM Treasury Green Paper (2002, p 2) declared that 'the concept of normal retirement age will vanish from tax legislation', indicating that 'retirement' will no longer be regarded as a specific contingency for which the state ought to make provision.

Healthcare

Unlike social security, designed to secure a national minimum income, the aim of the National Health Service (NHS) was to make optimum standards universal. So what Bevan meant when he said that the sound of a dropped bedpan in Tredegar would reverberate around the Palace of Westminster was that achieving equal standards in healthcare was the responsibility of Ministers accountable to Parliament and that such equality was the only way to guarantee high standards for everyone. "We have got to achieve," he said, "as nearly as possible a uniform standard of service for all – only with a national service can the state ensure that an equally good service is available everywhere" (Bevan, 1946, quoted in Thane, 1996, p 29). Nevertheless, the price of a national health service was to allow considerable professional autonomy, with resource distribution strongly influenced by professional networks interpreting need in accordance with the relative prestige of different branches of medicine.

This professional/bureaucratic healthcare delivery model was unsettled in the late 1980s when a healthcare quasi-market was introduced. The NHS was split into purchasers and providers, with the providers competing for contracts issued by purchasers – general practitioner (GP) fund-holders and health authorities. In opposition, New Labour criticised this division because not all patients belonged to fund-holding general practices, hence a two-tier NHS had been created and the purchaser–provider split, with the involvement of commercial organisations as providers, was 'back-door privatisation'. In office, New Labour modified the NHS quasi-market in the direction of 'partnerships' between purchasers and providers via 'soft', 'relational' and 'network-based' contracts and compacts (Bovaird, 2004; Fyfe, 2005), with the central state shaping the system via performance indicators and targets. GP funding was replaced by larger Primary Care Trusts that commissioned 'secondary' care and directly employed health visitors, midwives and community nurses. However, towards the end of its first term, 'exit' politics (see **Box 3.2**) began to feature more strongly in New Labour's modernisation programme (Newman and Vidler, 2006). In 2004, the Prime Minister, Tony Blair, said: "We are proposing to put an entirely different dynamic in place to drive our public services: one where the service will be driven not by the managers but by the user – the patient, the parent, the pupil and law-abiding citizen" (Blair, 2004). New Labour's 2005 Manifesto (Labour Party, 2005 p 63) gave an assurance that "by the end of 2008, patients whose GPs refer them for an operation will be able to choose from any hospital that can provide that operation to NHS medical and financial standards".

> **Box 3.2:** *Exit, Voice and Loyalty*
>
> In *Exit, Voice and Loyalty*, Hirschman (1972) made a distinction between 'exit' and 'voice' as ways in which consumers can influence an organisation's behaviour. 'Exit' involves taking custom elsewhere so that the supplier eventually goes out of business. 'Voice' involves complaining to the management about the quality of its product in the hope that it will improve. If, over time, an organisation has fostered loyalty to itself from its customers, the exercise of 'exit' politics will be delayed as customers allow time for their 'voice' to have an impact.

After the 2005 General Election, 'contestability', a euphemism for competition, began to feature in New Labour's references to the NHS. GPs would be encouraged to take part in 'practice-based commissioning', a new term for GP fund-holding, the supply of 'independent treatment centres' would be increased and a national tariff system for supplier payments – with funds gravitating to the best-performing organisations – would be set up (DH, 2006). In effect, a new quasi-market – the state supplies the cloth but the tailoring is bespoke – started to be constructed, in which NHS Foundation Hospitals would play an important role. The 2003 Health and Social Care Act established NHS Foundation Hospitals (or Trusts) as independent public benefit corporations modelled on diluted cooperative and mutual traditions. The majority of their governors are elected by people invited to become Trust 'subscribers' and the Trusts have a degree of independence from the NHS 'command–and–control' system. They can accept patients from a variety of purchasers according to legally enforceable contracts.

State finance/state provision: local government

It is now conventional to classify local government as 'state' because its members are elected by universal franchise, it has statutory duties related to the local 'public good' and it possesses the power to impose local taxation. However, local government has a long tradition of independence from the central state and its history contains episodes of bitter local/central conflict, most recently in the 1980s when several prominent New Labour Ministers cut their political teeth in the clash between 'local socialism' and 'market liberalism' (Boddy and Fudge, 1984).

In the 'classic' welfare state, local government had an extensive role in direct welfare provision: it supplied education at all levels from pre-school to polytechnics, owned over six million council houses and offered personal social services and domiciliary healthcare. In making this provision, it exercised considerable autonomy (Griffith, 1966), but, over the past 25 years, local government has lost many of its direct provider functions. As Blair has said:

> The days of the all-purpose local authority that planned and delivered everything are gone. They are finished. Local authorities will still deliver some services but their distinctive leadership role will be to weave and knit together the contribution of the various local stakeholders. (Blair, 1998, p 13)

Moreover, what remains of the local government provider role has been subject to more intensive central management. The 1999 Local Government Act substituted the competitive tendering introduced by the Conservatives with the requirement that every local authority "must make arrangements to secure continuous improvement in the way in which its functions are exercised, having regard to a combination of economy, efficiency and effectiveness" (Local Government Act, 1999, Section 3.1) and gave central government the power to set performance targets and standards on which 'best value' would be assessed. Local government service provision is now surrounded by centrally determined targets and performance indicators that must be absorbed into various local strategies and brought together in a comprehensive performance assessment (see **Box 3.3**).

Box 3.3: Examples of New Labour's performance indicators

Social service performance indicators include:
- stability of placements of children looked after by reference to the percentage of children looked after on 31 March in any year with three or more placements during the year (BV49);
- intensive home care per 1,000 population aged 65 or over (BV53);
- percentage of items of equipment delivered within seven working days (BV56);
- the number of adults and older people receiving direct payments per 100,000 population aged 18 years or over (BV201).

Housing performance indicators include:
- the number of private sector vacant dwellings that are returned into occupation or demolished during 2003/04 as a direct result of action by the local authority (BV 64);
- local authority rent collection and arrears: proportion of rent collected (BV 66a);

- satisfaction of tenants of council housing with the overall service provided by their landlord, with results further broken down by (i) black and minority ethnic and (ii) non-black and minority ethnic tenants (BV 74);
- the average length of stay in (i) bed and breakfast accommodation and (ii) hostel accommodation of households which include dependent children or a pregnant woman (BV 183). (Department for Communities and Local Government, 2006a)

For some commentators, this detailed intervention has meant the erosion of local democracy to extinction point. Local government has been declared a 'policy-free zone' (Maile and Hoggett, 2001, p 512) and compared to a branch of a big retailer (Stoker, 2004, p 107), and the Audit Commission (2005, p 2) has claimed that "council housing might more accurately be labelled 'national' housing".

State finance/market provision

Market provision involves service delivery through the mechanisms of supply and demand. Whereas privatisation is a necessary condition for market forces to operate, full market provision must also involve competition for customers between suppliers based on the search for profit to be distributed between shareholders. Customers pay the market price for their service, but the state may assist their consumption either by tax concessions or direct consumer subsidies.

In the 1950s, the Conservative Party attempted to stimulate market forces in welfare provision by enhanced existing tax concessions and introducing new ones. In addition, 'contracting out' of the contributions necessary to receive the state earnings related pension was allowed if a person contributed to an approved occupational pension or, under a scheme introduced by the Conservatives in 1988, to a 'personal pension' supplied by a private pension provider. In the pensions arena, this tax policy contributed to the 'mixed economy of welfare', but, because it also reflected the 'social divisions of welfare', it produced a "highly unequal current pensioner income distribution" (Pensions Commission, 2005, p 2). Although some tax expenditures, for example, tax relief on mortgage interest, have been abolished the 'fiscal welfare state' remains extensive. The Inland Revenue (2005) has estimated that, in 2004/05, 'tax expenditures' – revenue forgone by tax concessions – were worth £61 billion, although this estimate needs to be treated with caution because it includes various tax credits, somewhat curiously treated in Treasury accounting procedures as tax expenditures rather than the direct state payments that most of them are. Housing benefit is an example of direct state finance to consumers to enable them to afford private provision. The White Paper *Housing: The*

Government's Proposals (Department of the Environment, 1987) signalled the government's intention to allow all rents – local authority, housing association and private landlord – to rise to market levels, with housing benefit, paid on a means-tested basis, allowing low-income households to afford these higher rents. Thus, housing benefit would become an entitlement that tenants could spend with a variety of landlords, each charging a market rent. In the event, only rents in the private landlord sector were allowed to increase to the full market level. Today there are two different sectors in the rental market: private landlords who charge market rents and social landlords who offer accommodation at 'sub-market' rents.

State finance/voluntary provision

Direct service provision by local government has been replaced by commercial provision underpinned by state assistance and by the voluntary sector, that is, non-profit, non-elected, single-purpose organisations. Bryce (2005) suggests that such 'non-profits' are characterised by their 'cognitive social assets' – their social purposes – and by their 'principal-agency' relationship with the state. Housing is a salient example of the way the state interacts with such 'non-profit' organisations. During the past 10 years, more local authority houses have been transferred to the voluntary sector than to private individuals under the Right to Buy. Given that New Labour's vehicles for NHS and educational reform – Foundation Trusts, Trust Schools and City Academies – bear a striking similarity to housing associations, the chosen agents for the receipt of local authority houses, stock transfer will be examined at length.

Stock transfer from local authorities to housing associations started in the late 1980s as a local government initiative. Southern rural districts started to transfer their houses to specially created housing associations in an attempt to prevent the loss of social housing in their areas and to circumvent restrictions on capital spending: new housing association tenants did not have the Right to Buy and housing associations were not subject to central borrowing constraints. Under New Labour, transfer was linked to the achievement of the decent homes target, which stated that all social sector houses should be upgraded to a specified standard by 2010. Stock transfer, plus the concentration of new-build social housing in the housing association sector, has transformed the formal ownership of the social housing stock. In the early 1980s, local government supplied 95% of the social housing in England. By 2004, the balance was 354 local authorities with 2,335,000 homes and 2,000 'registered social landlords' - mainly housing associations - with 1,665,000 dwellings (DCLG, 2006b). In 2005, private developers were allowed to bid for government grants to build 'affordable' housing, thereby extending the 'mixed economy' in the supply of social housing.

Social housing now appears to be the most pluralistic welfare sphere and a potential model for a more 'mixed economy of welfare' in other welfare domains. However, the stock transfer process has been accompanied by significant changes in the central state's regulatory activities - as the voluntary sector has expanded into the local state's domain, the central state has permeated the voluntary sector. Resources for the registered social landlord sector are distributed by unelected Regional Housing Boards dominated by central government officials. Individual rent levels are determined by a nationally set formula, housing associations are inspected by the Audit Commission and their everyday activities are directed towards achieving centrally set targets and performance indicators. As Malpass (2000, p 259) has stated, housing associations "are little more than agents of the state and the voluntary element has been reduced to marginal and largely symbolic importance, providing a fig-leaf for those who really hold the power".

State finance/informal 'neighbourhood' provision

New Labour's review of the Conservatives' area-focused programmes reached the conclusion that they had been ineffective, in part because "community commitment had not been harnessed" (SEU, 1998, p 4). This diagnosis was reflected in a new initiative, New Deal for Communities (NDC), launched in 1998, that concentrated on nurturing social capital - the collective value of all the social networks and the inclinations that arise from these networks to do things for each other. The NDC emphasis on local involvement in decision making to generate social capital reflected an attempt to create a new level of governance – the neighbourhood. As yet, there is a dearth of information on NDC outcomes, but an early official evaluation identified a number of concerns. These included community engagement costs in terms of "burn-out of key local community players; intra-community tensions; the demands placed on the time and resources of NDC employees and agencies" (ODPM, 2003, p 1), indicating that state attempts to harness neighbourhood social capital may founder on the diversity of the social capital located in a particular district. Nevertheless, the idea of neighbourhood has retained a central place in New Labour's social policies because enhanced returns are expected from combining neighbourhood investment and community involvement. New Labour's 2005 Manifesto promised enhanced powers for neighbourhood governance, including community funds for neighbourhoods to spend on local priorities, the ability to own community assets such as recreation facilities and powers to trigger action in response to antisocial behaviour.

Market finance/state provision

The capital and revenue finance necessary for central and local state expenditure is obtained by taxation and by borrowing from the private sector. The problems generated by Labour's 'tax and spend' policy in the 1970s, when loans had to be secured from the International Monetary Fund, prompted New Labour to adopt a 'prudent' approach to the Public Sector Borrowing Requirement. Two rules were set out to govern state borrowing:

> The golden rule states that, on average over the economic cycle, the Government should borrow only to invest and not to fund current expenditure. So to accord with the rule, the average surplus on current budget over the cycle should be positive....

> The sustainable investment rule requires that public sector net debt, as a percentage of GDP, will be held, over the economic cycle, at a stable and prudent level. (HM Treasury, 2005, p 1)

These rules leave the Chancellor ample room for manoeuvre but, in the long term, they impose constraints on public borrowing to maintain the confidence of the financial institutions in the Chancellor's economic management. One reason for the transfer of local government functions to the voluntary sector is that voluntary sector borrowing does not count as part of the public sector borrowing requirement. The Private Finance Initiative (PFI) is another way round this borrowing constraint.

PFI incorporates a variety of schemes, but the basic idea is that a private supplier enters into a contract with a public body to build and/or operate a facility (for example, a school, hospital, or rented houses). The private organisation supplies the finance – hence the capital spending and other up-front costs of a project do not count as part of the public sector borrowing requirement in the year it starts to operate – whereas the public body specifies the nature of the facility and leases it, usually over a 30-year period. The initiative reflects the complexity of state–public relationships, as the management of a PFI facility is private but financial guarantees are made by the state that specify the objectives of the provision. PFI could equally well be classified as state finance/private provision.

PFI conveniently allows the state to 'live now and pay later', but it also generates 'public–private partnerships' and provides the opportunity to introduce a wider variety of management styles into the public sector. It has become a major way to finance capital projects, with total annual payments for PFI initiatives signed by 2003 amounting to £6.7 billion (Emmerson et al, 2004). Given the private sector management of PFI facilities and that PFI contracts have first call on 'commissioner' resources, the initiative has major implications for long-term social service governance.

The state and the redistribution of income

A distinguishing characteristic of the state is its ability to impose compulsory taxation and use the resources for its chosen purposes. In raising and spending resources, the state has the capacity to redistribute real incomes and, according to some authors, this redistributive role – directed to promoting social justice by favouring the 'least advantaged' – is more important than whether the state is involved in direct service provision (Rawls, 1971). Since the early 1960s, the government has attempted to estimate the redistributive impact of the tax/ benefit system. Households are divided into five – sometimes 10 – categories according to equivalised 'initial' income, that is, income from market transactions such as employment and investment, taking into account the composition of each household. Cash benefits are then added to give 'gross' income and direct taxes are deducted to produce an estimate of 'disposable' income. At the next stage, indirect taxes are subtracted to produce 'post-tax income' and the value of benefits in kind, such as education and healthcare, are then added to give 'final income'. Under New Labour, inequalities at all stages of the distributive process have remained broadly stable at the level inherited from the Conservatives in 1997 (Jones, 2006), indicating that, as yet, New Labour's 'social investment' state has had no impact on inequality.

New Labour/New State?

Ranelagh (1991, p ix), in his account of Margaret Thatcher's first visit to the Conservative Research Centre after she became Party leader, states that "… the new Party leader reached into her briefcase and took out a book. It was Friedrich von Hayek's *The Constitution of Liberty*. Interrupting our pragmatist, she held the book up for all of us to see. 'This,' she said sternly, 'is what we believe', and banged Hayek down on the table".

Hayek's work supplied the ideas that informed the policies of the Thatcher/ Major governments, but there is no similar publication through which New Labour's ideology can be identified. Indeed, it has been said that New Labour is 'pragmatic' (Shaw, 2004), uses different catchphrases – 'stakeholder society', 'communitarianism', 'Third Way', 'social exclusion' – at different times (Hindmoor, 2005) and is essentially concerned with what works in winning elections (Stoker, 2004). However, although there is no contemporary synthesis of the various elements in New Labour's programmes – its gurus, Giddens and Etzioni, are sociologists interested in identifying trends, not political theorists setting out a normative order (Hale, 2004) – it is possible to identify such a blend.

Social inclusion

'Social inclusion' is about the distribution of the human and social capital necessary for an inclusive society based on promoting equal opportunities rather than equality of outcome. Promoting social inclusion via social investment features as objective 1 in the targets set in the 2004 Spending Review for all the relevant departments of state:

- "... reduce inequalities between the level of development achieved by children in the 20% most disadvantaged areas and the rest of England" (Objective 1: Department for Education and Skills, HM Treasury, 2004, p 11);
- "Substantially reduce mortality rates by 2010: from heart disease and stroke related disease by at least 40% in people under 75, with at least 40% reduction in the inequalities gap between the fifth of areas with the worst health and deprivation indicators and the population as a whole" (Objective 1: Department of Health, HM Treasury, 2004, p13);
- "Tackle social exclusion and deliver neighbourhood renewal ... in particular narrowing the gap in health, education, crime, worklessness, housing and liveability outcomes between the most deprived areas and the rest of England, with measurable improvement by 2010" (Objective 1: Office of the Deputy Prime Minister, HM Treasury, 2004, p 17).

Obligations and rights

New Labour believes that, in the past, there has been too much emphasis on rights and therefore it has been reluctant to create new statutory entitlements to scarce resources. Indeed, some existing entitlements have been abolished, for example, the right to a home improvement grant if the claimant's property is below a certain standard and household income is below a specified threshold. Such rights have, in part, been substituted by targets and performance indictors set by the 'core executive'. The abolition of the right to a home improvement grant, for example, was replaced by the target, set by the Office of the Deputy Prime Minister, that 70% of vulnerable householders in private housing sector would have a decent home by 2010. Thus, in effect, targets and performance indicators represent a set of citizenship expectations. These expectations have been accompanied by the attachment of obligations to the receipt of state-financed services in the communitarian belief that, via 'conditional welfare', civil virtues will become internalised by citizens because the state has expressed its formal disapproval of such uncivil behaviour (see **Box 3.4**).

Box 3.4: New Labour: examples of attaching obligations to rights

- Work-seeking behaviour is expected from disabled people if, under the proposals contained in *A New Deal for Welfare: Empowering People to Work*, (DWP, 2005), they are to obtain the same benefit level provided by incapacity benefit.
- Sure Start maternity grant can only be claimed if the applicant can demonstrate that she has received advice on the health needs and general welfare of her new baby and, if the claim is made before the baby is born, on maternal health. There is a certificate on the back of the claim form to certify that such action has been taken that must be signed by a health service professional.
- The 2002 Homelessness Act contains a clause that restricts the rights of a homeless person to housing if "he, or a member of his household, has been guilty of unacceptable behaviour serious enough to make him unsuitable to be the tenant of the local authority ..." (2002 Homelessness Act, Section 2C)

Supply diversity

If the 'core executive' specifies key objectives and if these key objectives are translated into targets that permeate downwards through the agencies responsible for implementation, the form of delivery – central state, local government, for-profit companies or non-profit voluntary organisations – is irrelevant to achieving the state's objectives. Indeed, state aims may be more easily attained by the incorporation of diverse suppliers into the 'big tent' of the state. The 'public interest' can be secured without public ownership and the challenge is how to combine 'knightly' public interest motivations with the self-interest of the 'knave' (Le Grand, 2003). Effectiveness in delivering central targets based on 'evidence' (Cabinet Office, 1999) becomes the main criterion for selecting participants in welfare delivery.

Conclusion

New Labour's policy lodestars - social inclusion, rights linked to obligations and supplier diversity – have a marked similarity to the 'New Liberalism' that influenced the 1906-14 Liberal Reforms. Based on British Idealism – "the dominant philosophy in Britain during the last decade of the 19th and beginning of the 20th century" (Panagakou, 2005, p 1) – the 'New Liberalism' emphasised attaching rights to obligations. Rights, so the New Liberals argued, are acquired by sharing a common purpose with others and hence cannot be divorced from the obligations involved in achieving that common purpose. This emphasis on the 'common good' also permeated prescriptions on the agencies to be involved in welfare delivery. Voluntary organisations – especially 'mutuals' of people both giving and receiving services – would provide the contexts within which citizens could internalise a sense of their interdependence. The state was the ultimate embodiment of this interdependence and its role was not to produce greater equality of outcome as desired by 'socialists' but to 'hinder hindrances' (Green, 1881, p 73) to a more cohesive society by investment in human and social capital.

Like the 'New Liberalism', New Labour has represented the state not as a specific set of institutions but as the pursuit the 'public interest' through social investment via a diversity of welfare suppliers. This is not a restricted state – it is an extensive state that, via its regulatory power, its ability to raise and distribute resources and its promulgation of 'citizenship discourse', permeates civil society at all levels.

Two problems in applying this concept of the state to contemporary welfare delivery have been identified. Some commentators have doubted the ability of the 'new public sector managerialism', operating in a 'mixed economy of welfare', to deliver the public interest, a diagnosis usually associated with 'governance' theory. 'Governance' theory argues that power has drained away from the central state externally to 'global' forces and internally to regional and local provider networks whose activities in a 'differentiated polity' are difficult to control (Rhodes, 1997). The globalisation thesis argues that international capital flows and trade liberalisation have forced governments to cut public expenditure and deregulate labour markets in order to make their countries more competitive. Thus, there is a convergence towards smaller welfare states, with each state forced to 'go with the grain' of 'global forces'. However, recent research (Castles, 2004; Navarro et al, 2004; Schettkat, 2005) has cast doubt on this thesis by identifying growth in welfare states over the alleged globalisation period, a lack of convergence and a strong political influence in countries where welfare states were changed.

The 'internal' dimension of 'governance' theory argues that, in 'steering' rather than 'rowing', the state depends on other agencies with the capacity to dilute the public interest. Thus, for example, it has been argued that housing associations, in concentrating on the performance indicators of minimising rent arrears and reducing antisocial behaviour, are evicting tenants and thereby passing their problems to other agencies (Sprigings, 2002). However, this view tends to underplay state financial power exercised via the 'top-down' system of targets, performance indicators and inspection. Managerialism is a technique – a means to steer 'rowers' towards a destination (Osborne and Gaebler, 1993) – and it can be applied to whatever objectives the central state so chooses. As Finlayson (2003, p 112) has stated: "Certainly a regime of assessment measures can change the culture and values of an organisation. But it cannot decide what to change those values to. That is a political decision". Critiques of a 'target culture' should not be confused with critiques of the chosen targets: if the 'core executive' wants to focus housing association attention on the prevention of eviction, it can do so by setting new targets and imposing financial penalties on the associations that do not meet their targets. A strong 'public interest' state would generate an extensive target and performance indicator portfolio, monitor them and impose financial sanctions on underachieving 'knaves'.

Second, there is the issue of how to reconcile choice and competition with the public interest. Blair has acknowledged that the identification of the state with the 'common good' limits the individual consumer choice that New Labour perceives as a growing expectation of the electorate (Hindmoor, 2005). Centrally determined targets, set in accordance with the public interest, impose a 'top-down' pattern on outcomes that is difficult to reconcile with the outcomes of choice as mediated through competition and the diverse social purposes of the voluntary sector (Driver, 2005). On the other hand, choice as reflected in market outcomes can undermine the public interest. Hospital choice, for example, reduces the collective interest in ensuring that the hospital serving a particular locality offers a high-quality service by allowing more informed consumers to 'exit' (Hirschman, 1972). Moreover internal markets limit the scope for inter-agency cooperative activity to achieve a common goal and magnify the possibility of 'cream skimming', that is, accepting only low-risk consumers to maximise agency performance. This 'cream-skimming' dilemma was reflected in the debate surrounding the White Paper, *Higher Standards, Better Schools For All: More Choice for Parents and Pupils* (DfES, 2005). The White Paper sought to enhance school autonomy by allowing schools, in future to be known as 'Trust' schools, to be able to set their own admissions policies subject to 'having regard to' the School Admissions Code of Practice set out in the 1998 School Standards and Framework Act. However, the Select Committee on Education and Skills (2006), the parliamentary committee that scrutinises government education policy, believed that such autonomy would lead to selection by income and ability unless admissions policy was more tightly regulated. This balance between the outcomes produced by welfare pluralism and those desired by advocates of the 'public interest' is at the heart of disputes about the state's role in welfare supply. Hayek (1976) identified markets as generating a 'catallaxy' - a spontaneous order without a collective purpose and hence without notions of social justice or the common good. However, if the state is seen as promoting the 'public interest', the principal–agency relationship involved in 'welfare pluralism' will be accompanied by a strong, regulatory state that, in essence, may not be different from the state as provider – a role often identified as the hallmark of the 'classic welfare state'.

Summary

- The state's role in social welfare supply is contested, with disputes relating to different views about the state's nature.
- There are a range of possible interactions between the central state and the other agencies involved in supplying welfare. In the 'classic' welfare state, each welfare domain – social security, healthcare, education, housing and personal social services – reflected different combinations of relationships.
- In the past 25 years, quasi-markets have been created to deliver welfare services and local government has lost many direct provider functions.
- The central state is increasingly 'steering' rather than 'rowing' the welfare system.
- The 'social investment' state now focuses on preventing the contingencies that generate the need for welfare provision.
- New Labour's new welfare 'settlement' involves encouraging non-state provision, promoting civic responsibility and empowering 'consumer-citizens' to determine the supply pattern.
- This detachment of the state from the direct delivery of welfare services has been accompanied by attempts to achieve social objectives via direct financial support, tax concessions, regulation, targets and performance indicators.

Questions for discussion

- Should schools be improved by 'exit' politics or by 'voice' and 'loyalty' politics?
- Is there a rationale for the provision of social services by local government?
- Are 'choice' and 'social inclusion' contradictory goals?
- Which services might 'neighbourhood' government supply?

Visit the websites of the following think-tanks. What is the role of the state endorsed by each think-tank?

- The Adam Smith Institute
- Catalyst
- Civitas
- Institute of Economic Affairs
- Institute for Public Policy Research

Further reading

The establishment of the National Assembly for Wales, the Scottish Parliament and the Northern Ireland Assembly in 1999 has produced a more devolved state structure in the United Kingdom. **McEwen and Parry (2005)** discuss the implications of devolution.

The State: Theories and Issues, edited by **Hay et al (2006)**, sets out various state theories that can be applied to social welfare.

Reinventing Government: How the Entrepreneurial Spirit is Transforming the Public Sector by **Osborne and Gaebler (1993**) supplies the rationale of New Labour's organisational reforms.

A More Equal Society?, edited by **Hills and Stewart (2005)**, examines the impact of New Labour's strategy in terms of poverty, inequality and social exclusion.

References

Audit Commission (2005) *Financing Council Housing*, London: Audit Commission.

Babb, P., Martin, J. and Haezewindt, P. (2005) *Focus on Social Inequalities, 2004 Edition*, London: Office for National Statistics.

Blair, T. (1998) *Leading the Way: A New Vision for Local Government*, London: Institute for Public Policy Research.

Blair, T. (2004) *Choice, Excellence and Equality*, Labour Party (www.labour.org.uk/news/tbpublicservices0604).

Boddy, M. and Fudge, C. (1984) *Local Socialism?*, Basingstoke: Palgrave Macmillan.

Bovaird, T. (2004) 'Public–private: from contested concepts to prevalent practice', *International Review of the Administrative Sciences*, vol 70, no 2, pp 199-215.

Brewer, M., Goodman, A., Shaw, J. and Sibieta, L. (2006) *Poverty and Inequality in Britain 2006*, London, Institute for Fiscal Studies.

Bryce, H.J. (2005) *Players in the Public Policy Process: Nonprofits as Social Capital and Agents*, New York, NY: Palgrave Macmillan.

Cabinet Office (1999) *Modernising Government*, Cm 4310, London: Cabinet Office.

Castles, F.G. (2004) *The Future of the Welfare State: Crisis Myths and Crisis Realities*, Oxford: Oxford University Press.

DCLG (Department for Communities and Local Government) (2006a) *Best Value Performance Indicators* (www.communities.gov.uk/index.asp?id=1136106).

DCLG (2006b) *Housing Statistics* (www.odpm.gov.uk/pub/10/Table104Excel37Kb_id1156010.xls).

DoE (Department of the Environment) (1987) *Housing: The Government's Proposals*, Cm 214, London: HMSO.

DfES (Department for Education and Skills) (2005) *Higher Standards, Better Schools For All: More Choice for Parents and Pupils*, London: DfES.

DH (Department of Health) (2006) *The NHS in England: The Operating Framework for 2006/7*, London: DH.

DWP (Department for Work and Pensions) (2004) *Simplicity, Security and Choice: Informed Choices for Working and Saving*, Cm 6111, London: The Stationery Office.

DWP (2005) *A New Deal for Welfare: Empowering People to Work*, London: DWP.

DWP (2006) 'Households below average incomes: 1994/5 to 2004/5' (www.dwp.gov.uk/asd/hbai.asp).

Driver, S. (2005) 'Welfare after Thatcherism: New Labour and social democratic politics', in M. Powell, K. Clarke and L. Bauld (eds) *Social Policy Review 17*, Bristol: The Policy Press, pp 255-73.

Emmerson, C., Frayne, C. and Love, S. (2004) *A Survey of Public Spending in the UK: Briefing Note No 23*, London: Institute for Fiscal Studies.

Finlayson, A. (2003) *Making Sense of New Labour*, London: Lawrence and Wishart.

Fyfe, N.F. (2005) 'Making space for "neo-communitarianism"? The third sector, state and civil society in the UK', *Antipode*, vol 37, issue 3, pp 536-57.

Green, T.H. (1881) *Liberal Legislation and Freedom of Contract*, London: Simpkin Marshall.

Griffith, J.A.G. (1966) *Central Departments and Local Authorities*, London: Allen and Unwin.

Hale, S. (2004) 'The Communitarian "Philosophy" of New Labour', in S. Hale, W. Leggett and L. Martell (eds) *The Third Way: Criticisms, Futures, Alternatives*, Manchester: Manchester University Press, pp 87-108.

Hay, C., Lister, M. and Marsh, D. (eds) (2006) *The State: Theories and Issues*, Basingstoke: Palgrave Macmillan.

Hayek, F.V. (1960) *The Constitution of Liberty*, Routledge: London.

Hayek, F.V. (1976) *Law, Legislation and Liberty*, Routledge: London.

Hills, J. and Stewart, K. (eds) (2005) *A More Equal Society?: New Labour, Poverty, Inequality and Exclusion*, Bristol: The Policy Press.

Hindmoor, A. (2005) 'Public policy: targets and choice', *Parliamentary Affairs*, vol 58, no 2, pp 272-86.

Hirschman, A.O. (1972) *Exit, Voice and Loyalty: Responses to Decline in Firms, Organizations and States*, Harvard, MA: Harvard University Press.

HM Treasury (2004) '2004 Spending Review: Public Service Agreements 2005-2008' (www.hm-treasury.gov.uk/spending_review/spend_sr04/psa/spend_sr04_psaindex.cfm).

HM Treasury (2005) 'Fiscal policy' (www.hm-treasury.gov.uk/documents/uk_economy/fiscal_policy/ukecon_fisc_index.cfm).

Inland Revenue/HM Treasury (2002) *Simplifying the Taxation of Pensions: Increasing Choice and Flexibility for All*, London: HMSO.

Inland Revenue (2005) 'Tax expenditures and structural reliefs' (www.hmrc.gov.uk/stats/tax_expenditures/table1-5.pdf).

Jones, F. (2006) 'The effects of taxes and benefits on household income, 2004-05', *Economic Trends*, no 630, London: Stationery Office, pp 1-47.

Labour Party (2005) *Britain Forward not Back*, London: Labour Party.

Le Grand, J. (2003) *Motivation, Agency and Public Policy: Of Knights and Knaves, Pawns and Queens*, Oxford: Oxford University Press.

McEwen, N and Parry, R. (2005) 'Devolution and the preservation of the United Kingdom welfare state', in N. McEwen and L. Moreno (eds) *The Territorial Politics of Welfare*, Abington: Routledge, pp 41-62.

Maile, S. and Hoggett, P. (2001) 'Best value and the politics of pragmatism', *Policy & Politics*, vol 29, no 4, pp 509-16.

Malpass, P. (2000) *Housing Associations and Housing Policy: A Historical Perspective*, Basingstoke: Macmillan.

Navarro, V., Schmitt, J. and Astudillo, J. (2004) 'Is globalisation undermining the welfare state?' *Cambridge Journal of Economics*, vol 28, no 1, pp 133-52.

Newman, J. and Vidler, E. (2006) 'Discriminating customers, responsible patients, empowered users: consumerism and the modernisation of health care', *Journal of Social Policy*, vol 35, no 2, pp 193-209.

Offer, J. (2006) *An Intellectual History of British Social Policy: Idealism versus Non-idealism*, Bristol: The Policy Press.

ODPM (Office of the Deputy Prime Minister) (2003) 'New Deal for Communities: Annual Review, 2001/2' (www.neighbourhood.gov.uk/docs/NDC_Ann_Review_2001-2.pdf).

OECD (Organisation for Economic Co-operation and Development) (2005) *Economic Outlook*, vol 2004/2, no 76, December, Paris: OECD.

Osborne, D. and Gaebler, T. (1993) *Reinventing Government: How the Entrepreneurial Spirit is Transforming the Public Sector*, Harlow: Addison Wesley.

Panagakou, S. (2005) 'The political philosophy of the British idealists', *British Journal of Politics and International Relations*, vol 7, no 1, pp 1-4.

Pensions Commission (2005) *A New Pension Settlement for the Twenty-First Century: The Second Report of the Pensions Commission; Executive Summary*, London: Pensions Commission.

Ranelagh, J. (1991) *Thatcher's People*, London: Fontana.

Rawls, J. (1971) *A Theory of Justice*, Oxford: Oxford University Press.

Rhodes, R.A.W. (1997) *Understanding Governance: Policy, Networks, Governance, Reflexivity and Accountability*, Buckingham: Open University Press.

Schettkat, R. (2005) 'Is labor market regulation at the root of unemployment?: the case of Germany and the Netherlands', *Fighting Unemployment*, February, pp 262-84.

Secretary of State for Social Security and Minister for Welfare Reform (1998) *New Ambitions for Our Country: A New Contract for Welfare*, Cm 3805, London: HMSO.

Select Committee on Education and Skills (2006) *The Schools White Paper: Higher Standards, Better Schools for All First Report of Session 2005-06: Vol. 1 Report, Together with Formal Minutes: House of Commons papers 633-I*, London: House of Commons.

Shaw, E. (2004) 'What matters is what works', in S. Hale, W. Leggett and L. Martell (eds), *The Third Way and Beyond: Criticisms, Futures, Alternatives*, Manchester: Manchester University Press.

SEU (Social Exclusion Unit) (1998) *Bringing Britain Together: A National Policy for Neighbourhood Renewal*, London: Cabinet Office.

Sprigings, N. (2002) 'Delivering public services under the new public management: the case of public housing', *Public Money and Management*, October-December, vol 22, no 4, pp 11-17.

Stoker, G. (2004) *Transforming Local Governance: From Thatcherism to New Labour*, Basingstoke: Palgrave Macmillan.

Thane, P. (1996) *Foundations of the Welfare State*, London: Longman.

Titmuss, R. (1971) *The Gift Relationship: From Human Blood to Social Policy*, London: Allen and Unwin.

Weber, M. (1979) *Economy and Society: An Outline of Interpretative Sociology*, Berkeley, CA: University of California Press.

four

Private welfare

Mark Drakeford

Overview

Welfare services in the United Kingdom have always been provided through a mixture of public and private organisations. The major changes to be traced during the 20th century and into the present lie in the shifting balance between the different forms of provision, in terms of ownership, finance and regulation. This chapter concentrates on the rise of privatisation and marketisation during the Thatcher governments of the 1980s, and the way in which these policy approaches have been adapted during the New Labour era. It traces the way in which welfare responsibilities that were previously accepted by the state have been transferred out of the public sector, and into the hands of individuals, new forms of provision and conventional private companies. In doing so, it traces the ways in which competing claims to advance the public interest depend on some complex interactions between issues of ownership, different models of funding provision and the role of regulation.

Key concepts

Privatisation • marketisation • commodification • ownership • responsibility • choice • consumerism • equality • finance • profit • regulation • inspection • mixed economy

Introduction

This chapter deals with the practical application of privatisation and marketisation to the provision of social welfare services. In an increasingly plural pattern of welfare provision, the commercial end of the mixed economy has moved from the margin to the mainstream of government thinking. The shift is well summed up by Henry Pitman, chief executive of the consultancy and professional support services company, Tribal – an organisation that did not exist in 2000 but which, by 2005, employed 2000 staff, with a turnover of £230 million, almost all of which is government money used to deliver public services through the private sector. Quoted in a *Financial Times* front-page story – 'Private share of state sector soars' (April 2005) – Mr Pitman traced the change in this way:

> There was plenty of out-sourcing in the 1980s and 1990s, but it was chiefly blue-collar jobs: cleaning, catering, street clearing and bin emptying, the things that people did not care about.

> But in the last few years, it has moved into the core areas: schools, failing local education authorities and independent treatment centres. Nothing is off-limits now, and the potential for the private sector is massive.

Just how massive was demonstrated in a 2005 report from the information and outsourcing analyst, Kable, which estimated that by 2007/08 private and voluntary sector bodies could deliver up to 18% of all public services in Britain, a growth of almost 80% over a three-year period (Kable, 2005). Timmins (2005) uses figures from another firm of analysts, Laing and Buisson, to illustrate the impact of this shift in the field of social welfare. They suggest that, by 2005, some 56% of all adult and children's personal social services were being provided by the private and voluntary sectors, a figure that had risen from 40% in 1997. In terms of the different forms of ownership set out in **Figure 1.1** of Chapter One, therefore, the focus here is firmly on those forms of welfare that are provided, or have come to be provided, outside the state, and on those closest to the commercial market, in particular. Of course, ownership is only one aspect of the three-dimensional approach to welfare pluralism adopted here. Later in this chapter, the interplay between ownership, finance and regulation will also be explored.

With the more central position that private provision now occupies comes a greater obligation to subject this dimension of welfare to proper scrutiny and critical attention. Privatisation, here, is taken to be the transferring of assets from public to private ownership and the reallocation of responsibilities from public to private spheres (see Land, 2004, for an elaboration of this distinction). The discussion concentrates on the approach to these issues that has developed during the two terms of New Labour government. Inevitably, it traces something of the legacy that the 1997 Blair administration inherited from the neo-liberal experiments of the Thatcher and Major years.

The idea of privatisation

If privatisation was one of the big 'new ideas' of the Thatcher era, it was one that did not emerge until well into the 1980s, and the sale of the great utilities of gas, electricity and water, that the policy began to be regularly and actively promoted as having a philosophical as well as a practical purpose. The arguments deployed were an amalgam of those that had been long developed – but largely uninfluential, at least in a British context – by writers such as Schumpter and Hayek. The former emphasised the intrinsic advantages private ownership was said to enjoy over ownership by the public sector, such as self-interest in business outcomes and careful stewardship of assets. The latter emphasised the primacy of markets, rather than state-owned monopolies, in the provision of services. The returns claimed for this approach included innovation, entrepreneurialism and cost reduction in a list of benefits – responsiveness, economy, choice and quality – that formed the privatisers' litany.

At the same time as the sale of public assets gathered pace in the United Kingdom of the 1980s, a parallel set of ideas emphasised a more general 'rolling back' of the state in which the allocation of responsibility for tackling social and economic problems was redistributed away from the state and towards the individual citizen. It is important, near the start of this discussion, to draw to the surface the ideological basis of these policy decisions. As Chapter One suggests, movements between public and private forms of welfare are more than simply moving the furniture around the drawing room. This holds true however the shift takes place, in terms of direct provision, funding regimes or regulatory arrangements. Private welfare involves an inevitable and intrinsic ideological component – a values-into-outcomes trajectory – not simply just another form of delivery. To put this in the crude terms of political debate, unemployment during the 1980s was portrayed largely as the responsibility of the unemployed who needed to 'price themselves into jobs', by accepting lower wages or making more effort to secure available work by 'getting on their bikes', while young people looking for a home were expected to adjust their expectations to whatever the market – rather than the local council – might provide. Public welfare has its own ideology, resting on the belief that providers – doctors, teachers, housing officers and so on – are motivated by an ethos of public service, rather than simply personal gain (see Le Grand, 2003, for a challenging account of this notion).

Privatisation and social welfare

The account of the development of privatisation, as previously discussed, emphasises the economic origins of the policy. As argued extensively elsewhere (Drakeford, 2000), however, the impact of three central strands – transfer of ownership, creation of markets and reallocation of responsibilities – was quickly felt in the sphere of social policy.

In terms of *ownership*, the Conservative government's Right to Buy policy, in which council house occupants were encouraged to purchase the homes they had hitherto occupied as tenants, represented the most direct transfer of property from public to private hands. Indeed, as Chapter One points out, typologies of shifting responsibility conclude that, without that transfer, the balance between public and private welfare in the United Kingdom remained almost unchanged. The late 1980s saw the emergence of new forms of ownership, which continued the transfer of social welfare assets from the state direct to new intermediate bodies, such as self-governing (or 'grant-maintained') schools and hospitals. These semi-autonomous organisations, membership of which was either wholly appointed (as in the case of hospital Trusts) or a mixture of elected and appointed members (as in the case of schools) had transferred to them buildings and other assets that were formerly in the direct ownership of the state. At the same time, responsibility was transferred for a range of decisions – over investment, access, development of future services, and so on – that had previously been assumed by elected politicians.

In terms of *market creation*, changes in the social welfare field were, perhaps, more distinctive and, from a theoretical perspective, more interesting. In the economic sphere, the government had moved to reposition goods such as gas and electricity, so that consumers could choose between suppliers in a fully competitive market, in the same way as shopping for baked beans or chewing gum. In the provision of goods such as education, healthcare and social work, however, the creation of fully competitive markets was not a practical possibility. In their place, quasi-markets (see Bartlett et al, 1998) were developed, either by encouraging existing suppliers to compete for customers (as between hospitals in the 'internal market' for healthcare) or by creating new and differentiated suppliers within the liberalised forms of ownership. A clear example of this strategy is to be found in the education field, where City Technology Colleges were heavily promoted by the Conservative government of the early 1990s, as injecting competition into the existing comprehensive school system through the creation of new rights of entry to non-public providers of services in what had been, hitherto, largely the preserve of state bodies. The idea was taken up with new enthusiasm, and considerable political difficulties, during the third New Labour administration, and Prime Minister Tony Blair's determination to liberalise the education market through a combination of specialist schools, faith schools and City Academies.

For the personal social services, local councils were to be transformed from direct suppliers of services into organisations that bought such services from others. A market was thus to be created in which local authorities acted as surrogates for users of social services themselves, pursuing what the privatisers claimed would be new opportunities for purchasing slicker, quicker, cheaper and better outcomes than would have been possible in the old monolithic pattern of state provision.

As for *personal responsibility*, the third strand in neo-liberal marketisation, the ideological impact for the individual user of social welfare services was two-fold. First, it suggested (see, for example, Green, 1993 and Marsland, 1996) that private provision was always and inevitably likely to be preferable to goods and services provided through the state. Second, it suggested that new measures would be needed to help bring home the advantages of the newly liberalised world, both to suppliers and consumers of welfare goods. Users of such services, especially, were to be encouraged to behave in ways that suited the new circumstances. The approach adopted was essentially that of the carrot and the stick. For the reasonably well-off, or well-circumstanced, the carrot was dangled in the form of favourable economic incentives to leave state systems and purchase privately. Thus, mortgage interest tax relief provided very substantial subsidies to private home owners, which, in the case of people buying their own council houses came in addition to the huge discounts at which such properties were able to be purchased; tax relief on private healthcare insurance produced record numbers of such policy-holders (Baggott, 1994), while in education, the Assisted Places Scheme fed children of the genteel poor into British public schools in unprecedented numbers (see Edwards and Whitty, 1997).

For those without the means to take advantage of these new opportunities, the second of the government's strategies – the stick – was far more in evidence. Among the privatisers and marketeers, it was common currency that the welfare state had produced not simply economic decline, but a parallel deterioration in the moral fabric of those who depended on it. State services were regarded as adding to the problems of society, rather than helping to solve social difficulties. In particular, the new orthodoxy regarded the recipients of such services as morally, socially and economically diminished by that receipt. The answer was a withdrawal of state support from those who had become accustomed to rely on it. Thus, the answer to homelessness became a withdrawal of rights from homeless people to permanent housing (see Kemp, 1992), the problem of disaffected young people solved by making it easier to exclude them completely and permanently from the education and benefit systems (see Hayden, 1997) and so on.

An example of the interplay between ownership, finance and the reallocation of responsibility is the government's brief and ill-fated experiment with nursery vouchers, in which parents were supplied with a cash-equivalent and made responsible for shopping around for provision – state, voluntary or private – that best suited their needs. For those able to 'top up' vouchers with funding of their own, the system generally provided a subsidy for the better-off, much as Titmuss described earlier fiscal welfare schemes. For the voluntary sector, the scheme had the effect of undermining long-established efforts to respond to local needs, as state schools amended admission criteria to hang onto funding that had previously arrived on a planned basis. For those economic actors with the least access to information, additional funding or physical mobility, the effect was to narrow choice while increasing responsibility (see Drakeford, 2000, for a more extended account of the nursery voucher experiment).

For individuals in these circumstances, the privatisation agenda had a new twist. The 'rolling-back' of the state had rolled forward a set of responsibilities into their own lives with which they were singularly ill equipped to deal. The social problems that, from Beveridge onwards, governments had been prepared to regard as a shared obligation, had been redefined as belonging only to those individuals whose capacity to deal with such difficulties was least well formed – and not only would this be better for the rest of society, it would be better for them too.

The ideological and practical impact of neo-liberal thinking on social welfare services in Britain during the 1980s was thus of a very high order. While the ascendancy of such thinking was greatest during the Thatcher years, the impact was far more long-lasting. The Major government that followed saw competition rather than cooperation as the key driver in the delivery of services, introducing changes that commentators such as Butler (1993, p 56) concluded "finally mark the break with the service structures erected by Bevan and Beveridge". The fundamental policy direction, further extending the neo-liberal agenda in welfare services and adding new layers to what Silburn (1992) calls the 'privatisation of risk', was thus set and formed the legacy that fell to the New Labour government, and to which this chapter now turns.

New Labour's first term

If the Conservative years of the 1980s had been sufficiently ideological to be capable of being summed up in a single word – 'Thatcherism' – the New Labour leadership adopted a radically different approach in making a positive virtue of what it claimed to be an absence of any guiding ideology. The new Prime Minister made his first major post-election speech at a run-down, inner-London housing estate on 2 June 1997. He used the occasion to reject government by 'dogma'. Instead, he said, his "approach will be different. We will find out what works and we support the successes and stop the failures. We will back anyone – from a multinational company to a community association – if they can deliver the goods." This was to be a government that would be "pragmatic and rigorous about what does and does not work".

In the earliest months of New Labour, pragmatism appeared to rule out competition as a means of improving social welfare services. In health, Ministers (DH, 1997) summed up the new approach in this way: "The government is dismantling the internal market. In place of competition, the NHS will work together for the benefit of patients". The language the new administration used to describe 'working together' was one of 'partnership'. Yet, while new social welfare markets were seldom promoted, existing examples – other than in health – were largely left unaltered, or positively developed. The field of education provides the most striking examples. Hostility to private education, as the purchase of privilege by a self-perpetuating elite, had long been a simple orthodoxy for many Labour figures (see, for example, Tawney, 1921; Crosland, 1961). Now, it was dismissed as an 'old prejudice' that needed to be buried (Department for Education and Employment, 1997). A £1 million grant followed, to 'foster links with independent schools' (Department for Education and Employment, 1998).

It was not long before what Page (2001, p 531) describes as New Labour's 'ideological commitment to the free market' began to come to the fore, while Powell (2000, p 54) concluded that "continuities with the Conservatives far outweigh those with Old Labour".

Box 4.1: John and private welfare

John lives with his wife and two children in their own home, which he bought from the council under the Right to Buy scheme. This private asset has risen in value well above inflation over the past 15 years. While he himself is an agnostic, he chose to send his children to a local Church of England primary school. His eldest son now attends a new City Technology College, following an interview with the headteacher, in which he was able to impress on her the family's commitment to regular attendance and educational achievement. John's wife is able to drop their son off at the school on her way to work, despite the fact that it lies at some distance, across the city, from where they live. John's mother lives in a privately run residential care home where the council pays her fees. John 'tops up' the local authority's funding, in order to buy some extra services for his mother that were previously provided as part of the council's contract, but were squeezed out when fees were renegotiated in the previous year. Last year, too, John's mother's need for a hip replacement became more urgent. With the help of his GP, he identified a Foundation Hospital, about 200 miles away, which was able to provide the operation at short notice. Although his mother would have preferred to have been treated locally, she agreed to travel because John's wife was able to take some time off work to transport her to the hospital and stay nearby until she was fit enough to travel home. At the hospital, a mix-up occurred in the complicated system for ordering an evening meal and something was delivered that John's mother did not like to eat. She complained to her daughter-in-law, who quickly found the Patient Advocacy Liaison Officer. The meal-ordering system remained the same, but John's mother's order was watched carefully during the rest of her stay.

Blair's second term

For a Labour government, even one as far removed from traditional roots as that led by Tony Blair, there are limits to the extent to which some arguments in favour of privatisation and marketisation can be adopted. Claims for the intrinsic advantages of private ownership are less often advanced by British Labour politicians, even of the newest variety. Yet, and particularly as the second New Labour term began in June 2001, one aspect of neo–liberalism provided a growing grip on the Blairite agenda – the argument that modern citizens demanded choice in the way that services were provided to them, and that choice was best secured through breaking up old public sector monopolies. The then Secretary of State for Health in England, Dr John Reid, devoted a whole speech to this theme during 2003 (Reid, 2003). He summarised the government's position in this way:

> With every generation, as people's expectations rise and their income follows suit, they will demand more power and flexibility over the manner in which they and their families are treated. In short, people will want choice for themselves and their families.... The main question, therefore, is not whether they can and should exercise choice, but whether we can ensure that choice can be exercised within the NHS, rather than only outside the NHS.

In presenting this case, Dr Reid was applying the argument of choice to a particular policy – that of the creation of 'Foundation Hospitals'[1] in England and one of the defining features of the second Blair administration. The notion of such hospitals did not appear in the Manifesto on which the second New Labour administration was elected. Rather, the term was first used in public debate in a speech delivered by the then Secretary of State for Health, Alan Milburn, to the New Health Network (Milburn, 2002). He emphasised the need to develop freedoms for successful NHS organisations and declared that the era of the 'NHS as a nationalised industry' was over. In its place, Foundation Hospitals would be pioneers in "a fundamentally different sort of NHS. Not a state run structure but a values based system: where greater diversity and devolution are underpinned by common standards and a common public service ethos".

The public debate that gathered around Foundation Hospitals concentrated mainly on issues of provision and ownership. In the parliamentary Bill through which they were set up, Foundation Hospitals were to be given the powers to generate surpluses, to trade in NHS and non-NHS services (Clause 14), to buy and sell land and other assets (Clause 18), to create commercial arms or join existing commercial ventures (Clause 17) and to employ staff on the conditions they choose. Once established, the new Foundation Trusts would assume ownership of NHS land, buildings and equipment that would thus cease to be owned by the NHS as a whole.

Neo-liberals described the policy enthusiastically as "the State abandoning the ownership of hospitals" (Bosanquet and Kruger, 2003, p 2). They continued that, "in practical terms", the change would see the reinstatement of the internal market. Foundation Hospitals meant that, by 2008, England would be "the only country in Europe to have all its hospitals operating in the independent sector".

Opponents criticised Foundation Trusts on the same terms. Far from patients being offered a greater choice of provider, the new Trusts would soon come to choose those patients who contributed most to their balance sheets. The freedom to define core activity more narrowly would be used to move away from recuperative services and thus, in a United Kingdom context, place access to such facilities in the realm of means-tested social care, rather than state-provided medical care. As Needham (2003, p 7) puts it, "Foundation Trusts have an incentive to redefine eligibility for NHS care at local level thereby introducing new charges for services which were once provided by the NHS". The result would be that poorer, sicker and less advantaged individuals would be least attractive to the new suppliers, and left to rely on poorer services in those hospitals that do not achieve Foundation Trust status.

The government disagreed. Such arguments were succinctly dismissed by Minister Reid:

> Some say poorer people do not want to exercise choice or are not
> able to do so. I disagree profoundly. That is patronising nonsense.
> (Reid, 2003)

Even so, not all members of the Cabinet were of the same view. The Chancellor used the muscle of the Treasury to place considerable limitations on the financial freedoms within which the new Trusts were to operate. The hospitals were to have no powers to make or retain profits from patients, to develop new insurance products or design their own ownership models. They were not to have the ability to borrow money against their assets off the public sector balance sheet, thus severely constraining their capacity to mimic private sector operators. This led to predictable and regular complaints from the new entrepreneurs of the Foundation Trust sector. By the middle of 2005, the Foundation Trust Network was calling for the abolition of the cap on the number of private patients Trusts can treat, for new freedoms to provide primary care services and to take over less successful Trusts, for obligations to meet national targets to be lifted and for a more liberal capital borrowing regime. It also proposed giving Foundation Hospitals the freedom to develop a money-making 'Debenhams model' of healthcare, in which 'branded boutiques' would provide Foundation-style services at other hospitals (see *Health Service Journal*, 2005).

The third aspect with which this chapter is concerned – regulation – saw Foundation Trusts come fully equipped with the sort of overseeing individual that had become the hallmark of the Blairite approach to welfare services. The new bodies were to be accountable to their local 'members' and to a Monitor – but not to the Department of Health. Klein (2005, p 58) traces some early tensions between what he describes as the 'conversion' of New Labour Ministers to localism and the actions of the Monitor in, for example, removing the chair of the Bradford NHS Foundation Trust and replacing him with the Monitor's own nominee. However these debates work themselves out over coming years, Klein's conclusion (2005, p 58) that reform had already delivered "a well funded lobby of semi-independent NHS barons" provides a fair reflection of the earliest achievements.

Box 4.2: Privatisation: the example of Hospital Trusts

The three main characteristics of the application of privatisation to social welfare services are to be found in the single policy of Foundation Hospitals and Trusts. They will take away assets from the public sector and make them the property of the new bodies; their most basic rationale lies in the creation of a market in healthcare in which patients are afforded new choices, but those choices will rely on individuals taking responsibility for decisions that were previously made on their behalf. While it is certainly true that the reforms retain a health service for all British citizens, the effect of profit seeking is likely to narrow the range of services offered, and items that are free of charge now will be made fee services in future. The public interest, in this model, is to be enforced through the third leg in the mixed economy of welfare, that of regulation, although the office of the regulator remains steadfastly outside any direct control of the public it has been set up to serve.

Going private: hospital treatment

If Foundation Hospitals tell us something important about the New Labour project, there is a different, but equally important, strand in its second-term thinking that shows a more direct willingness not simply to mimic the market, but to join it.

Here, just one example – Independent Diagnostic and Treatment Centres – will have to stand as an example of this wider trend.

As early as October 2000, six months before the end of the first Blair term, the Department of Health (DH, 2000) was celebrating the fact that "the relationship between the NHS and the private sector was today put on a formal footing for the first time".

By 2001, Health Secretary, Alan Milburn, announced the government's intention not simply to formalise relationships with the private sector, but to bypass the NHS itself in favour of private providers for the administration's new diagnostic and treatment centres. He was in active negotiations with BUPA, Britain's largest private healthcare supplier, but made it clear that "other private providers from home or abroad" (DH, 2001) were being solicited to carry out treatment on NHS patients.

During 2002, such providers were being actively courted. In June, Mr Milburn entertained Ophthalmology Network Organisation (based in Switzerland), Deluca Medical (based in France), German Medicine Net (based in Germany), Germedic (based in Germany) and Capio (based in Sweden) in order to make clear that it was now "an explicit objective of Government health policy to shift towards greater plurality and diversity in the delivery of elective services" (DH, 2002). In signing a concordat between the private sector and the NHS, Minister Milburn declared that a rubicon had been crossed in the use of private medicine (Powell, 2003, pp 735-6).

In 2003, Junior Health Minister, John Hutton, was able to confirm at a leading private sector health conference that the diagnostic and treatment centre programme was to be renamed the Independent Sector Treatment Centre (ISTC) programme, with new overseas and UK-based private healthcare providers in 26 areas across England, and the government ready to invest around £2 billion over the next five years in the programme (Laing and Buisson, 2003).

Throughout 2004, the Department of Health acted to provide the detail of this general policy. In January (DH, 2004a), two centres were announced, with five more in February (DH, 2004b). In May (DH, 2004c), John Hutton set out the government's intention to commission a further eight ISTCs – over and above those announced in 2003 – from the private sector firm, Capio Healthcare. By the end of 2004, the Department of Health (DH, 2004d) was confident that 10% of all NHS elective surgery in England would be carried out in the private sector, where ISTCs now employed more than 1,000 staff. Behind that figure, of course, lay a series of issues to do with employment law, the transfer of staff from one undertaking to another and the enduring efforts of the private sector to extract profits by lowering the conditions of service of employees. The social division of labour, and the mixed economy of welfare, are intimately connected in private provision. The enthusiasm with which large-scale capitalist enterprises have re-entered the residential care market (to be discussed later) is partly, at least, founded on the new concentrations of poorly paid, indifferently trained and supported staff, employed on the reduced terms and conditions that are to be found in the sector. Such market mechanisms do not bypass ISTCs, the difference here being the direct hand the government has in their establishment and organisation.

At the start of 2005, a celebratory in-house Department of Health report (DH, 2005a) found that more than 120,000 patients had been treated in the ISTC programme "at a rate up to eight times faster than traditional NHS providers". NHS groups described this observation as 'gratuitous' and misleading (BMA, 2005), and a conclusion that entirely ignored the different contexts – such as case mix – in which the two sectors operate. The NHS Confederation (2005), representing senior managers, warned that the rise of treatment centres was now threatening the viability of existing NHS hospitals, because of the enforced diversion of elective work to the private sector. Dr Reid reacted to such a possibility with what might best be described as insouciance, telling a gathering of London journalists that such hospitals would be allowed to close (*Guardian*, 2005), a highly unlikely outcome in practical politics and one that his successor as Health Secretary in Labour's third term, Patricia Hewitt, took an early opportunity to dismiss (Hewitt, 2005). Her in-tray was soon to become dominated by the consequences the Confederation had predicted, as Trusts ran up unprecedented deficits and responded by laying off thousands of staff.

Going private: residential care

This chapter now turns to the private sector engagement in the residential and nursing home market, a development that marks the United Kingdom out from almost every other European Union member state, with only France having followed this same path, and that on a reduced scale, and which, for our purposes, provides an illustration of the practical operation of privatisation in this dimension of social welfare.

The private care home market went through a boom in the early 1990s, with companies attracted by the guaranteed demand stream represented by an ageing population, matched by what appeared to be a guaranteed stream of payment by the public sector and a shortage of beds.

Ten years later, the market had gone through turbulent times. Of the 20 or so large-scale nursing home operators listed at the peak, only one fully listed operator, Care UK, remained. Market analysts Laing and Buisson reported (2003) that total capacity had fallen by 13% since its peak in 1996, albeit with evidence that (Laing and Buisson, 2004) the pace of decline in the sector had slowed and that the growing number of elderly people in the population continued to underpin the long-term prospects for the sector.

It was in this context that, in the second half of 2004, the market moved to a wave of consolidations – or, as the *Financial Times* described it, "frenzied private equity activity in the sector" (*Financial Times*, 2004). That activity was underpinned by the sector's new attractiveness to private equity groups, based on steady cash flows, large property portfolios (Essex, 2004) and "its power to generate cash, the growth opportunities offered by an ageing population, the debt markets' willingness to fund deals and the prospect of further consolidation" (Smith, 2004a). Moreover, as Smith (2004b) disarmingly puts it, with 61% of all residents paid for by local authorities (Laing and Buisson, 2004), "healthcare has proved attractive to private equity groups because governments or their agencies often end up paying the bills". With such substantial funding for residential care coming from the public purse, the government has made attempts to persuade a reluctant population to make better self-provision for future old age. The challenge it faced is illustrated in Johnstone's 2005 survey, which takes as its starting point that "the public's track record in voluntary planning for future care costs is very poor" and that "any form of voluntary scheme is unlikely to succeed" (p 1). Among a lengthy list of potential private means of funding future care needs are long-term care insurance (despite the withdrawal, in 2004, of most of these products from the market, by the main providers of such insurance), investment-based plans (which have suffered the same market failure), annuities and equity release schemes. Johnstone's conclusion (2005) was that failure to regulate the financial services sector adequately had eroded public confidence in its products, thus reducing their use. The interplay between the different elements in the mixed economy of welfare is thus well illustrated. The issue of regulation, in relation to private sector provision, needs some exploration of its own, and this now follows.

If New Labour was agnostic in its attitude towards ownership, it was far more certain in its approach to regulation. It inherited a Conservative model of audit and inspection that combined a focus on economy as well as effectiveness. While the new government talked a different talk, emphasising quality, autonomy and diversity, in practice, as Humphrey concludes (2002, p 468), "the grip of centralised command and control" was actually tightened, with a "massive expansion of the regulatory apparatus" under New Labour (Humphrey 2003, p 5). Regulation and inspection were to provide the means by which the public interest could be secured, even while ownership remained outside the public sector.[2]

In the field of social care, the rapid growth of private sector provision had led even the third, and most radical, Thatcher administration to strengthen regulation of residential care. The 1990 NHS and Community Care Act brought both local authority and private residential homes within the ambit of a semi-autonomous set of Inspection Units located within social services departments. Thereafter the actual pattern of regulation has undergone a series of changes. In 1995, the Conservative government set up a review of the 1990 Act system, ostensibly designed to look for ways of simplifying and lightening the regulatory burden. For England, the incoming New Labour government set up the

National Care Standards Commission under the 2000 Care Standards Act, with a remit to inspect against a set of National Minimum Standards. It, too, was short-lived, being overtaken in April 2004 by the Commission for Social Care Inspection, created as a consequence of the 2003 Health and Social Care (Community Health and Standards) Act. The ink was barely dry on the new headed notepaper, however, before being overtaken by another round of 'simplification', in which the Department of Health set out to review its suite of arm's-length bodies and concluded that a merger between the Health and Social Care Commissions was now necessary (DH, 2005b).

What does all this tell us about the role of regulation in an era of welfare pluralism? Shifting patterns of ownership in social welfare services mean that while regulation has moved centre-stage, its practical application to private sector providers has not proved easy. As Balloch et al (2004, p 372) point out, "the regulatory process faces, and will be likely to continue to face, difficulties in putting on pressure for the raising of standards in a sector severely constrained by market forces". In the residential care market, for example, enforcing minimum standards produces costs that have either to be absorbed by home owners, or passed on to residents or their local authority sponsors.

A considerable body of literature now exists in relation to the pattern of regulation and inspection that has grown up over the past 20 years. A general conclusion seems to have emerged that, whatever the underlying explanation, regulation has failed to deliver the improvements in service delivery and quality that were hoped for it. Whether the reasons for that failure be the stultifying, trust-destroying nature of the regulatory state (see O'Neill, 2002) or the incomplete nature of the regulatory experiment (see Moran, 2001), the dissatisfaction with its results seems widespread.

Nor was this shifting cocktail of ownership, funding and regulation confined to the residential care of older people. Writing in the *Financial Times* in July 2004, Jonathon Guthrie commented approvingly on the opportunities now available in relation to people with "serious mental handicaps" who were "becoming business assets, as the state contracts out healthcare work to private companies". As he pointed out:

> ... one attraction of running homes for the mentally disabled is that local authorities have limited scope to chisel down fees. Wide variation in mental conditions means charges are negotiated individually for each resident with the local authorities, which pay the bills.

> In contrast, care homes for the elderly tend to be stuck with a fixed tariff for each inmate [sic], making it more of a commodity business. (Guthrie, 2004)

Against this background, it is unsurprising to find Laing and Buisson (2004) reporting that mental health, generally, continued to be the strongest growth area of independent sector hospital services, increasing by 7% (real terms) in 2003 to be valued at £537 million. According to their report, "robust spending on independent sector treatment by NHS agencies has continued to be the market's main driving force", with fully 67% of the sector's revenues accounted for by NHS spending. An indication of the direction of public policy travel may be found in Laing and Buisson's conclusion that "Market leader Priory Healthcare broke new ground in 2003 by securing a three-year contract to provide the Ministry of Defence with all its mental health requirements, the first time any government agency has outsourced all its mental health services".

Does all this matter to users of services? The Blairite orthodoxy is that those on the receiving end are indifferent to the operation of the mixed economy of welfare. What matters, it claims, is not who owns services, or the mechanisms by which they are provided, but the quality of the results. Certainly, it is true that the manoeuvrings of high finance, with millions of pounds, and the lives of thousands of people being traded in auction deals in the private residential homes sector reported here, seldom reached the wider public. Yet, during the period in which a new "golden age for healthcare investors" was dawning (Essex, 2004), the issue of residential care of older people was hardly ever out of the headlines. In Birmingham, for example, the city council, with 29 local authority homes in its area, embarked on a public inquiry into its plans to privatise or close the units, in an effort to recoup a £28 million overspend in its social services budget (*Birmingham Evening Mail*, 2005). As over-spends in social services departments began to bite, in the second half of the financial year 2005/06, decisions to shut care homes caused disquiet from one end of Britain to the other. In Devon, the Conservative MP described plans of the Lib Dem controlled county council to reduce residential care homes as 'a sick joke' (*Herald Express*, 2005). In Stoke-on Trent, 250 pensioners, carers and union members marched to the Conservative-dominated council headquarters to hand in a 5,000-name petition against the Older People's Strategy, which included shutting nine care home (*The Sentinel*, 2005). In Durham, the chair and the secretary of the Labour Group resigned as the executive tried to force through the end of direct council residential care for the elderly (*Northern Echo*, 2006). In Northumberland, a veteran councillor was suspended for passing confidential information to relatives about care home closures (*The Journal*, 2006a).

The views of relatives, perhaps, cast most direct light on the ordinary citizen's reaction to the commodification of care. Angela Bolam, whose 94-year-old mother lives at one of the Durham homes destined to be transferred out of council ownership, said:

> To talk about 'best value' when you are considering elderly people's homes and welfare it's like the council is putting it on a par with street cleaning and grass cutting. It's all about saving money. (*The Journal*, 2006b).

For some parts of the public, at least, ownership really does appear to matter. To echo the first chapter of this text once again, public reaction suggests an understanding that public and private provision are not simply functional equivalents: they are, indeed, based on different principles, and those different principles lead to different outcomes.

Box 4.3: Jill and public welfare

Jill lives alone with her 13-year-old daughter. Her partner deserted them three years ago. Following many months in a single room at a bed and breakfast, during which her claim to be unintentionally homeless was exhaustively investigated, they were allocated a council flat on a peripheral estate where crime levels are high and levels of repairs and maintenance are low. Jill's daughter did badly in her Key Stage Two tests, which coincided with her father's disappearance and moving to bed and breakfast. The nearest school to her new home is a 'specialist' school, but her application was turned down by letter, because her results did not show sufficient 'aptitude' for the specialism the school offered. Jill is a practising Roman Catholic and would have liked her daughter to attend a secondary school of that denomination. Unfortunately, the only one available was situated at the other end of town. The local council had recently taken advantage of new 'flexibilities' provided by the New Labour government to charge for school transport and Jill had reluctantly concluded that she could not afford the weekly bus fare. Instead, her daughter attends the local estate school. Staff are excellent and highly committed, but the school suffers from falling rolls and planning blight. The curriculum on offer has had to be reduced and the range of extra-curricular activities, for which children have to pay, has had to be set at a level that local parents can afford.

Jill is waiting for a knee operation. Her GP has put her on the waiting list of the local 'no-stars' Trust, because Jill will need to be as close as possible to home, even when the operation becomes available. She knows that it might have been possible to have been treated more quickly elsewhere, but has no money to pay for travel and other incidental costs, nor is she willing to leave her daughter at home alone.

Jill's father suffers from the progressive onset of Alzheimer's disease. His private care home, where he was settled and happy, had informed her that they were no

---

longer able to look after him, because of the level of care required. He was moved, therefore, to another private provider, where Jill has not been satisfied by standards of care. More services can be purchased, over and above those provided by the local authority fee, but a dispute has taken place between the local health service and the council as to who should pick up the bill. As a result, no extra care has been provided. Jill has attempted to complain about the system, which has left her father, and others, in this position. The home could only provide a leaflet, which turned out to be out of date. The local council directed her to the Citizens' Advice Bureau for help. The volunteer there has compiled a lengthy list of possible organisations to contact – the local medical committees, the Social Services Inspectorate, the Care Standards Inspectorate, the Commission for Health Improvement, to name but a few. Jill knows that, one day, when she has more time and energy, she will get round to making sure her voice is heard.

Conclusion

This chapter has traced the continuing impact the marketising agenda has produced on British social welfare policy for a quarter of a century. New Labour politicians may have come at the subject from a different angle to that espoused by the Thatcherites, but many of the same claims made for privatisation in the 1980s have resurfaced in new guises since 1997. Indeed, during the second Blair administration, the pace of reform quickened and deepened. The impact of commodification can already be seen in the privatisation of routine elective surgery and the marketisation of private residential care: profit lines and market movements become an integral part of the bottom line of health and social care provision in a way hitherto unimagined in post-1945 welfare services.

In all of this, the greatest casualty has been one of the cardinal founding principles of the British welfare state, that of equality. The model of the relationship between the government and the individual, which regards that individual as a consumer rather than as a citizen, inevitably privileges those people who are already best placed to exercise their advantages as market actors. The articulate, the well-informed and the relatively better-off are able to use these benefits in order to secure for themselves better health services, better education and better social welfare services, more generally than others in the population. The agenda of choice brings with it, its proponents claim, a series of benefits. The dangers to what Mohan (2003) has called 'egalitarian public services', based on a collective sense of public good and a determination to advance the interests of those least able to fend for themselves, are far less frequently articulated, but remain real and are, as yet, unresolved.

Notes

[1] One of the most radical measures of the Blair government was found in the devolution of power to new democratic institutions in Scotland, Northern Ireland and Wales. Health was one of the responsibilities transferred to these new bodies. Thus Foundation Hospitals refer to a policy only being introduced in England, the other institutions having decided against such a development.

[2] Of course, the extensive literature on regulation suggests a series of less worthy motives for the growth in the regulatory state, including 'blame avoidance' through the delegation of activities which might prove electorally unpopular. See Hood (2002) for a general discussion of these issues.

Summary

- The delivery of social welfare services by the voluntary and private sectors has grown significantly in the United Kingdom over the past quarter of a century.
- The privatisation and marketisation of public services began under Mrs Thatcher and has been continued, albeit in rather different ways, under New Labour.
- Privatisation in the social welfare field takes a variety of different forms. It can mean transferring ownership of assets from the state to shareholders or new forms of local citizenship, such as school governing bodies or Foundation Trusts. It can mean purchasing services, such as domiciliary and residential care, from the private or independent sector, rather than providing them directly by the state itself. The interplay between funding and provision is complex and can take many different forms.
- Privatisation also involves redrawing the boundaries of responsibility, with the state withdrawing from roles previously undertaken, and relocating them within the sphere of individual responsibility.
- Where the state relies on private providers, the role of regulation and inspection takes on a new importance in securing compliance with minimum standards for users. Patterns of regulation have changed regularly and rapidly over the past 15 years, and are yet to achieve a secure confidence in their effectiveness.
- There are a number of tensions inherent in the shift of responsibility from public to private spheres. The claims made for choice, responsiveness and efficiency can be difficult to reconcile with public fondness for local services and are positively inimical to the pursuit of greater equality.

Questions for discussion

- What makes for the most effective welfare markets – private ownership or competition and choice between providers, whoever they may be?
- Can the state enforce minimum standards in welfare services through regulation rather than direct provision?
- Which provides the best motivation for providing quality welfare: profit or public service?

Further reading

Bartlett et al (1998) provides an excellent summary of policy changes in this field during the 1980s and 1990s, applying the reforms to specific social welfare services.

Drakeford (2000) is a comprehensive account of the way in which marketisation and privatisation has been implemented in British social policy, including impacts on individuals as well as organisations.

Land (2004) offers a concise overview of the application of privatisation in social welfare since 1979, including developments under New Labour.

Electronic resources

The best source of the most up-to-date debates in this area is to be found in the websites of the major policy think-tanks. Catalyst (www.catalystforum.org.uk/) for example, provides a wealth of material from a left-of-centre perspective, generally sceptical of the benefits claimed for private provision of welfare. The Centre for Policy Studies (www.cps.org.uk/) comes at these issues from the opposite side of the ideological spectrum, generally supportive of policies and actions that favour private sector services in the welfare field and that 'roll back the state'.

References

Baggott, R. (1994) *Health and Health Care in Britain*, London: Macmillan.

Balloch, S., Banks, L. and Hill, M. (2004) 'Securing quality in the mixed economy of care: difficulties in regulating training', *Social Policy and Society*, vol 3, no 4, pp 365-73.

Bartlett, W., Roberts, J.A. and LeGrand, J. (1998) *A Revolution in Social Policy: Quasi-market Reform in the 1990s*, Bristol: The Policy Press.

Birmingham Evening Mail (2005) 'Inquiry on future of care homes', 11 January.

BMA (British Medical Association) (2005) 'Treatment centres threaten NHS Trusts', Press Release, 7 January.

Bosanquet, N. and Kruger, D. (2003) *Strong Foundations: Building on the NHS Reforms*, London: Centre for Policy Studies.

Butler, J. (1993) 'A case study in the National Health Service: working for patients', in P. Taylor-Gooby and R. Lawson (eds) *Markets and Managers*, Buckingham: Open University Press, pp 54-68.

DfEE (Department for Education and Employment) (1997) 'Burying old prejudices with £500,000 boost for private/state school partnerships – Byers', Press release 393/97, 26 November.

DfEE (1998) '£1 million to foster links with independent schools – Morris', Press release 459/98, 7 October.

DH (Department of Health) (1997) 'Frank Dobson announces action to "end ther two tier National Health Service"', Press release 97/091, 9 May.

DH (2000) 'NHS to use spare private capacity', Press release, 31 October.

DH (2001) 'NHS and BUPA negotiate new public private partnership', Press release, 4 December.

DH (2002) 'New role for overseas and independent healthcare providers in England', Press release, 25 June.

DH (2004a) 'New treatment centre for Cheshire, Merseyside and Worcestershire', Press release, 16 January.

DH (2004b) 'New treatment centres across the South East will treat 5,000 patients a year', Press release, 17 February.

DH (2004c) 'Treatment centre programme delivering real results for patients', Press release, 13 May.

DH (2004d) *Information on Independent Sector Procurement by the NHS in England*, London: DH.

DH (2005a) 'Treatment centre success contributing to lowest ever waiting list since comparable records began', Press release, 7 January.

DH (2005b) 'Reid confirms planned merger of Healthcare Commission and Commission for Social Care Inspection', Press release, 16 March.

Drakeford, M. (2000) *Privatisation and Social Policy*, London: Longman.

Edwards, T. and Whitty, G. (1997) 'Marketing quality: traditional and modern versions of educational excellence', in R. Glatter, P.A. Woods and C. Bagley (eds) *Choice and Diversity in Schooling: Perspectives and Prospects*, London: Routledge, pp 29-43.

Essex, M. (2004) 'Golden age for healthcare investors', *Financial Times*, 7 November.

Financial Times (2004) 'EAC in Euros 100m nursing home sale', 6 December.

Financial Times (2005) 'Private share of state sector soars', 18 April.

Green, D. (1993) *Reinventing Civil Society: The Rediscovery of Welfare without Politics*, London: Health and Welfare Unit, Institute for Economic Affairs.

Guardian (2005) 'Unpopular hospitals could close', 3 February.

Guthrie, J. (2004) 'Homes for the mentally ill embrace a new commercialism', *Financial Times*, 27 July.

Hayden, C. (1997) *Children Excluded from Primary School: Debates, Evidence, Responses*, Buckingham: Open University Press.

Health Service Journal (2005) '"Boutique" model mooted', 7 July, p 6.

Herald Express (2005) 'MP's concern for residential homes', 23 December.

Hewitt, P. (2005) 'Investment and reform: transforming health and healthcare', Annual health and social care lecture, London: London School of Economics and Political Sciences.

Hood, C. (2002) 'The risk game and the blame game', *Government and Opposition*, vol 37, no 1, pp 15-37.

Humphrey, J. (2002) 'Joint reviews: retracing the trajectory, decoding the terms', *British Journal of Social Work*, vol 33, no 3, pp 463-76.

Humphrey, J. (2003) 'New Labour and the regulatory reform of social care', *Critical Social Policy*, vol 23, no 1, pp 5-24.

Johnstone, S. (2005) *Private Funding Mechanisms for Long-term Care*, York: Joseph Rowntree Foundation.

Kable (2005) *UK Public Sector Outsourcing: The Big Picture to 2007/08*, London: Kable Market Intelligence Services.

Kemp, P. (1992) 'Housing', in D. Marsh and R.A.W. Rhodes (eds) *Implementing Thatcherite Policies: Audit of an Era*, Buckingham: Open University Press, pp 65-80.

Klein, R. (2005) 'Transforming the NHS: the story in 2004', in M. Powell, L. Bauld and K. Clarke (eds) *Social Policy Review 17*, Bristol: The Policy Press, pp 51-68.

Laing and Buisson (2003) *Value of the Care Home Market*, London: Laing and Buisson.

Laing and Buisson (2004) *Care of Elderly People Market Survey 2004*, London: Laing and Buisson.

Land, H. (2004) 'Privatisation, privatisation, privatisation: the British welfare state since 1979', in N. Ellison, L. Bauld and M. Powell (eds) *Social Policy Review 16*, Bristol: The Policy Press, pp 251-69.

Le Grand, J. (2003) *Motivation, Agency and Public Policy: Of Knights and Knaves, Pawns and Queens*, Oxford: Oxford University Press.

Marsland, D. (1996) *Welfare or Welfare State?: Contradictions and Dilemmas in Social Policy*, Basingstoke: Macmillan.

Milburn, A. (2002) 'Redefining the National Health Service', Speech to the New Health Network (www.doh.gov.uk/speeches/jan2002milburnnhn.htm), accessed 17 January 2004.

Mohan, J. (2003) *Reconciling Equity and Choice? Foundation Hospitals and the Future of the NHS*, Catalyst Working Paper, London: Catalyst.

Moran, M. (2001) 'Not steering but drowning: policy catastrophes and the regulatory state', *Journal of Political Science*, vol 32, no 2, pp 391-413.

Needham, C. (2003) *Citizen–consumers: New Labour's marketplace democracy*, London: Catalyst.

NHS Confederation (2005) 'Treatment centres bring faster treatment but must be coordinated with existing NHS services', Press release, 7 January.

Northern Echo (2006) 'Labour chiefs resigns in care home closures row', 30 March.

O'Neill, O. (2002) *A Question of Trust – the Reith Lectures*, Cambridge: Cambridge University Press.

Page, R. (2001) 'New Labour, the third way and social welfare: "phase two" and beyond', *Critical Social Policy*, vol 21, no 4, pp 513-46.

Powell, M. (2000) 'New Labour and the third way in the British welfare state: a new and distinctive approach?', *Critical Social Policy*, vol 20, no 1, pp 39-60.

Powell, M. (2003) 'Quasi-markets in British health policy: a longue durée perspective', *Social Policy and Administration*, vol 37, no 7, pp 725-41.

Reid, J. (2003) 'Choice', Speech to the New Health Network, London: Department of Health.

Silburn, R. (1992) 'The changing landscape of poverty', in N. Manning and R. Page (eds) *Social Policy Review 4*, London: Social Policy Association, pp 134-53.

Smith, P. (2004a) 'NHP agrees £564 million bid from US buy-out group Blackstone', *Financial Times*, 30 November.

Smith, P. (2004b) 'Allianz unit wins Four Seasons auction', *Financial Times*, 6 July.

Tawney, R.H. (1921) *The Acquisitive Society*, London: Fontana.

The Journal (2006a) 'Punished for trying to save care homes', 10 March.

The Journal (2006b) 'Care homes closure puts lives at peril', 30 January.

The Sentinel (2005) 'Cost of children's care sparks city cash crisis', 9 December.

Timmins, N. (2005) Growth of the service provision business', *Financial Times*, 18 April.

five

Voluntary and community sector welfare

Pete Alcock and Duncan Scott

Overview

This chapter discusses what is meant by the voluntary and community sector in the context of social policy in the UK. It examines the problems that have been encountered in defining and measuring the sector, and the importance of its relations with other sectors. Then it discusses the development of the current policy context, in particular the significant changes experienced over the past decade. This is followed by a description of the size and shape of the sector, illustrated by three short vignettes. Finally, the chapter considers the future prospects for the sector in the context of the new emerging mixed economy of the 21st century.

Key concepts

Voluntary and community sector • civil society • public service delivery • civic renewal

Introduction

Defining the voluntary and community sector in the UK involves reflection on the nature of modern British society itself. Since the recognition and development of 'the market' and 'the state' as the key organisational dimensions of a developed capitalist state, there has also been identification of another dimension, generally referred to as civil society. Of course, as commentators on civil society have pointed out, quite what set of social relations and social institutions is encompassed by this term is open to dispute – or at least debate (see Deakin, 2001). And this is a debate that remains an ongoing and relevant one for politicians and policy planners at the start of the new century (for instance, Jochum et al, 2005). All seem to be agreed, however, that civil society is somewhere in between, and separate from, the market and the state.

The relationships encompassed by civil society extend beyond the voluntary and community sector; but they would certainly include it. Voluntary and community-based social action, and the organisations and agencies within which this takes place, are essential elements of civil society. These organisations are not part of the state, they have no formal public status; and they are not part of the market, they do not exist only to trade and produce an economic profit (although many voluntary organisations do produce, buy and sell goods). For these reasons, the sector is also sometimes referred to as what it is not – see **Box 5.1**.

Box 5.1: Key terms

Sectoral status
- Non-statutory – not created by legal statute
- Non-governmental – not owned or controlled by government
- Charitable – with legally approved charitable status
- Independent – self-governing or controlled
- Third sector – a sector among others
- Third Way – between the state and private interests

Core purposes
- Non-profit – not distributing profits to shareholders
- Philanthropic – providing help for others
- Mutual/self-help – providing help for members
- Communitarian – providing a collective base for activity

Bigger pictures
- Social capital – the strengths of social relationships
- Civil society – active citizenship outside the state and the market

The wide (and increasing) diversity of voluntary and community organisations, to be discussed later, means that the overall utility of the notion of this as a 'sector' of activity within a mixed economy of welfare is inherently problematic. This diversity prompted one set of commentators to suggest that the task of defining and classifying the sector was 'inherently impossible', and it led, too, to them famously referring to it as 'a loose and baggy monster' (Kendall and Knapp, 1996). It certainly suggests that the search for an endogenous definition of the sector may ultimately be a fruitless one; and it is interesting that exogenous approaches, implied in the definitions in **Box 5.1**, have commonly been taken up. This has led some to a focus on 'tension fields' (Evers and Laville, 2004) rather than on any essential characteristics – commonly represented as a triangular inter-sectoral landscape, as in **Figure 5.1**.

The place of the voluntary and community sector is thus in between, and overlapping with, the other three sectors of welfare provision. Within this schema, some voluntary organisations will be clearly in the centre of the voluntary and community sector triangle, but others (perhaps many) will be operating on and around the boundaries with the other sectors; and here the tensions between definition and operation may well be of political and practical, as well as theoretical, significance – in particular for those working within them or seeking to access the services they provide. Our approach to analysis of the sector must embrace this inter-sectoral location and the tensions to which it gives rise. Just such tensions also explain why **Figure 5.1** is inevitably an oversimplification. Organisations located at points 1, 2 and 3 will not be static, nor will they necessarily be so homogeneous in values and structure as to be permanently moored in one location.

Figure 5.1: *Inter-sectoral landscapes*

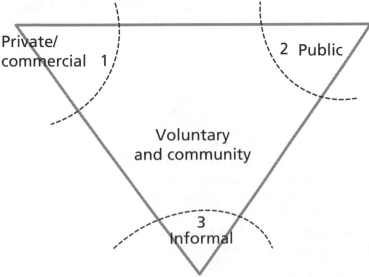

For example, an organisation such as the Big Issue operating in the social enterprise field on the boundaries of commercial activity (1 in **Figure 5.1**) will experience contradictory organisational tensions to reconcile its social mission, in relation to homeless people, with commercial imperatives associated with drives for profit in its magazine sales (see Pharoah et al, 2004). Similarly Age Concern working with the state to deliver public services (2 in **Figure 5.1**), while influenced by resource issues such as the organisational impact of funding flows, has increasingly been circumscribed by contractual elements relating to the size, shape and consistency of services (see Alcock et al, 2004). Finally, groups such as local childminders and pre-school groups, overlapping with informal networks (3 in **Figure 5.1**), are likely to be characterised by the ways in which relatively informal social reciprocities (when people exchange resources, mostly of their time and skills, for little or no monetary gain) are agreed and maintained or disputed (see later, and Scott, 2003).

The voluntary and community sector is not one of these organisations, but all; and analysis of the sector must focus on the tensions and differences between them. Despite these definitional tensions, however, academic researchers have attempted to define, map and measure the voluntary sector, both on a national and international basis. Within the UK, the National Council for Voluntary Organisations (NCVO) produces a regular biennial *Almanac* of the voluntary sector, the most recent being Wilding at al (2006a). This relies on existing data on the scale and structure of the sector from official sources, principally the Charity Commission and Companies House. It is therefore biased towards a record of the larger and more formal organisations, in particular those that have sought and obtained charitable status. Many smaller community-based organisations, especially those operating at the informal sector interface, are not therefore covered by this. Nevertheless, the data are fascinating and important. They reveal, for instance, that in 2003/04 the sector had a total income of £26.3 billion, assets grossing £70.1 billion, and a workforce of 608,000 paid employees (Wilding et al, 2006b, p 3).

Box 5.2: The voluntary and community sector

The term voluntary and community sector (VCS) is adopted for a number of reasons:

- since 1997, it has been the favoured term of policy makers;
- it emphasises the voluntary dimension – even the larger, more formal organisations that employ paid workers still espouse voluntary principles in their use of unpaid trustees;
- it emphasises the community dimension – the majority of VCS agencies operate locally and rely on volunteers.

On an international level, the most significant research is that based in the Johns Hopkins University in the US. This research has developed and operationalised an International Classification of Non-profit Organisations (ICNPO), which is then used by researchers in different countries to map and measure voluntary organisations there (see Salamon and Anheier, 1997; Salamon et al, 1999; Anheier and Kendall, 2001). This approach uses what has been termed a 'structural operational definition' (Kendall and Knapp, 1996, pp 17–18), with four linked themes:

- formality
- independence
- non-profit distribution
- voluntarism.

As with the NCVO *Almanac*, these themes inevitably exclude many key elements of the sector, including those not formally independent of the state, cooperatives that do operate with profit and loss accounts and (again) smaller community-based organisations. Nevertheless, from this the Johns Hopkins researchers have produced the 12-point ICNPO classification – see **Box 5.3**.

Box 5.3: ICNPO classification

- Culture and recreation
- Education and research
- Health
- Social services
  - children; youth; families; disability; older people (5)
  - self-help; multi-purpose social service (2)
  - support, standards, governance (1)
- Environment
- Development and housing
- Law, advocacy and politics
- Philanthropic intermediaries and voluntarism promotion
- International activities
- Religion
- Business and professional associations, trade unions
- Others

(Kendall and Knapp, 1996, pp 269-73)

The Johns Hopkins studies and much other academic debate and research on the sector are discussed and summarised by Kendall (2003) in a review of the sector, which focuses particularly on the changing nature of relations between voluntary organisations and the state and on the structure and operation of voluntary organisations in the housing, social care and environmental fields. Kendall's analysis provides a good basis for a thorough understanding of the sector and a useful starting point for investigation into the particular role of the sector within the mixed economy of welfare. This is most importantly the case because the sector is a key locus of social policy. Voluntary and community organisations have developed and delivered social policy and continue to do so. What is more, these organisations are themselves the focus of policy action, in part, as will be seen, to support their role as policy providers. Within the mixed economy of welfare, the policy role of the voluntary and community sector is a critically important one; and it is a role with a long history.

Development

The early historical development of the voluntary and community sector (VCS), in particular its relations with the developing state provision of welfare, has been summarised in Chapter Two by Stewart (see also Lewis, 1995, 1999). As Stewart and Lewis make clear, this has been a changing relationship, with Lewis identifying a number of major shifts in the terms of this – for example from the 'parallel bars' (where the state and the voluntary sector operated in separate but complementary fields) to the 'extension ladder' (where voluntary activity aimed to build on basic state services), approaches identified by the Fabian authors Sidney and Beatrice Webb. Even Beveridge, often characterised as the architect of state welfare provision, identified a significant role for voluntary activity in this extension ladder model (Beveridge, 1948).

This history also reveals that the diversity and difference that characterises the sector today has, in fact, always been a feature of voluntary action. In particular, the distinction between philanthropy and mutuality can be found in the 19th-century roots of the sector. For instance, there was a stark difference then between the charitable provision of welfare services to the poor and needy orchestrated by the Charity Organisation Society (Humphries, 1995) and the mutual self-help approach of the Friendly Societies providing insurance-based support for workers threatened with breaks in employment (Gosden, 1961).

At the end of the 20th century, however, another major shift in the relations between the voluntary sector and the state was under way, resulting in particular from some of the broader political and policy debates about a new mixed economy of welfare discussed in the other chapters in this book. For the voluntary and community sector, this meant that the profile of voluntary action and voluntary organisations within political debate and policy practice began to rise significantly, placing the sector at the forefront of many of the developing debates about the reform and delivery of public services. One of the consequences of this new profile was the introduction of new policy initiatives to support the sector and improve its relations with government and other agencies.

For instance, in the early 1990s, the Conservative Prime Minister, John Major, gave his personal support to a new government programme to promote volunteering, called the Make a Difference initiative (see Davis Smith, 2001). But at this time, it was the move towards competitive tendering and outsourcing of contracts for service delivery that had the greatest impact on state and voluntary sector relations.

The use of contracting as the basis for the planning and delivery of services was experienced across public provision, and was underpinned by New Public Management concerns with accountability, delivery and value for money (see Ferlie et al, 1996). However, it was the impact of the community care legislation of 1990 that had probably the greatest direct impact on the voluntary sector. Under this, social services departments and National Health Service agencies were enjoined to work collaboratively in the development of local provision for health and social care, but to look to a range of organisations (public, private and voluntary) to deliver these, the idea being that the statutory bodies would then enter into contracts with these other agencies for the delivery of specific services for specific groups over specific time periods.

This led to a significant change in the nature of the funding relationships between government (particularly local government) and voluntary organisations – a shift from support to regulation and control. Throughout most of the 20th century, most public funding for voluntary organisations was provided in the form of *grants*. These would be fixed sums of money over specific periods of time, often only annual; and they would be provided in order to support the activities of the organisation in question. But the grant would not specify particular activities and payment would not be conditional on successful performance of these. The move to *contracts* changed this, for contract funding was awarded in order to achieve the provision of particular services and was conditional on agreement to provide these in an acceptable form. Contracts are mutually binding agreements that may even have formal legal status, backed up, in principle at least, with formal legal enforcement – referred to by some critics as the growth of a new 'contract culture' within the sector (Russell and Scott, 1997; Billis and Glennerster, 1998).

It was within this wider context of a new phase in relations between the state and the voluntary sector that the NCVO established an independent commission (chaired by Nicholas Deakin) to conduct a review of the role of the sector into the 21st century. The report of the Commission concluded in particular that relations with the state were now of critical importance to the development and operation of the sector and contractual funding for service provision was an important and growing feature of this. In such a context, therefore, it suggested that both parties would benefit from some formalisation and regularisation of relations – preferably through the establishment of a negotiated 'concordat' that could underpin all future contracts and other funding arrangements (Deakin Commission, 1996).

Policy context

There is no doubt that, as other contributors to this book have pointed out, under Labour the notion of the mixed economy of welfare has been more widely and more enthusiastically embraced than at any time in recent policy development, captured more generally in Prime Minister Tony Blair's commitment to the pursuit of a 'Third Way' for politics and policy development, avoiding a focus solely on either the state or the market (Blair, 1998). One of the core features of Labour's Third Way has been its commitment to the promotion of what is now called 'civic renewal' and the open embracing of the civil society dimension of social relations, as discussed earlier. This draws, indirectly at least, on some of the communitarian writings of US commentators like Etzioni (1995, 2000) and on the research of the US political scientist Putnam on the role of 'social capital' in the promotion of social relations (Putnam, 1993, 2000). The literature on this and civil society more generally has been usefully summarised by Deakin (2001); and recent NCVO research has explored the importance of social capital for an understanding of the potential contribution of voluntary action to social relations (Jochum, 2003; Yates and Jochum, 2003).

For the purposes of state and voluntary relations, in particular, what has flowed from these political developments has been a renewed commitment within government to recognition of the role that the sector plays within society generally and in the delivery of public services in particular. Blair has commented on a number of occasions on the importance of including voluntary action within government policy planning, and at the 2004 NCVO Annual Conference, the Chancellor, Gordon Brown, talked of the "transformation of the third sector to rival the market and the state, with a quiet revolution in how voluntary action and charitable work serves the community". This statement has not just been a rhetorical one, however; significant commitments have been made by the government to support the voluntary sector, both through institutional development and investment of resources.

The Voluntary Services Unit within the Home Office, which had been the main source of government funding and support for the sector in general in the latter part of the 20th century, was expanded and relaunched in 1999 as a new Active Communities Unit (ACU) with a much larger budget and a commitment to investment in 'modernising' the infrastructure of the sector. The concordat idea recommended by the Deakin Commission was implemented through the establishment of a formal Compact to govern relations between the sector and the state, developed by the Home Office (1998). This was followed in many places by the establishment of local compacts between local government and voluntary sector representatives (see Craig et al, 2002); and since then, there have been further developments at the national level with the establishment of a permanent Compact Working Group.

The Compact is now to be developed further. There has been the publication of an additional statement on 'Funding and Procurement' providing guidance and a code of practice for these (Home Office, 2005a). This was followed by a process of consultation on a new form of relationship, called Compact Plus, under which selected voluntary organisations would be 'kitemarked' and encouraged to enter into a formal relationship with the state agencies, through which contracts for service delivery could be managed (Home Office, 2005b).

Much of this contracting and compacting activity within the new 'contact culture' has had beneficial impacts. Nevertheless, the waves of increased government interest in VCS have also inevitably been accompanied by increased scrutiny. The stress on Best Value, the measurement and reporting of inputs and outputs, the extension of charitable status (from four categories to 12), and the expansion of National Audit Office monitoring of how the voluntary and public sectors interact, can all be seen as sites for increased state regulation of the sector and the organisations operating within it.

However at the same time, the government has also made more formal commitments to civic renewal with the establishment in 2003 of a Civil Renewal Unit, based in the Home Office, and the publication of a strategy document on *Building Civil Renewal* (Home Office, 2003) outlining plans for support for capacity building within communities. A central feature of these plans now formally refers to the VCS. A guide to these plans and the broader debate about civil renewal and active citizenship has recently been provided by the NCVO (Jochum et al, 2005).

Thus the expansion of involvement of the sector in the delivery of mainstream public services has continued, and yet a wider role in the civic renewal agenda has been developed. These shifts in the nature of relations between the voluntary sector and the state at the beginning of the new century have massively increased both the scale and the profile of the sector within political and policy planning. This was recognised formally in the Home Office's Public Service Agreement, which included a specific target to increase voluntary and community sector activity, including increasing community participation, by 5 per cent by 2006. Underpinning these developments, the government's spending review of 2002 included a 'Cross Cutting Review' of the role of the voluntary and community sector in service delivery (HM Treasury, 2002).

The Cross Cutting Review was steered by a Ministerial group, chaired by the then Financial Secretary to the Treasury, Paul Boateng. It included five working groups focusing on:

- service delivery;
- social and community enterprise;

- capacity;
- funding relationships;
- development of the Compact.

In the Comprehensive Spending Review report that followed, the section on the role of the voluntary sector opened with the statement that:

> The Government needs a voluntary and community sector that is strong, independent and has the capacity, where it wishes, to be a partner in delivering world-class public services. To help achieve this, the Government will increase funding to build capacity in the sector and increase community participation. (HM Treasury, 2002, ch 30)

The review therefore proposed increases in funding for the ACU from £35 million in 2002/03 to £65 million in 2005/06, and announced a range of other new initiatives – see **Box 5.4**.

Box 5.4: Cross Cutting Review

- A new *Future*builders investment fund, worth £125 million over three years, to tackle the barriers to effective service delivery and to modernize the sector through the purchase or development of physical assets (such as buildings) or intangible assets (such as intellectual property), or the provision of one-off development funding by grants or loans.
- A commitment to implement fully the Compact and its attendant Codes, through the appointment of a senior official in each government department to 'champion' engagement with the sector.
- An acceptance that overhead costs should be covered within the contracts for delivery of public services.
- A commitment to maximise the added value provided by the voluntary sector by involving it in both the planning and delivery of public services.
- A commitment for all government departments to adopt a strategic approach to capacity building. (HM Treasury, 2002)

The *Future*builders fund revealed a commitment by government to take a lead in developing the capacity of the sector through strategic investment, and was clear evidence of the changed nature of relations between the state and the voluntary sector under Labour at the start of the 21st century. And it was quickly followed by another initiative called ChangeUp (Home Office, 2004). The aim of this is to provide support for the development of expertise within the sector and for the work of infrastructural agencies, in particular at the local level. The funding for this included £80 million for initial support for a capacity-building framework, followed by £70 million over the two years from 2006 to 2008, under the leadership of a new agency called Capacity Builders (Home Office, 2005c). It also included the formal establishment of a number of 'hubs' of expertise to provide advice and guidance to the sector, initially covering six areas of activity and funded by £16.5 million over two years:

- performance improvement;
- workforce development;
- ICT;
- governance;
- financing voluntary and community sector activity;
- recruiting and developing volunteers.

There can now be no doubt therefore of the commitment by government to an increasingly high profile for the voluntary sector backed up by the allocation of resources to support this.

These developments were the subject of a review by the National Audit Office in 2005, focusing on the role of the Home Office in working with the 'third sector' (NAO, 2005).

This concluded that, although much had been done by government, and by the sector itself, to improve relations and develop the capacity of the sector, many strategic and practical problems remained in the management of relations between the two. Recommendations for further action and improvement were made, which have largely been accepted by government, although they have led to some debate within the sector itself.

Since then there have also been significant changes in the structure of organisational responsibility for relations between the VCS and the state. In May 2006 primary responsibility for relations with the sector was transferred from the Home Office to the Cabinet Office, with the Active Communities Unit (by now a Directorate) moving into a new Office of the Third Sector. Responsibility for fiscal policy for the sector, including charitable funding, remains within the Treasury, however, in a Charity and Third Sector Finance Unit. The Treasury has also, in conjunction with the Cabinet Office, initiated a further joint review of the VCS, as part of the 2007 Comprehensive Spending Review round. Responsibility for support for social enterprise has been transferred to a new Social Enterprise Unit in the Department of Communities and Local Government. Despite the restructuring, therefore, fragmentation of responsibility still remains.

The problem for the voluntary and community sector with all of this new government concern and policy action on state and voluntary sector relations is that it is to a significant extent predicated on assumptions about the nature of the sector and its primary activities and needs that do not recognise or respond to the very diversity of voluntary and community action discussed earlier.

For those organisations that are engaged in ongoing and (perhaps) contractual relations with the state over the development or delivery of services, the work of the Home Office, the Compact, *Future*builders and ChangeUp is a potentially important element of a developing and improving engagement – evidence that the mixed economy of welfare now encompasses managed and supported relationships between the public and voluntary sectors. However, for those organisations that are not regularly engaged in formal relations with the state – in particular the smaller community-based self-help groups that probably make up the majority of voluntary and community action in practice – such policy intervention is largely irrelevant.

Thus some in the sector have openly embraced the new service delivery and public funding climate, for instance the proponents of a Voluntary Finance Initiative, aimed at ensuring solid funding for those service-delivery voluntary and community bodies involved (Ormerod et al, 2003; ACEVO, 2004). Others, including the NCVO, the major national infrastructure body for the sector, adopt a more cautious approach. Indeed, the NCVO points out that two thirds of respondents in a recent survey believed that there had been too much emphasis on the VCS as a service-delivery mechanism (Brindle, 2005).

There is something of a contrast here, too, with the rhetoric of commitment to the role of the sector in the promotion of civil renewal (Home Office, 2003). Deepening service-delivery roles, it is argued by some, could erode public trust in voluntary bodies, and weaken the capacity of these same agencies to maintain high standards of accountability and user-sensitivity (Paxton and Pearce, 2005). These are the core ingredients that enable the VCS to play a vital role in civil renewal and community cohesion in the first place, and yet in practice it has received considerably less financial investment from government.

Indeed, the new policy context may even be threatening to many voluntary and community organisations. It can threaten by omission, suggesting that organisations not actively involved in Compact and Compact Plus are not worthy of policy interest or support. And it can threaten by commission, implying that all organisations should embrace the new structures and guidance in order to establish their status as members of the sector. The policy context of the new mixed economy therefore now recognises the importance of engaging actively in relations with the voluntary and community sector; but it may not be able to embrace the 'loose and baggy monster' with which it is seeking to engage.

Description

It is difficult to under-emphasise the importance of this diversity within the voluntary and community sector, in particular to political and policy-making audiences that see a role for the sector within a mixed economy welfare policy. A role for the sector implies distinction and definition, it implies relationship and regulation, it implies contracting and compacting and it implies support and sustainability. In each case an implicit question remains – of what? As discussed earlier, attempts to define the sector often do so relatively, in terms of distinction from, and in relation to, other sectors of welfare provision. Attempts to map or measure the sector rely on the implicit definitions contained in official statistics or international classifications.

However, these approaches inevitably exclude many voluntary and community organisations – indeed they may in practice exclude most. The NCVO *Almanac* contains information on 169,000 general charities (Wilding et al, 2006b, p 3). But other measures suggest numbers way beyond these, for instance Westall (2005, pp 76-8) talks of:

- 220,000 organisations in the wider 'not-for-profit' sector (including sports, arts and housing);
- 100,000 community groups;
- 600,000-900,000 micro groups.

Policy concern and quantitative measurement are perhaps inevitably going to focus primarily on the larger and more formally established voluntary organisations that are registered as charities or companies, or are contracting with or funded by the public sector. And within this context the evidence suggests that a small number of larger organisations are dominant here, at least in financial terms, with 14 'super charities', each with incomes of over £100 million a year, more than 10 per cent of the overall income of the sector (Wilding et al, 2006b, pp 6-7). In the context of the triangle of inter-sectoral landscapes in **Figure 5.1**, these are likely to be those organisations in the top right corner operating around the borders with the public sector.

However, there is a much wider range of organisations, with a wider range of structures and problems, making significant contributions in practice to the mixed economy of welfare. Qualitative research by the authors and colleagues over a number of years has explored the range of voluntary sector organisations, their experiences of the national policy context and their changing relations with the state (Russell et al, 1993, 1995; Russell and Scott, 1997; Scott et al, 2000; Alcock and Scott, 2005). The following three examples have been drawn from this research to outline some of the policy and practice issues associated with the different inter-sectoral boundaries within the mixed economy.

Box 5.5: Tumble Tots – informal/VCS

It is just getting light when a young woman pushes her child in his buggy past the window, two minutes later the scene is repeated. A few minutes go by and two women walk briskly back without buggies. One hour later and the human traffic intensifies as primary and secondary school pupils straggle off to their respective destinations. Then, at about 9.15 am, there is another, smaller tidal wave of young mothers tugging 3- and 4-year-olds to pre-school. The final episode in all these 'outward' journeys occurs when some pre-schoolers are shunted from one side of the Community Centre to the other, from voluntary, non-profit pre-school to commercial, for profit 'Tumble Tots'. The welfare mix, for one sub-category of the classification system, is at work.

The earliest buggies are en route to paid childminders, some 'hidden' from officialdom, others inspected, supported and regulated by local authority social services departments. The pre-school group will normally be managed by a committee of parents (usually mothers) on an entirely voluntary basis, the committee will employ paid part-time workers as circumstances allow, and these will be helped by a rota of volunteers from the mothers with children in the group. 'Tumble Tots' is typical of for-profit play/nursery provision and will be owned and managed as a small business. (Scott, 2003, p 301)

The main organisational dimensions of these informal and small group worlds centre on a mesh of micro-reciprocities and voluntary commitments. Most childminders know each other and operate a 'bush telegraph' about the changing contexts of their work – new customers, links with pre-school, impending inspection and so on. Pre-schools range from the purely voluntary to a mix of paid workers, with parental presence on the management committees. Different degrees of formality are necessary to maintain and manage the pre-school relationship, including volunteer rotas, fundraising, negotiation with local primary schools, and responding to changing regulatory regimes.

All these recurrent activities present organisational challenges, which are met by a mix of informal, implicit responses intermingled with smaller amounts of formality (lists on noticeboards, introductory leaflets, annual reports). In poorer neighbourhoods, much of the administrative burden may be undertaken by programme workers from agencies such as Sure Start; whereas in middle England networks of middle-class women follow their children through pre-school into the ascending layers of formal education.

The extent to which the informal/formal resource mix is sufficient for the mesh of tasks varies within and between agencies. Much depends on degrees of continuity in key volunteers, stability of premises, financial flows, relationships with the host community association and changing regulatory requirements. Sudden new policy demands can exert pressure on the informal relationships that sustain the pre-school sector and lead to other unintended outcomes. Pre-schools can become one of the most important sources of social capital in local neighbourhoods. The young mother decides to train as a welfare worker as a result of time spent volunteering, and the committee members develop friendships that result in their becoming more prominent players in the wider community. Yet increasing regulation by public authorities can threaten the viability, and even the desirability, of such fragile organisational forms.

Box 5.6: Small Potatoes – private/VCS

Small Potatoes was established in 1992 to offer a commercial response to the problems of hard-to-employ groups such as ex-offenders and homeless people. It buys produce from local wholesalers and then employs over 200 people to sell this at local markets and on the streets. The work opportunities business began as a company limited by guarantee with a charitable trust, but has since been restructured on two occasions, first, to separate the charitable trust from the business arm and second, to merge with another social enterprise involved in a diversity of social and regeneration contracts, providing local social and healthcare services. Current turnover (2004) is around £5 million, with nearly 140 paid workers and volunteers as trustees. The company is housed in modern, spacious, three-storey premises in a regeneration area of a large city; nearby are a number of fashionable shops and bars. A bold mural spans two floors within a central atrium, and on it are the names of the hundreds of individual and corporate sponsors.

Attempting to combine both social and economic objectives presents perhaps the central challenge for such organisations, as the beneficiaries are both economic units and clients. Each individual enters into a two-year franchise agreement, whereby, in addition to selling vegetables as independent traders, they are required to become involved in supervision sessions and training activities. There are thus continuing disagreements between senior managers responsible for economic and social goals, respectively (Pharoah et al, 2004, p 35). One of the latter commented (about her sales services colleague): "we had some really difficult sessions ... I was struggling to work with what I saw as different cultures and value systems" (Pharoah et al, 2004, p 46). These cultural and value differences also influence, even threaten, the external relations of Small Potatoes. A senior manager talked of the constant risk that their public image as a (relatively) successful agency could be disrupted by the street trading behaviour of their clients.

While informal childminding networks and pre-school groups often grow in relatively unplanned ways, more complex and larger-scale organisations such as Small Potatoes need more formal systems. Social enterprises such as these can take up to 10 years to build a core of experienced workers and enough of a reputation to attract major funding. Many initiatives fail during this period. The ability to deploy successfully social and financial skills is neither universally distributed nor easily acquired. Moreover, even as the organisation becomes more formalised, there is still evidence that the capacity to respond to uncertainty is central; the popular term 'social entrepreneur' is not simply a description of someone who is a rational go-between (literally an intermediary). There is also convincing evidence that the inter-sectoral borderlands between the private sector and VCS are characterised as much by informal, contingent and competitive behaviour as by formal planning and cooperation (Pharoah et al, 2004, p 70).

> **Box 5.7:** Family Friends – public/VCS
>
> "When I came back to work from having flu, the forms were on my desk. They are about 25 pages long – look at them! They want strategic plans, business plans, budgets and God knows what else.... And this is just one of the forms. And we've got 3 weeks to do it. And there's £7 million being thrown at this programme – where has it suddenly come from?
>
> … There is a flurry of activity. This is where we go wrong in the voluntary sector. In my opinion, it would be much healthier for the whole of the voluntary sector to turn round and say 'This is totally unrealistic, this is stupid. Take it away, we don't want any of it'. Funders would then have to re-think how they do things. But you won't get that – you'll get people rushing to fill in forms and create projects." (Scott et al, 2000, p 50)

Family Friends is a voluntary organisation that aims to promote the welfare of families with at least one child under five years. It experienced major funding increases at the end of the 1990s, as the government's emphasis on family and first years gained momentum. In 1999-2000, the social services grant increased by over 30% to almost £130,000, with comparable increases coming from the then Department of Education. All of this funding paid for six full-time and three part-time staff, coordinating 115 volunteers. Its experience of sudden public sector contracts is captured in the above excerpt from an interview with the senior organiser.

Of course, detailed empirical case studies, such as those on the impact of public sector contracting on voluntary and community agencies, provide a mixed picture. Despite the post-influenza scepticism of the Family Friends organiser, a number of the interviewees in our many studies were positive about the advantages of contractually based services. Instead of chasing a huge range of small grants, larger and defined arrangements brought degrees of stability and status. But the picture was indeed mixed. Even within a single agency some workers and volunteers differed in their views about impact. For example, it became clear that younger staff often adopted more careerist and instrumental views about their motives and aspirations. And, even when it became apparent that contracts frequently marginalised volunteers in a strategic sense (they played little or no part in the decisions relating to contracting), many were positive about their new 'busyness' (for instance, Russell and Scott, 1997).

Future prospects

The size and diversity of the voluntary and community sector mean that any attempt to include it in a mapping of the mixed economy of welfare will inevitably be to some extent partial and incomplete. This does not mean, of course, that 'a little knowledge is a dangerous thing'. Indeed, the quantitative and qualitative measurement and description of the sector that has increasingly taken place in academic research over the past decade or so means that we do know much about the size and shape of the sector and the roles that it plays within welfare policy. We know more; but we are also more aware of how little we know (Kendall, 2003, p 232).

Diversity and difference within the sector is not just an academic issue, however. It is also of critical importance to the political debates and the policy planning that are now taking place to support and develop a mixed economy of welfare in 21st-century Britain. As discussed earlier, the policy context is now one in which significant expectations are entertained by government about the roles for the sector and significant investments are being made in support and development for the sector to fulfil these roles. In one sense, therefore, the future prospects for the sector are both positive and extensive. But in practice the complexity of the sector and the tensions within the policy process make these future prospects rather more contradictory.

For a start, there are some very different expectations of the roles that the sector might play within the new development and delivery of welfare. On the one hand, there is the expectation that voluntary activity and the voluntary ethos can in itself contribute to civic renewal and a revitalisation of civil society. This draws on the Putnam (1993, 2000) notion of voluntary action as a core element in the measurement and promotion of social capital, and is now openly championed by the Home Office in its attempt to build 'civil renewal' (Home Office, 2003). However, in practice, relatively little in the way of public resources has been provided to support this more general role for the sector; and there is little recognition of the problems of transforming the concerns of particular voluntary organisations into a more general contribution to the enhancement of socio-structural relations.

There is something of a contrast here with the more specific support that is now provided for capacity building, promotion of good practice and infrastructural support for organisations involved in the delivery of public services. Futurebuilders, ChangeUp and the Compact have involved significant investments of both financial and political capital by government. It is too early as yet for any informed judgement of the impact of these on the sector, and on the citizens for whom it is now providing services, although, as the National Audit Office review revealed, many practical problems so far remain and further actions and improvements are needed (NAO, 2005).

The future prospects for VCS in this new policy climate therefore are likely to depend on whether these extensive, and consistent, expectations are maintained and how these practical problems are addressed. And these are likely to depend themselves on the future development of relations within the sector and between the sector and the public, private and informal sectors with which it interlinks. There are increasing signs that whatever the government's principled commitment to a Third Way here, in practice it is disproportionately favouring for-profit organisations, particularly in relation to health service delivery – traditionally an area employing VCS organisations. However, it is perhaps too early to tell if the growing mix of pragmatic privatisation here will directly affect organisations in the sector. In summary, there are nevertheless both endogenous and exogenous pressures here; and the location of voluntary action 'between the state and the market' will remain of central importance to its future development.

Conclusion

That VCS must adapt to a changing social, political and economic climate is, of course, neither unique nor new; but there is a concern within the sector (or at least within major infrastructural organisations such as the NCVO) that the current drive towards increased public service delivery within a more fragmented and demanding consumer market will pose challenges for many organisations. These are summarised in another publication from the NCVO on the challenges facing voluntary action in the 21st century (Robb, 2005, p 9):

> Will our sector just be left to fit round this new consensus in the places neither the public or private sectors feel comfortable or profitable? Can the various strands of the broader third sector find enough common cause to unite and genuinely place their values and view of the world alongside the other two?

At the same time, challenges will come from inter-sectoral relations. On the boundaries with the private sector, the ability of major social enterprises such as housing associations to balance commercial viability with independence and accountability is growing. But it is on the boundaries with the state where many of the most difficult challenges of the new political economy lie. In large part, this is because of inconsistencies and contradictions within the public policy itself. These include an imbalance in investment between service delivery and civil renewal at central government level, with little more than rhetoric following the latter, and a continuing gap between central government policies on compacting and mainstreaming and evidence of inadequate practices within local authorities and other local state agencies. On the ground, relations are still problematic (for instance, Alcock et al, 2004).

They also, however, include ambivalence within some sections of government and the public sector over the commitment to the mixed economy of public welfare, with voluntary organisations increasingly playing a role once occupied by arms of the central and local state – for instance in some Labour controlled local authorities. A sustainable mixed economy of welfare will ultimately rely as much on political change and policy reform in the public sector as it will on the capacity building and organisational development of the voluntary and community sector, as other contributors to this volume have pointed out. As discussed earlier, the history of voluntary action in the past century was played out to a large extent against the changing political and policy context of public welfare. In the new century, the future prospects for the sector are likely to be just as closely linked to the latest version of the ever-changing welfare mix.

Summary

- There are difficulties and disagreements in defining and measuring the voluntary and community sector.
- The sector is very diverse, and this is reflected in the roles and structures of the different voluntary organisations and community groups.
- Understanding the operation of the sector involves appreciation in particular of the 'inter-sectoral landscapes' within which it operates.
- The policy context for the sector has been changing significantly and rapidly in recent years and the profile of VCS within the mixed economy of welfare has been increasing dramatically.
- The growth of government support for the sector has given rise to contradictory pressures, whose impacts vary depending on the different types of organisation.

Further reading

The best source of data on VCS is the biennial *Almanac* from the National Council for Voluntary Organisations **(Wilding et al, 2006a, 2006b)**.

The most comprehensive overview of the policy context of VCS in the UK is **Kendall (2003)**.

A range of perspectives and issues can be obtained from reading the essays in **Harris and Rochester (2001)**.

Policy debate on VCS organisations delivering public services is succinctly discussed in **Paxton et al (2005)**.

Electronic resources

Centre for Civil Society – an academic site with links to UK and comparative analysis in developing countries (www.lse.ac.uk/collections/ccs).

Charities Aid Foundation – charitable giving and financial trends (www.cafonline.org).

Community Development Exchange – community-based practice (www.cdx.org.uk).

Community Development Foundation – policy-related research and practice in relation to community development (www.cdf.org.uk).

National Council for Voluntary Organisations – the main coordinating agency for information and policy development within the English voluntary sector (www.ncvo-vol.org.uk).

Office of the Third Sector – coordination of government policy is now based in the Cabinet Office (www.cabinetoffice.gov.uk/the_third_sector).

Volunteering England – research, information and policy development in relation to volunteering (www.volunteeringengland.org).

Voluntary Sector Studies Network – the main academic association for researching VCS (www.vssn.org.uk).

References

ACEVO (Association of Chief Executives of Voluntary Organisations) (2004) *Communities in Control*, London: ACEVO.

Alcock, P. and Scott, D. (eds) (2005) *'Close Work': Doing Qualitative Research in the Voluntary Sector*, West Malling: Charities Aid Foundation.

Alcock, P., Brannelly, T. and Ross, L. (2004) *Formality or Flexibility: Voluntary Sector Contracting in Social Care and Health*, London: National Council for Voluntary Organisations.

Anheier, H. and Kendall, J. (eds) (2001) *Third Sector Policy at the Crossroads: An International Non-profit Analysis*, London: Routledge.

Beveridge, W. (1948) *Voluntary Action: A Report on Methods of Social Advance*, London: Allen and Unwin.

Billis, D. and Glennerster, H. (1998) 'Human services and the voluntary sector: towards a theory of comparative advantage', *Journal of Social Policy*, vol 27, no 1, pp 79-98.

Blair, T. (1998) *The Third Way*, London: Fabian Society.

Brindle, D. (2005) 'Happy days ... but a rosy future?', *Guardian*, 28 September.

Craig, G., Taylor, M., Wilkinson, M. and Monro, S. (2002) *Contract or Trust? The Role of Compacts in Local Governance*, Bristol: The Policy Press.

Davis Smith, J. (2001) 'Volunteers: making a difference?', in M. Harris and C. Rochester (eds) *Voluntary Organisations and Social Policy in Britain: Perspectives on Change and Choice*, Basingstoke: Palgrave, pp 185-99.

Deakin, N. (2001) *In Search of Civil Society*, Basingstoke: Palgrave.

Deakin Commission (1996) *Meeting the Challenge of Change: Voluntary Action into the 21st Century, Report of the Commission on the Future of the Voluntary Sector in England*, London: National Council for Voluntary Organisations.

Etzioni, A. (1995) *The Spirit of Community: Rights and Responsibilities and the Communitarian Agenda*, London: Fontana Press.

Etzioni, A. (2000) *The Third Way to a Good Society*, London: Demos.

Evers, A. and Laville, J.-L. (eds) (2004) *The Third Sector in Europe*, Cheltenham: Edward Elgar.

Ferlie, E., Ashburner, L., Fitzgerald, L. and Pettigrew, A. (1996) *The New Public Management in Action*, Oxford: Oxford University Press.

Gosden, P. (1961) *The Friendly Societies in England 1815-1875*, Manchester: Manchester University Press.

Harris, M. and Rochester, C. (eds) (2001) *Voluntary Organisations and Social Policy in Britain: Perspectives on Change and Choice*, Basingstoke: Palgrave.

HM Treasury (2002) *The Role of the Voluntary and Community Sector in Service Delivery: A Cross Cutting Review*, London: HM Treasury.

HM Treasury (2003) *Futurebuilders. An Investment Fund for Voluntary and Community Sector Public Delivery: Proposals for Consultation*, London: HM Treasury.

Home Office (1998) *Compact on Relations between Government and the Voluntary and Community Sector in England*, Cm 4100, London: Stationery Office.

Home Office (2003) *Building Civil Renewal: Government Support for Community Capacity Building and Proposals for Change*, London: Home Office.

Home Office (2004) *ChangeUp: Capacity Building and Infrastructure Framework for the Voluntary and Community Sector*, London: Home Office.

Home Office (2005a) *Funding and Procurement: Compact Code of Good Practice*, London: Home Office.

Home Office (2005b) *Strengthening Partnerships: Next Steps for the Compact, A Consultation Document*, London: Home Office.

Home Office (2005c) *Developing Capacity: Next Steps for ChangeUp*, London: Home Office.

Humphries, R. (1995) *Sin, Organised Charity and the Poor Law in Victorian England*, Basingstoke: Macmillan.

Jochum, V. (2003) *Social Capital: Beyond the Theory*, London: National Council for Voluntary Organisations.

Jochum, V., Pratten, B. and Wilding, K. (2005) *Civil Renewal and Active Citizenship: A Guide to the Debate*, London: National Council for Voluntary Organisations.

Kendall, J. (2003) *The Voluntary Sector*, London: Routledge.

Kendall, J. and Knapp, M. (1996) *The Voluntary Sector in the UK*, Manchester: Manchester University Press.

Lewis, J. (1995) *The Voluntary Sector, the State and Social Work in Britain*, Cheltenham: Edward Elgar.

Lewis, J. (1999) 'Reviewing the relationship between the voluntary sector and the state in Britain in the 1990s', *Voluntas*, vol 10, no 3, pp 255-70.

NAO (National Audit Office) (2005) *Home Office: Working with the Third Sector*, London: The Stationery Office.

Ormerod, P., Kay, J., Mayo, E. and Hutton, W. (2003) *Replacing the State? The Case for Third Sector Public Service Delivery*, London: Association of Chief Executives of Voluntary Organisations.

Paxton, W. and Pearce, N. (2005) 'The voluntary sector and the state', in W. Paxton, N. Pearce, J. Unwin and P. Molyneux *The Voluntary Sector Delivering Public Services: Transfer or Transformation?*, York: Joseph Rowntree Foundation, pp 3-36.

Paxton, W., Pearce, N., Unwin, J. and Molyneux, P. (2005) *The Voluntary Sector Delivering Public Services: Transfer or Transformation?*, York: Joseph Rowntree Foundation.

Pharoah, C., Scott, D. and Fisher, A. (2004) *Social Enterprise in the Balance: Challenges for the Voluntary Sector*, West Malling: Charities Aid Foundation.

Putnam, R. (1993) *Making Democracy Work: Civic Traditions in Modern Italy*, Princeton, NJ: Princeton University Press.

Putnam, R. (2000) *Bowling Alone: The Collapse and Revival of American Community*, New York, NY: Simon and Schuster.

Robb, C. (ed) (2005) *Voluntary Action: Meeting the Challenges of the 21st Century*, London: National Council for Voluntary Organisations.

Russell, L. and Scott, D. (1997) *Very Active Citizens? The Impact of Contracts on Volunteers*, Manchester: University of Manchester.

Russell, L., Scott, D. and Wilding, P. (1993) *Funding the Voluntary Sector: A Case Study from the North of England*, Manchester: University of Manchester.

Russell, L., Scott, D. and Wilding, P. (1995) *Mixed Fortunes: The Funding of the Voluntary Sector*, Manchester: University of Manchester.

Salamon, L. and Anheier, H. (1997) *Defining the Nonprofit Sector: A Cross-national Analysis*, Manchester: Manchester University Press.

Salamon, L., List, R., Toepler, S., Sokolowski, S. and associates (eds) (1999) *Global Civil Society: Dimensions of the Non-profit Sector*, Baltimore, MD: Johns Hopkins Centre for Civil Society Studies.

Scott, D. (2003) 'The role of the voluntary and non-governmental sector', in J. Baldock, N. Manning, and S. Vickerstaff (eds) *Social Policy*, Oxford: Oxford University Press, pp 293-326.

Scott, D., Alcock, P., Russell, L. and Macmillan, R. (2000) *Moving Pictures: Realities of Voluntary Action*, Bristol: The Policy Press.

Westall, A. (2005) 'Exploring diversity: the links between voluntary and community organisations, social enterprise, and cooperations and mutuals', in C. Robb (ed) *Voluntary Action: Meeting the Challenges of the 21st Century*, London: National Council for Voluntary Organisations, pp 69-93.

Wilding, K., Clark, J., Griffith, M., Jochum, V. and Wainwright, S. (2006a) *The UK Voluntary Sector Almanac 2006*, London: National Council for Voluntary Organisations.

Wilding, K., Clark, J., Griffith, M., Jochum, V. and Wainwright, S. (2006b) *The UK Voluntary Sector Almanac 2006: The State of the Sector (Summary)*, London: National Council for Voluntary Organisations.

Yates, H. and Jochum, V. (2003) *It's Who You Know That Counts: The Role of the Voluntary Sector in the Development of Social Capital in Rural Areas*, London: National Council for Voluntary Organisations /The Countryside Agency.

six

Informal welfare

Hilary Arksey and Caroline Glendinning

Overview

Families, friends, neighbours and other informal networks constitute very substantial sources of welfare. This chapter focuses on one particular type of informal welfare – the help, largely unpaid, provided by the close relatives and friends of sick or disabled children, adults and older people. To set the chapter in context, details of the adult unpaid carer population are provided. Next, policies for carers that have been introduced since the mid-1990s are outlined and evidence is presented about their impact on improving support for carers. Finally, the impact of these policies is discussed and reasons for their limited impact are explored.

Key concepts

Informal sector • community care • informal care giving • carer legislation • National Strategy for Carers • disabled people's movement • carers as a free resource

Introduction

Welfare, in its broadest sense, is provided by a wide range of organisations and individuals, over and above the services that are funded or arranged by the welfare state. Voluntary organisations are major providers of information, advice and more direct services, particularly to people whose circumstances are relatively unusual. Often such organisations are funded by national or local government to provide this support. For example, voluntary organisations provide services for disabled and older people, and for their carers; they represent the interests of disabled and older people and carers to the planners and funders of services; and many voluntary organisations also offer valuable opportunities to meet others in similar situations so that information and common experiences can be shared.

However, an even more significant source of non-statutory welfare is the help provided by relatives, friends and neighbours. The help that is provided by these people is often termed 'informal' as it comes not from formal organisations but derives from different types of close relationships between individuals: kinship relationships between family members; the mutual obligations that develop between neighbours, friends and within communities; or the support that is exchanged between people in similar situations through self-help and other networks. Many of these relationships are characterised by reciprocity – the explicit or implicit assumption that the help that is given is in return for support given in the past, or that it will be returned at some time in the future. Reciprocity is one of the main foundations of care-giving relationships (Qureshi and Walker, 1989).

In many instances, these mutual obligations are highly generalised or non-specific. For example, the care that parents provide for their children when young may lead those children to wish to return that care by supporting their parents in their old age; Finch and Mason (1993, p 51) refer to this indirect exchange as 'generalised reciprocity', in which "there is simply the expectation that repayment will be made at some point". Some people may prefer to give help to, or receive help from, friends and relatives rather than formal services, reflecting strongly held normative beliefs about the 'proper thing to do' in the context of valued personal relationships (Williams, 2004). Thus, for example, some parents needing care for their children while they are at work may prefer to obtain this from grandparents, siblings or other parents, believing that this is 'better' than formal services provided by local authority or private sector nurseries (Skinner and Finch, 2006). Similarly, some older people may be reluctant to receive help from local authority services, preferring instead to receive help with personal care and daily living activities from their spouses or children.

Because informal welfare is rooted in close relationships within families and between friends, it is difficult to identify and quantify through surveys and other research. However, there is one kind of informal welfare that has received considerable attention from researchers and policy makers since the 1970s – the support that is provided by families, friends and neighbours for disabled or chronically sick adults and frail older people (Ungerson, 2003). This is generally termed 'informal care'.

Indeed, the majority of the support required by disabled adults and frail older people is provided by close relatives, other family members, friends and neighbours on an informal basis. This is particularly the case if the help that is needed is very intensive, or involves intimate care (Walker, 1995; Pickard, 2001).

As early as 1968, Richard Titmuss questioned the meaning of the term 'community care' (Titmuss, 1968). In particular, he was concerned that people with mental health problems were being discharged from hospitals into the community without adequate provision and argued for a major expansion in community-based formal social services (Titmuss, 1968). In the following years, feminist researchers revealed the extent of the unpaid care provided for sick, disabled and older people (Oakley, 1974; Martin and Roberts, 1984; Baldwin and Twigg, 1991; Fine and Glendinning, 2005). They argued that, in reality, community care policies depend on women in their roles as unpaid carers and serve to reinforce women's disadvantaged position in the labour market (Finch and Groves, 1983; Ungerson, 1987).

Successive governments responded only slowly to these critiques. In 1976, a new cash benefit, the Invalid Care Allowance (now called Carers Allowance) was introduced for working-age men and single women who had no income from paid work because they were caring for a relative. Married women were not eligible, on the grounds that they would be at home in any case and only became eligible for the benefit in 1986 following a test case in the European Court. In 1988, the Griffiths Report, *Community Care: Agenda for Action*, emphasised the need to support informal carers (Griffiths, 1988). The second priority of the subsequent 1989 White Paper, *Caring for People*, was to increase levels of practical support for carers (DH, 1989). This was particularly important as the White Paper's proposals, enacted in the 1990 NHS and Community Care Act, aimed to promote care in the community rather than institutional settings for disabled adults and older people – a measure that in practice meant care at home by family members. Since the 1990s, policy measures have continued to encourage care in the community but, as discussed later, the welfare provided by informal carers has increasingly been incorporated into the welfare mix through legislation and other initiatives.

The state welfare system would not be able to cope without informal care (DH, 2005), and future demand for informal care is likely to increase rather than decrease (Pickard et al, 2000). Although people may live longer in the future, this does not necessarily mean that their later years will be spent in good health (Kelly et al, 2000), suggesting that needs for additional support in older age are likely to increase rather than diminish. Encouraging and sustaining the informal care provided by family and friends is one way that policy makers can continue to deliver community care without substantial additional financial resources (Parker and Clarke, 2002). One estimate of the cost to the state of replacing the support provided by informal carers in the UK is £57 billion – roughly equivalent to the cost of the NHS (Carers UK, 2002).

The next section briefly summarises evidence on the numbers and characteristics of informal carers.

Carers – who are they?

Throughout the past 20 years, families – and particularly women within families – have provided the bulk of the support needed by disabled and frail older people (Qureshi and Walker, 1989; Maher and Green, 2002; Parker and Clarke, 2002). Despite recent increases in women's labour market participation, female relatives are still more likely than male relatives to be providing support.

Estimates of the volume of unpaid care are available from large-scale data sets such as the British Household Panel Survey (BHPS), the General Household Survey (GHS) and the 2001 Census. Analysis of the GHS for 2000 showed that there were around 6.8 million adult carers in Britain (Maher and Green, 2002). Nearly one carer in 20 (4%) spent 20 or more hours per week on care-giving activities. While women were more likely to be carers than men (18% compared with 14%), men nevertheless constituted four out of 10 carers. However, only 3% of men spent at least 20 hours per week on caring tasks, compared with 5% of women.

The 2001 Census asked everyone whether they provided care for someone who was sick, disabled or elderly. The Census figures are likely to be more accurate because they are based on a complete rather than a sample enumeration of the population (Hirst, 2005). They are also useful for providing information about the geographical distribution of the carer population. **Box 6.1** gives an overview of care giving by individuals of all ages in England and Wales.

Box 6.1: Care giving in England and Wales in April 2001

The Census showed that in England and Wales in April 2001:
- There were 5.2 million carers of all ages, one in 10 of the population; about 175,000 of these individuals were young carers (aged between five and 17).
- Below the age of 65, women were more likely than men to be carers; above the age of 65, men were more likely than women to be carers.
- Of the total population of carers, 68% cared for up to 19 hours per week; 11% for 20-49 hours per week; 21% for 50 or more hours per week. Seven per cent of young carers, the majority of whom were aged 16 to 17, cared for 50 hours a week or more.

- Among 16- to 74-year-olds, only about half of carers who spent between 20 and 49 hours caring per week were in employment, compared with about six out of 10 non-carers. Among those caring for 50 or more hours per week, only three out of 10 had paid jobs.
- People in their 50s were most likely to be providing care: more than one person in five aged 50-59 had caring responsibilities. Although the proportion then declined with age, significant numbers of people aged 75 and over had caring responsibilities.
- Many carers were not in good health themselves, especially older carers and carers providing more than 50 hours of care per week.
- Wales had a higher proportion of carers than any English region (11.7%).
- In England, the North East had the highest proportion (11%) of carers, followed by the North West (10.8%); London had the lowest proportion (8.5%).
- Among women, Pakistani, Bangladeshi and White British groups were most likely to be carers; among men, Indian, Pakistani, Bangladeshi and White British groups were most likely to be carers.

Sources: National Statistics Online website; Becker, 2004; Arksey et al, 2005; Buckner and Yeandle, 2005a; Young et al, 2005.

Carers are a very diverse group (Eley, 2003). Buckner and Yeandle (2005b) found that, across the UK, more than 1.5 million carers are aged 60 or over. Of these, almost 350,000 carers are 75 or over, and more than 8,000 are 90 or over. As age increases, men are more likely than women to be care givers and the amount of care they provide also increases; at 85 and above, over half of male carers and almost half of female carers provide 50 hours or more of care each week.

At the other end of the age scale, the 2001 Census indicates that there are 150,000 young (under age 18) carers in England and Wales (Dearden and Becker, 2004), nearly 5,500 of whom are between five and seven years old. The majority is much older, the largest proportion being 16 or 17 years old. However, the definition of young carers is highly contested, with many researchers and disabled people arguing that research and policy should focus on providing adequate formal services for disabled parents so that they do not have to rely on their children for support (Keith and Morris, 1995; Olsen and Tyers, 2004).

The GHS and Census provide only 'snapshot' figures. However, the BHPS shows there is a steady turnover among the carer population; each year a third of co-resident carers and 40% of carers living in another household become carers and similar proportions cease to be carers (Hirst, 2002).

New Labour's policy response to carers

What measures has New Labour introduced to support informal carers? Apart from the Invalid Care Allowance (discussed earlier), the first piece of legislation specifically aimed at carers – the 1995 Carers (Recognition and Services) Act – was implemented shortly before New Labour came into power. Since then, three further measures have been enacted (**Box 6.2**). It is important to note, however, that no additional funding was provided for local authorities to implement the new legislation, although resources were made available for the National Strategy for Carers. Other health and social care policies, for instance, Standard Six of the National Service Framework for Mental Health (DH, 1999b), have also emphasised the need for services to support carers.

Box 6.2: Policy landmarks for carers

1. 1995 Carers (Recognition and Services) Act
2. 1999 National Strategy for Carers
3. 2000 Carers and Disabled Children Act
4. 2004 Carers (Equal Opportunities) Act

Carers' organisations, in particular Carers UK, have been highly effective in achieving policy recognition and rights for carers; indeed, the UK is one of the few countries in the European Union in which carers have legal rights to services of their own, rather than indirectly through the person they are supporting. However, these policy measures all aim to support carers in their caring role, rather than offering families a choice between informal care and statutory services. In some other countries, for example, Germany, policies and funding arrangements offer frail older people and their relatives a clear choice between informal support, formal services, or a combination of the two (Glendinning and Igl, forthcoming).

In the 1995 Carers (Recognition and Services) Act, a 'carer' was defined as someone who provides, or intends to provide, 'a substantial amount of care on a regular basis', a rather circular 'definition' that has continued to be used ever since. The Act, which covered England, Scotland and Wales, gave carers entitlement to an assessment of their own circumstances and needs arising from their care-giving role. However, this entitlement depended on the person receiving care having first had an assessment of his or her own needs. Local authority social services practitioners, responsible for assessing both carers and those needing support, then had to decide whether services for the latter should be provided (which could indirectly benefit the carer). In other words, carers had a right to be assessed, but not to be provided with specific services, in their own right.

The National Strategy for Carers was the first carers' policy initiative introduced by New Labour (DH, 1999a). The strategy related primarily to England; the Scottish Executive (1999) and the National Assembly for Wales (2000) subsequently published their own strategies. The national strategy was underpinned by principles of choice, consumer control, access to paid work and social inclusion – hallmarks of New Labour's approach to welfare (Lloyd, 2000). The strategy had three main elements: information for carers; support for carers; and care for carers (see **Box 6.3**).

As part of the national strategy, the government introduced the Carers Special Grant in England to fund new services allowing carers a break from caring (DH, 1999a). Short-term breaks are regarded as particularly important in supporting carers, although the benefits depend on such breaks also being acceptable to the people they are supporting. Partly for this reason, evidence on the effectiveness and cost-effectiveness of short-term breaks has been difficult to establish (Arksey et al, 2004). This is the only time that resources have been provided specifically for carers' services. The Carers Special Grant – £140 million over three years – was 'ring-fenced', meaning that local authorities could use it only for services that enabled carers to take a break. The grant has continued to be renewed, at increased levels of funding, on a regular basis, although the ring-fencing was removed in 2004.

Box 6.3: Summary of key points in the National Strategy for Carers

- Charter setting out new standards relating to long-term care services.
- Good health information, including government information on the internet and carer information available from NHS Direct.
- Carers to be involved in planning and providing services.
- Local carers' organisations to be consulted.
- Carers' right to have their own health needs met.
- New legislation to extend local authorities' powers so they can address carers' needs directly.
- New grant of £140 million over three years to help carers take a break.
- More carer-friendly employment policies, with the government taking a lead.
- Consideration of the scope for extending New Deal to help carers return to work.
- A second pension for carers, intended to give carers of pensionable age an additional £50 by the year 2050.
- Support for carers' centres and other neighbourhood services.
- Help for young carers, including help at school, and those caring for disabled children.
- A new question in the 2001 Census on carers to increase information.

In the context of the new devolution settlement, the 2000 Carers and Disabled Children Act covered England and Wales only. This legislation implemented some of the measures proposed in the National Strategy for Carers (DH, 1999a). The Act strengthened carers' rights by giving them rights to an assessment of their needs, irrespective of whether the person needing support had received an assessment or services; moreover, local authorities could provide services for carers in their own right, rather than simply to (and via) the person needing support.

The 2000 Act also gave local authorities powers to provide carers with direct cash payments. Direct payments enable individuals to purchase their own support, rather than receiving services arranged by the local authority; they offer increased choice and control and flexibility over when and how services are received, and from whom (Spandler, 2004; Leece and Bornat, 2006). Disabled people can use a direct payment to employ a relative living in a different household to provide their care or, exceptionally, a relative living in the same household. In addition, carers can receive direct payments to purchase services that will provide them with their own support, such as employing someone to do household tasks like cleaning or gardening that they are unable to do themselves because of shortage of time. One-off direct payments can be made too, to pay for services such as education and training courses, driving lessons, holidays, taxi and train fares and stress-reducing therapies (Fletcher, 2006).

The 2004 Carers (Equal Opportunities) Act, which came into force in England and Wales in April 2005, had wider ambitions than the preceding measures, as it aimed to address the social exclusion experienced by many carers. It built on the two preceding Acts by placing a duty on local authority social services practitioners when conducting carers' assessments to consider carers' desires and ambitions to take part in paid work, education, training or leisure activities, and to provide appropriate information, advice and support. The Act also requires local authorities to cooperate with other agencies such as providers of education and training. Although implicit in previous carers' legislation, the 2004 Act made New Labour's policy emphasis on carers' participation in paid work explicit.

To illustrate the changes in policies for carers, **Box 6.4** compares service provision for Anne and Jessie before and after New Labour came to power. Anne is in her early 50s and provides regular and substantial amounts of support for her mother Jessie, who is 95 and has limited mobility. Anne lives round the corner from Jessie. She would like to return to paid work now that her children have grown up, but she is currently spending a lot of time looking after Jessie. Anne does all her mother's housework and laundry, as well as providing her with company.

Box 6.4: Case example of changes over time in carer support

Before New Labour came to power

Anne could ask for a carer's assessment, but only at the same time as Jessie was being assessed or reassessed. She would not be entitled to any services in her own right, but the local authority could decide to provide services to Jessie, which could indirectly benefit Anne.

After New Labour came to power

Anne can ask for a carer's assessment, regardless of whether Jessie has an assessment or receives any statutory services. Anne's assessment must take account of her wishes in relation to training, education, employment and leisure activities. The local authority could agree to provide, as a carer's service, cleaning and laundry services for Jessie; or day care for Jessie so that Anne could take a paid job. Anne could be given a direct payment to buy a washing machine to do Jessie's laundry, or a mobile phone to keep in contact with her mother while she is at work. Anne might also have a break from caring, if Jessie would agree; Jessie could go into a residential home for a week or Anne could be given a direct payment to pay a neighbour to look after her mother while she goes on holiday.

Source: Adapted from DH, 2001, p 33.

Financial support for carers

Care giving often has adverse effects on carers' finances (Macgregor and Hill, 2003). Reasons include additional disability-related expenditure, such as special diets requiring more expensive food; extra heating; specialist equipment and extra transport costs. Where a carer shares the same household as the person he or she is supporting, the carer will also experience the impact of these extra costs (Glendinning, 1992a). Many carers living in a separate household from the person they are supporting will also help out financially or have extra expenses because, for example, they have extra transport costs arising from frequent visits or do not have time to 'shop around' for bargains.

Caring also frequently has a negative impact on carers' incomes (Baldwin, 1985; Carmichael and Charles, 1998; Carers National Association, 2000). Earnings can be affected if carers' ability to work is restricted by the level of care they provide. To accommodate the two activities, they may have to change from full-time to part-time work, or reduce the number of hours worked. The financial legacy of caring can also penalise carers' future pension incomes (Hancock and Jarvis, 1994; Ginn and Arber, 2000; Evandrou and Glaser, 2003).

Some financial support is available for carers; as noted earlier, the Carers

Allowance (formerly Invalid Care Allowance) was introduced in 1976 for men and single women of working age, extended to married women in 1986 and to people over retirement age in 2003. Compared with other countries, the UK is unusual in providing a cash benefit to which carers have an independent entitlement. In many other countries, payment for informal carers is 'routed' through the allowances received by the person receiving care (Glendinning and McLaughlin, 1993; Ungerson, 1997; Glendinning, 2006). However, the eligibility criteria for Carers Allowance are restrictive. The allowance is intended for carers who have (almost) no earnings or income from other social security benefits because they are providing very substantial amount of care. Carers must be providing at least 35 hours a week of care, have only minimal earnings from part-time work or be in education for a maximum of 21 hours a week, and must be looking after someone receiving a benefit in respect of their disability. Above all, the level of the Carers Allowance is very low – below the minimum for means-tested benefits – and cannot be received at the same time as another social security benefit. Carers, some of whom will have given up well-paid jobs to support a close relative, regard the level of the allowance as unacceptably low. The level of the benefit, divided by the 35-hours-a-week-care qualifying criterion, yields an hourly rate for caring that is well below the legal minimum wage. Moreover, the earnings limit acts as a disincentive to carers who might otherwise want to find part-time work that fits in with their care commitments (Arksey et al, 2005). Although carers receiving the allowance also receive credits towards their state pensions, the value of this protection is questionable in the context of policies that encourage increasing reliance on occupational and private pensions.

Apart from extending eligibility for Carers Allowance to retired carers, little has been done over the past two decades to improve levels of financial support for carers and reduce their very significant risks of poverty in the short and longer terms (Evandrou and Glaser, 2003). One of the most important ways in which these risks can be reduced (and, at the same time, carers' well-being sustained) is for carers to be able to stay in paid work while caring. New regulations were introduced in the 2002 Employment Act that give parents of disabled children under 18 the right to request (but not necessarily to be given) flexible working arrangements; this right will be extended to carers of adults from April 2007. For carers themselves, flexibility over the time and location of work and an entitlement to paid leave to cope with emergencies are essential in keeping a paid job (Arksey et al, 2005).

What difference have New Labour policies made for carers?

A flurry of research was conducted following the implementation of the 1995 Carers (Recognition and Services) Act. The evidence showed the Act had made only limited progress in improving the provision of information and publicity regarding carers' rights, increasing the number of carers' assessments or increasing the services offered to carers following an assessment (CNA, 1997; CNA/ADSW/ADSS, 1997). On the contrary, the number of carers' assessments was low; carers were not always aware that an assessment had taken place so they could not actively contribute; and few carers received written results of the assessment (CNA, 1997; Dearden and Becker, 1998; SSI, 1998; Robinson and Williams, 1999; Seddon, 1999; Arksey et al, 2000).

The National Strategy for Carers (DH, 1999a), with its aim of improving choice and flexibility for carers, was welcomed as an important development (Holzhausen and Pearlman, 2000). However, it was criticised for not recognising the poverty faced by many carers (Holzhausen and Pearlman, 2000); nor did it adequately address the complex nature of caring relationships or take account of the needs and wishes of those receiving care (Lloyd, 2000), an issue to be discussed later.

Research evidence does not show that assessment practice and the provision of information improved significantly in the wake of the 2000 Carers and Disabled Children Act either (Keeley and Clarke, 2002; Clark, 2003; Macgregor and Hill, 2003; Arksey et al, 2005). One piece of research undertaken by Carers UK suggested that carers' assessments, mainly for carers of adults with a physical disability, had led to an increase in community care services for the disabled person (Macgregor and Hill, 2003). However, a telephone survey of 10 local authorities for the same study indicated that only a handful of carers were receiving carers' services (such as taxi fares to attend carer support groups/ evening classes, driving lessons or a holiday) in their own right.

Research shows that carers can benefit from the provision of direct cash payments, either to the person receiving care or to carers themselves to purchase help (Macgregor and Hill, 2003; Stainton and Boyce, 2004). For instance, one study of direct payments found that the flexibility they offered had allowed some carers to continue shift working; this would not have been possible with traditional services (Stainton and Boyce, 2004). Furthermore, alternative support purchased with direct payments by carers or disabled people may be more reliable than conventional services and therefore require fewer interventions from family members if conventional services are not delivered on time. However, the number of carers obtaining direct payments themselves for carers' services remains low, with only 2,327 carers recorded as receiving direct payments in September 2004 increasing to 3,630 by March 2005 (CSCI, 2005). Moreover, there are major variations between local authorities in the numbers of carers receiving direct payments in their own right (Fletcher, 2006).

Barriers to providing effective support to carers

As detailed earlier, the impact of the new rights for carers has been limited. This section of the chapter suggests some reasons why supporting carers may be problematic and the effectiveness of the recent New Labour policies has been restricted.

The primary target of support: the carer or the person receiving care?

Opinion is divided as to who should be the primary target of policy – carers or disabled and older people themselves. The National Strategy for Carers states that "helping carers is one of the best ways of helping the people they care for" (DH, 1999a, p 12). However, the number of carers' assessments and levels of services provided specifically for carers both remain low (Parker and Clarke, 2002). One possible explanation is that practitioners find it difficult to balance the rights of both carers and disabled or older people (Scourfield, 2005).

It is all too easy for practitioners and policy makers to assume that the needs and interests of carers and older or disabled people are harmonious and that similar outcomes are sought by each. This is not necessarily the case, and focusing on carers may neglect the perspectives, interests and concerns of disabled and older people themselves. Thus, as the profile of carers has risen on the political and policy agendas, disabled people and their organisations have increasingly argued that this overlooks their rights for choice, control and self-determination. Indeed, the disabled people's movement has argued for many years that the very terms 'care' and 'carer' carry connotations of dependency, implying that disabled people are a 'burden' and less able to make choices for themselves (Morris, 1993; Shakespeare, 2000). Moreover, a focus on carers, as distinct from disabled and older people, has been criticised as failing to recognise the reciprocity that underpins many care-giving relationships. It also overlooks the fact that many disabled adults and older people also care for others at the same time as needing support in their own personal and daily activities (Morris, 1993).

In their analysis of community care policy, Parker and Clarke (2002) draw attention to the wealth of evidence that conventional social care services – help with personal care, domestic help, employment and other meaningful activities – for disabled adults and older people are the most effective way of supporting carers. This is because replacing informal care with formal paid services has the potential to reduce the need for informal care from family and friends. A similar conclusion was reached by Pickard's (2004) review of evidence on the effectiveness and cost-effectiveness of support for carers. However, there is little evidence to suggest that replacing some of the help provided by informal carers with formal services necessarily leads to an overall reduction in the support provided by relatives and friends, at least so far as older people are concerned. Experience in Scotland, where a policy of free personal care for older people has recently been introduced, shows that support from services can help carers to sustain care giving for longer, and to devote their time to providing social support such as outings rather than more mundane and intrusive tasks like intimate personal tasks, if this is their preferred choice (Bell and Bowes, 2006).

Conceptions of carers in policy

On the basis of research with health and social care practitioners, Twigg and Atkin (1994) developed a typology of the relationships between carers and service providers. They shed light on the degree to which carers are seen as a 'free' resource and their well-being is the central focus of policy and practice (Pickard, 2001). The first model, 'carer as resource', treats carers instrumentally as a taken-for-granted resource; promoting carers' well-being is only important to the extent that it sustains care giving. Carers' well-being receives slightly more attention in the 'carer as co-worker' model. However, in the third model, 'carer as co-client', carers' interests and well-being are valued outcomes of policy and practice in their own right. In the fourth model, the 'superseded carer', the need for support from an informal carer is dispensed with by the provision of services that meet all the support needs of the older or disabled person. According to Pickard (2001), current policies for carers are primarily based on the 'carer as resource' model, with some secondary elements of the 'carer as co-client' model. Until such time as the conceptual model underpinning policy shifts, it is likely that carers will continue to experience negative outcomes in their health, employment and finances.

Competing priorities: care giving versus employment

Many individuals are caught in the crossfire between needing to work and wishing to care. The likelihood of taking on care-giving responsibilities increases with age; the peak age for starting a caring role is between 45 and 64 years (Hirst, 2002). In other words, many carers are in paid work when older relatives begin to need substantial levels of support. Research evidence shows that some carers do give up paid work altogether because of the extent of their commitments and the lack of appropriate formal services, especially those providing 20 hours care or more a week (Arber and Ginn, 1995; Carmichael and Charles, 1998; Speiss and Schneider, 2003; Arksey et al, 2005). However, the majority of working-age carers combine some paid work and care, even though this is difficult (Parker, 1990; Glendinning, 1992b; Hancock and Jarvis, 1994; Joshi, 1995).

Policies towards carers and employment reflect conflicting priorities. The National Strategy for Carers (DH, 1999a) indicated that carers should be able to give up work to care altogether if that is their wish. However, those carers who do decide to leave work are not supported with adequate income maintenance or pension protection. The strategy also discussed at length how carers could combine work and care, or return to work once caring commitments cease, but offered no new measures to facilitate these objectives. The 2005 Carers (Equal Opportunities) Act builds issues about employment for carers into legislation, which means that practitioners must consider carers' wishes relating to training and paid work when conducting assessments. However, research shows there is still a long way to go before social services practitioners recognise that it is legitimate for carers to take part in paid work and are sympathetic towards providing the necessary services that are acceptable to both the carer and the person needing support to enable this to happen (Arksey et al, 2005).

Conclusion

Since New Labour came to power, policy measures have been introduced that acknowledge the role that carers play in supporting disabled and older people and aim to support carers in this role. The three Acts of Parliament and the National Strategy for Carers (DH, 1999a) all reinforce the notion that the government values the work of informal carers. However, the extent of the value attached to informal care is highly circumscribed. First, New Labour policies, like those of previous governments, aim primarily to sustain carers in their existing roles of providing sometimes very substantial amounts of help and support to disabled and older people. There is little evidence that policies aim actively to encourage or incentivise relatives and friends to take on new supportive activities. However, there is also little evidence of policies that aim to provide comprehensive formal support services to older and disabled people and their relatives that would offer both parties real choices between formal services and informal care. Such policies would require major investment in statutory support services and direct payments that had the potential to provide most of the support needed by severely disabled or very frail people. The only exception to this conclusion can be found in Scotland, where the introduction of free personal care has allowed some carers to relinquish responsibility for providing personal care and concentrate on providing other types of support instead (Bell and Bowes, 2006).

Nor is there much evidence of policies that offer carers real choices between paid work and largely unpaid informal care, or policies that are consistent with the government's determination to increase the numbers of women and older people in paid employment in order to meet the demands of a competitive economy. Such policies would require high levels of formal services to replace the support provided by informal carers; active training and re-entry measures to assist those who have been out of the labour market for a time; and entitlements to flexible working arrangements and periods of paid leave from work, to make it easier to combine work and informal care. A more flexible system of cash benefits to encourage carers to maintain contact with the labour market, rather than being available only to those who have left the labour market entirely as at present, would also be consistent with New Labour's policies of promoting paid work as a route out of social exclusion.

Moreover, local implementation of New Labour's policies remains patchy and piecemeal. Shortcomings may reflect the fact that local authorities have been given additional responsibilities in relation to informal carers but no additional resources, apart from extra funding under the Carers Special Grant for short-term breaks.

It is therefore difficult to avoid the conclusion that policies for informal carers are bounded by a major dilemma. While espousing a discourse of choice and independence, the volume of welfare provided informally by friends and relatives is indispensible; major economic constraints limit the extent to which formal services can be expanded to replace the very substantial amounts of informal welfare provided. Hence, policies tend to reflect an instrumental approach to carers, treating them as a resource that needs to be sustained rather than replaced by formal services. It is only when the level of informal welfare provided by carers threatens to become insupportable that carers may be treated as co-clients – hence the focus of many policies on those carers who provide more intensive levels of support (20 hours plus a week) and on identifying through carers' assessments those who, without some acknowledgement of their own needs, might be at risk of being unable to continue providing support. Thus under New Labour, carers remain a largely unpaid workforce, doubly disadvantaged by the costs of care giving and a reduced or lost income from paid work. It is therefore ironic that this very substantial source of informal welfare puts carers at risk of poverty and social exclusion.

Summary

- The majority of care for sick, disabled or older people is provided in the community by the informal sector (of close family members, relatives, friends and neighbours).
- Reflecting changing demographics, the future need for informal care givers is likely to increase rather than decrease.
- According to the 2001 Census, 5.2 million individuals of all ages (including young carers) have care-giving responsibilities in England and Wales. While the majority care for 19 hours a week or less, more than 30% fulfil substantial caring demands of 20 hours per week or more.
- Since the mid-1990s, there has been an increasing amount of policy interest in informal carers in the UK; the New Labour government elected in May 1997 has enacted a number of new policy initiatives designed to improve support for care givers.
- Measures include three Acts of Parliament – the 2000 Carers and Disabled Children Act; the 2004 Carers (Equal Opportunities) Act; and the 1995 Carers (Recognition and Services) Act – and the National Strategy for Carers. The Carers Special Grant was introduced to provide improved respite care services and short-term breaks for carers and the person receiving care.
- Direct financial support is only available for carers who have no, or only minimal, earnings or income from benefits. Moreover, the level of this financial support is very low; measures to protect carers from poverty in their own old age are rudimentary; and few carers have access to workplace rights that could help them combine paid work and care giving.
- Research evidence shows that some progress has been made in terms of improved support for carers, but that this is not consistent throughout all local authorities.
- A number of reasons help explain why New Labour policies for carers have not realised their full potential. These include: conflicts and ambivalence in terms of whether the primary target of support should be carers or those in receipt of care; an instrumental focus on carers arising from conceiving of them as a free resource; competing priorities for carers to continue to provide care but also to remain in, or return to, the paid workforce.

Questions for discussion

- To what extent have women and men been affected by informal caring?
- What are the boundaries between formal and informal support for disabled and older people? How much support should be provided by the state and how much by the family?

- How far have successive New Labour administrations moved towards getting a balance between caring as a family or a state responsibility?
- Why is it necessary to give equal consideration to the choices and rights of carers and those of the people they are looking after?

Further reading

Howard's (2001) *Paying the Price: Carers, Poverty and Social Exclusion* is a concise and accessible text focusing on the diverse pressures carers may face that could lead to financial hardship and limit their social inclusion. The work draws on empirical research to explore a range of income issues for different groups of carers, including young carers under age 18, working-age carers and carers over state pension age. The author makes suggestions to improve services for carers, as well as recommendations for financial improvements to carers that would tackle carer poverty.

The most comprehensive source of recent material on carers currently available is **Stalker (2003)**. This is an edited book that highlights the full scope and diversity of care giving and offers some new ways of thinking about current debates and policy concerns. Authors focus on the positive aspects of caring, and point to the reciprocity and interdependence that can characterise many care-giving relationships. Especially useful is the first chapter, which offers a brief review of key concepts and debates in the care-giving literature. Some of the other topic areas covered include: caring relationships; carers and assessment; the diversity of carers; and carers and employment.

Electronic resources

There are two main carers' organisations in the UK. Both provide information about carers and offer information and advice for carers in a wide range of situations and circumstances. Both organisations also speak out on behalf of carers and campaign for better recognition and support for carers at national and local levels:

Carers UK: www.carersuk.org/Home

Princess Royal Trust for Carers: www.carers.org/

See also:

www.carers.gov.uk/

www.employersforcarers.org.uk/

www.carersinformation.org.uk/

References

Arber, S. and Ginn, J. (1995) 'Gender differences in the relationship between paid employment and informal care', *Work, Employment and Society*, vol 9, no 3, pp 445-71.

Arksey, H., Hepworth, D. and Qureshi, H. (2000) *Carers' Needs and the Carers Act: An Evaluation of the Process and Outcomes of Assessment*, York: Social Policy Research Unit, University of York.

Arksey, H., Jackson, K., Croucher, K., Weatherly, H., Golder, S., Hare, P., Newbronner, E. and Baldwin, S. (2004) *Review of Respite Services and Short-term Breaks for Carers for People with Dementia*, York: Social Policy Research Unit, University of York.

Arksey, H., Kemp, P., Glendinning, C., Kotchetkova, I. and Tozer, R. (2005) *Carers' Aspirations and Decisions around Work and Retirement*, Department for Work and Pensions Research Report no 290, Leeds: Corporate Document Services.

Baldwin, S. (1985) *The Costs of Caring: Families with Disabled Children*, London: Routledge and Kegan Paul.

Baldwin, S. and Twigg, J. (1991) 'Women and community care', in M. Maclean and D. Groves (eds) *Women's Issues in Social Policy*, London: Routledge, pp 117-35.

Becker, S. (2004) 'Carers', *Research Matters*, August special issue, pp 5-10.

Bell, D. and Bowes, A. (2006) *Financial Care Models in Scotland and the UK*, York: Joseph Rowntree Foundation.

Buckner, L. and Yeandle, S. (2005a) *We Care – Do You?*, London: Carers UK.

Buckner, L. and Yeandle, S. (2005b) *Older Carers in the UK*, London: Carers UK.

Carers UK (2002) *Without Us …? Calculating the Value of Carers' Support*, London: Carers UK.

Carmichael, F. and Charles, S. (1998) 'The labour market costs of community care', *Journal of Health Economics*, vol 17, no 6, pp 747-65.

Clark, J. (2003) *Independence Matters: An Overview of the Performance of Social Care Services for Physically and Sensory Disabled People*, London: Department of Health.

CNA (Carers National Association) (1997) *Still Battling? The Carers Act One Year On*, London: CNA.

CNA (2000) *Caring on the Breadline: The Financial Implications of Caring*, London: Carers National Association.

CNA/ADSW/ADSS (Carers National Association/Association of Directors of Social Work/Association of Directors of Social Services) (1997) *In on the Act? Social Services' Experience of the First Year of the Carers Act*, London: CNA.

CSCI (Commission for Social Care Inspection) (2005) *Social Care Performance 2004-05*, London: CSCI (www.csci.org.uk/council_performance/paf/dis_report_2004-05.pdf, accessed 6 February).

Dearden, C. and Becker, S. (1998) *Young Carers in the United Kingdom: A Profile*, London: Carers National Association.

Dearden, C. and Becker, S. (2004) *Young Carers in the UK: The 2004 Report*, London: Carers UK.

DH (Department of Health) (1989) *Caring for People: Community Care in the Next Decade and Beyond*, Cm 849, London: HMSO.

DH (1999a) *Caring about Carers: A National Strategy for Carers*, London: DH.

DH (1999b) *National Service Framework for Mental Health*, London: DH.

DH (2001) *Carers and Disabled Children Act 2000: Practice Guide*, London: DH.

DH (2005) *Independence, Well-being and Choice: Our Vision for the Future of Social Care for Adults in England*, Cm 6499, London: DH.

Eley, S. (2003) 'Diversity among carers', in K. Stalker (ed) *Reconceptualising Work with 'Carers': New Directions for Policy and Practice*, London: Jessica Kingsley, pp 56-71.

Evandrou, M. and Glaser, K. (2003) 'Combining work and family life: the pension penalty of caring', *Ageing and Society*, vol 23, part 5, pp 583-602.

Finch, J. and Groves, D. (eds) (1983) *A Labour of Love: Women, Work and Caring*, London: Routledge and Kegan Paul.

Finch, J. and Mason, J. (1993) *Negotiating Family Responsibilities*, London: Routledge.

Fine, M. and Glendinning, C. (2005) 'Dependence, independence or interdependence? Revisiting the concepts of "care" and "dependency"', *Ageing and Society*, vol 25, no 4, pp 601-21.

Fletcher, M. (2006) 'Carers and direct payments', in J. Leece and J. Bornat (eds) *Developments in Direct Payments*, Bristol: The Policy Press, pp 171-85.

Ginn, J. and Arber, S. (2000) 'The pensions cost of caring', *Benefits*, issue 28, April/May, pp 13-17.

Glendinning, C. (1992a) *The Costs of Informal Care: Looking Inside the Household*, London: HMSO.

Glendinning, C. (1992b) 'Employment and community care: policies for the 1990s', *Work, Employment and Society*, vol 6, no 1, pp 103-11.

Glendinning, C. (2006) 'Paying family care givers: evaluating different models', in C. Glendinning and P.A. Kemp (eds) *Cash and Care: Policy Challenges in the Welfare State*, Bristol: The Policy Press, pp 127-40.

Glendinning, C. and Igl, G. (forthcoming) 'Long-term care', in G. Naegele and A. Walker (eds) *Social Policy in Ageing Societies: Britain and Germany Compared*, Basingstoke: Palgrave Macmillan.

Glendinning, C. and McLaughlin, E. (1993) *Paying for Care: Lessons from Europe*, Social Security Advisory Committee Research Paper no 5, London: HMSO.

Griffiths, R. (1988) *Community Care: Agenda for Action*, London: Department of Social Services.

Hancock, R. and Jarvis, C. (1994) *The Long Term Effects of Being a Carer*, London: HMSO.

Hirst, M. (2002) 'Transitions to informal care in Great Britain during the 1990s', *Journal of Epidemiology and Community Health*, vol 56, no 8, pp 579-87.

Hirst, M. (2005) 'Estimating the prevalence of unpaid adult care over time', *Research Policy and Planning*, vol 23, no 1, pp 1-15.

Howard, M. (2001) *Paying the Price: Carers, Poverty and Social Exclusion*, London: Child Poverty Action Group.

Holzhausen, E. and Pearlman, V. (2000) 'Carers' policies in the UK', *Benefits*, vol 28, April-May, pp 5-8.

Joshi, H. (1995) 'The labour market and unpaid caring: conflict and compromise', in I. Allen and E. Perkins (eds) *The Future of Family Care for Older People*, London: HMSO, pp 93-118.

Keeley, B. and Clarke, M. (2002) *Consultation with Carers Good Practice Guide*, London: The Princess Royal Trust for Carers.

Keith, L. and Morris, J. (1995) 'Easy targets: a disability rights perspective on the "children as carers" debate', *Critical Social Policy*, vol 44/45, pp 36-57.

Kelly, S., Baker, A. and Gupta, S. (2000) 'Healthy life expectancy in Great Britain: 1980-96, and its use as an indicator in United Kingdom government strategies', *Health Statistics Quarterly*, vol 7, pp 32-7, Autumn.

Leece, J. and Bornat, J. (2006) *Developments in Direct Payments*, Bristol: The Policy Press.

Lloyd, L. (2000) 'Caring about carers – only half the picture?', *Critical Social Policy*, vol 20, no 1, pp 136-50.

Macgregor, G. and Hill, M. (2003) *Missed Opportunities: The Impact of New Rights for Carers*, London: Carers UK.

Maher, J. and Green, H. (2002) *Carers 2000*, London: The Stationery Office.

Martin, J. and Roberts, C. (1984) *Women and Employment: A Lifetime Perspective*, London: HMSO.

Morris, J. (1993) *Independent Lives: Community Care and Disabled People*, Basingstoke: Macmillan.

National Assembly for Wales (2000) *Caring about Carers: A Strategy for Carers in Wales. Implementation Plan*, Cardiff: National Assembly for Wales.

Oakley, A. (1974) *The Sociology of Housework*, Oxford: Basil Blackwell.

Olsen, R. and Tyers, H. (2004) *Think Parent: Supporting Disabled Adults as Parents*, London: National Family and Parenting Institute.

Parker, G. (1990) *With Due Care and Attention: A Review of Research on Informal Care*, London: Family Policy Studies Centre.

Parker, G. and Clarke, H. (2002) 'Making the ends meet: do carers and disabled people have a common agenda?', *Policy and Politics*, vol 30, no 3, pp 347-59.

Pickard, L. (2001) 'Carer break or carer-blind? Policies for informal carers in the UK', *Social Policy & Administration*, vol 35, no 4, pp 441-58.

Pickard, L. (2004) *The Effectiveness and Cost-effectiveness of Support and Services to Informal Carers of Older People: A Review of the Literature*, London: Audit Commission.

Pickard, L., Wittenberg, R., Comas-Herrera, A., Davies, B. and Darton, R. (2000) 'Relying on informal care in the new century? Informal care for elderly people in England in 2031', *Ageing and Society*, vol 20, no 6, pp 745-72.

Qureshi, H. and Walker, A. (1989) *The Caring Relationship: Elderly People and their Families*, Basingstoke: Macmillan.

Robinson, C. and Williams, V. (1999) *In Their Own Right*, Bristol: Norah Fry Research Centre, University of Bristol.

Scottish Executive (1999) *Strategy for Carers in Scotland*, Edinburgh: Scottish Executive.

Scourfield, P. (2005) 'Understanding why carers' assessments do not always take place', *Practice*, vol 17, no 1, pp 15-28.

Seddon, D. (1999) *Carers of Elderly People with Dementia: Assessment and the Carers Act*, Bangor: Centre for Social Policy Research and Development, University of Wales.

Shakespeare, T. (2000) 'The social relations of care', in G. Lewis, S. Gewirtz and J. Clarke (eds) *Rethinking Social Policy*, London: Sage Publications.

Skinner, C. and Finch, N. (2006) 'Reciprocity, lone parents and state subsidy for informal childcare', in C. Glendinning and P.A. Kemp (eds) *Cash and Care: Policy Challenges in the Welfare State*, Bristol, The Policy Press, pp 187-201.

Spandler, H. (2004) 'Friend or foe? Towards a critical assessment of direct payments', *Critical Social Policy*, vol 24, no 2, pp 187-209.

Speiss, C.K. and Schneider, A.L. (2003) 'Interactions between care-giving and paid work hours among European midlife women, 1994 to 1996', *Ageing & Society*, vol 23, no 1, pp 41-68.

SSI (Social Services Inspectorate) (1998) *A Matter of Chance for Carers? Inspection of Local Authority Support for Carers*, London: Department of Health.

Stainton, T. and Boyce, S. (2004) '"I have got my life back": users' experience of direct payments', *Disability and Society*, vol 19, no 5, pp 443-54.

Stalker, K. (ed) (2003) *Reconceptualising Work with 'Carers': New Directions for Policy and Practice*, London: Jessica Kingsley.

Titmuss, R.M. (1968) 'Community care: fact or fiction?', in R.M. Titmuss (ed) *Commitment to Welfare*, London: Allen and Unwin, pp 104-9.

Twigg, J. and Atkin, K. (1994) *Carers Perceived: Policy and Practice in Informal Care*, Buckingham: Open University Press.

Ungerson, C. (1987) *Policy is Personal: Sex, Gender and Informal Care*, London: Tavistock.

Ungerson, C. (1997) 'Social politics and the commodification of care', *Social Politics*, vol 4, no 3, pp 362-81.

Ungerson, C. (2003) 'Informal welfare', in P. Alcock, A. Erskine and M. May (eds) *The Student's Companion to Social Policy* (2nd edn), Oxford: Blackwell Publishing, pp 200-6.

Walker, A. (1995) 'The family and the mixed economy of care – can they be integrated?', in I. Allen and E. Perkins (eds) *The Future of Family Care for Older People*, London: HMSO, pp 201-20.

Williams, F. (2004) *Rethinking Families*, London: Calouste Gulbenkian Foundation.

Young, H., Grundy, E. and Kalogirou, S. (2005) 'Who cares? Geographic variation in unpaid caregiving in England and Wales: evidence from the 2001 Census', *Population Trends*, vol 120, pp 23-33, Summer.

seven

Tax welfare

Adrian Sinfield

Overview

Since 1999, the pattern of tax welfare in the United Kingdom has been undergoing major change. The tax system now plays a significant part in the strategies to reduce poverty, especially child poverty, and to assist those on low pay. Replacing and extending major social security benefits, it is delivering resources to those who previously gained nothing from its workings. However, changes to tax welfare on pensions are likely to reinforce its traditional impact, continuing to promote wider inequalities and at the same time working to diminish the role of the welfare state in the mixed economy of welfare. This chapter will focus on these two developments and assess the implications.

Key concepts

Tax welfare • social division of welfare • tax expenditure • tax benefit • tax allowance • tax credit • upside-down benefit

Introduction

The idea of fiscal or tax welfare was introduced by Richard Titmuss, the first professor of social administration in the United Kingdom, in his lecture on 'the social division of welfare' (Titmuss, 1958, ch 2, and in Alcock et al, 2001, part 2, ch 2), first delivered on 1 December 1955. Titmuss used the term 'fiscal' but the more familiar 'tax' is now generally used. In challenging the conventional wisdom of substantial redistribution through the welfare state, he identified two other forms of intervention that also affected the distribution of welfare and resources – tax welfare and occupational welfare (see Chapter Eight).

By giving reliefs from tax, the state can encourage particular activities or provide benefits. "Allowances and reliefs from income tax, though providing similar benefits and expressing a similar social purpose in the recognition of dependencies, are not, however, treated as social service expenditure" (Titmuss, 1958, p 44; Alcock et al, 2001, p 65). As a result, tax is foregone that would otherwise have been collected. The term *tax expenditure* is used in contrast to public expenditure to cover such losses of revenue, whether concerned with welfare or any other objective (for a discussion of the concept, see Surrey, 1973; OECD, 1996, pp 16-18).

Box 7.1: Key terms

Tax welfare – benefits or subsidies received through tax or related systems such as National Insurance.

Tax expenditure – loss of revenue through tax or related systems as a result of favourable treatment of particular types of activities or groups of taxpayers.

Tax relief – income designated not subject to income tax.

Tax benefit – resource obtained through some form of tax relief.

Tax allowance – relief given against gross income, thus reducing taxable income.

Tax credit – relief deducted from the tax bill, thus reducing tax liability. Can be refundable so that it is paid to the individual, if the tax bill is nil or lower than the credit.

The most common form of tax expenditure has been the tax allowance where the size of the tax benefit depends on the individual's marginal rate of tax (see **Box 7.2**). It therefore works as an 'upside-down' benefit: it delivers more to those whose needs in social policy terms are likely to be fewer in contrast to the downward or horizontal, over-the-lifetime operation of welfare state income provision (Surrey, 1973, p 37). This is the reverse of the targeting of means-tested measures in public policy. Use is now also being made of tax credits, which are not regressive in this way and can be made progressive (see **Box 7.2**).

Tax expenditures operate relatively invisibly, with little parliamentary or independent scrutiny. They are not included in the public expenditure statistics, which are the subject of much debate and discussion. What control there is of this spending through the tax system rests with the Chancellor of the Exchequer and the Treasury which has long "reserved its sole proprietorship of 'budget' matters such as tax expenditures and national insurance contributions" (Deakin and Parry, 2000, p 47).

Box 7.2: Tax allowances and tax credits

The value of a *tax allowance* is determined by the marginal rate of tax – that is, the rate of tax to which a taxpayer's highest income is subject. Most taxpayers, on the standard rate of 22%, pay £220 less tax on an allowance of £1,000 but a higher-rate taxpayer gains £400 from the 40% rate. Someone with a low income and only paying tax at 10% will only save £100 – and if their tax liability would have been less than £100 or zero, they will only receive that smaller amount or nothing.

A *tax credit* is deducted from the individual's tax liability, not from pre-tax income. For most people, there is no change from a £1,000 tax allowance if the credit is set at £220. The one in nine currently paying higher rate tax, however, would receive no more than the rest, losing £180. The credit can also be made 'refundable'. Anyone whose tax bill is less than £220 has the remaining amount paid to them so that they lose none of the value. Those on a low income paying no income tax get the full tax credit paid to them. Current tax credits have a more complicated form of withdrawl, but the principle remains the same.

The cost of major tax expenditures and related National Insurance ones is substantial. In 2005-06, the income tax reliefs that provided benefits comparable to social welfare made up four fifths of the published income tax reliefs excluding the personal allowance (HMRC, 2006, Table 1.5, revised). They totalled £24 billion, equivalent to some 18% of the income tax actually collected.

The relative amount of revenue foregone by tax expenditures has fallen for two reasons. Tax rates have come down – the top rate to 40% from a peak of 83% in 1979, even 98% with the additional 15% investment charge; and the basic rate to 22% from 35%. The number of specific tax reliefs has also been reduced. In particular, two major and costly social policy tax reliefs, the married couple's allowance and mortgage interest relief, have been phased out, although the capital gains tax exemption for any gains from selling one's home remains considerable.

Tax benefits now fall into three categories (see **Table 7.1**). Well over half the cost supports benefits over and above public welfare benefits. About a quarter

Table 7.1: *Major tax and other reliefs related to social policy, United Kingdom, 1994-95, 2004-05 and 2005-06 (estimates in £ millions)*

	1994-95	2004-05	2005-06
I Beyond public welfare			
Income tax			
Married couple's allowance additional to personal allowance	3,500	ended	–
Age-related allowance	725	2,200	2,300
Additional allowance for one-parent family	260	ended	–
Exemption of first £30,000 paid on termination of employment	1,600	1,000	1,000
Relief for non-state pensions	9,200	12,300	13,700
Relief for mortgage interest	3,500	ended	–
National Insurance contributions relief			
Employer contributions to approved pensions	np	6,700	7,400
Contracted-out rebate on occupational	7,110	7,080	7,270
and on personal pension schemes	245	2,700	2,300
Capital Gains Tax			
Gains arising on disposal of only or main residence	850	13,000	12,500
II Exemptions of welfare state benefits			
Child benefit	650	1,060	1,090
Long-term disability benefits	1,410	1,080	1,090
III Tax credits			
Child Tax Credit	–	3,300	3,600
Working Tax Credit	–	1,100	1,000

Sources: HM Treasury (1995) and HMRC (2006, table 1.5 revised), on basis of revenue foregone. np – not published.

exempts some social benefits from tax – Child Benefit, war pensions and long-term disablement benefits. The remaining fifth comprises the new development for the United Kingdom – virtually a combination of social and tax rights through tax credits.

The move to tax credits

Tax welfare has generally been neglected in most social policy analysis. The move to tax credits has received more attention, largely, perhaps, because they developed from social security benefits central to the welfare state.

In 1909, child tax allowances were brought in for the poorest of the best-off, that is, those at the bottom of the then very small proportion of the population paying any income tax. By 1920, the benefit had been extended to all taxpayers. The welfare state family allowance only began in 1946, and then not for the first child. In comparison, the child tax allowance was always for all dependent children, was age-related and could be paid for longer. It had an upside-down effect and its cost to the Exchequer was greater than that of family allowance. After much campaigning building on Titmuss's analysis, both tax and family allowances were merged in the late 1970s into Child Benefit.

Current support for children through the tax system has taken a very different form. A task force was established by the newly-elected Labour government in 1997 to help "streamline and modernize" the tax and benefit systems "so as to fulfil our objectives of promoting work incentives, reducing poverty and welfare dependency, and strengthening community and family life" (HM Treasury, 1998, p 5, quoted in Millar, 2003, pp 128-9).

In 1999, the refundable Working Families Tax Credit (WFTC), administered by the Inland Revenue, replaced the Department of Social Security benefit, Family Credit, which had in 1988 replaced the Family Income Supplement of 1971. Together with credits for disabled and older workers, WFTC aimed to support the government's 'work first' strategy to reduce poverty. Tax credits had been considered in the early 1970s, but the impetus for WFTC owed much to the Earned Income Tax Credit in the United States (Howard, 1997).

Two arguments were presented for the shift to income tax: "a tax credit will associate the payment in the recipient's mind with the fact of working, a potentially valuable psychological tool ... a payment through the tax system, associated with the recipient's work, is likely to prove more acceptable to society at large" (HM Treasury, 1998, p 8, quoted in Millar, 2003, p 129). This second concern – to win the support of, or at least avoid alienating, powerful groups in society opposed to expanding welfare – was probably dominant. The political problem of how to transfer more support to families in poverty was all the greater given that social security and its recipients of working age had been systematically stigmatised, and often demonised, by previous Conservative governments (Cook, 1997).

In 2003, these credits and some more social security benefits were replaced by the more extensive Working and Child Tax Credits (WTC and CTC), the second intended to reach more than four out of five children. With the exception of the universal Child Benefit, all other central government financial support for children ended. The 2004 increase in CTC the following year directed significantly greater benefit to children in low-income families – what the government calls 'progressive universalism'. At this stage, the experience of Australia and Canada was also influential (Battle et al, 2000).

Box 7.3: Child Tax Credit

Child Tax Credit is paid weekly or monthly to the main carer and consists of basic elements for the family and for each child (£1,690 in 2006-07), increased for disabled and severely disabled children. These will increase at least in line with earnings up to the end of this Parliament but the family element of £545 (doubled for the first year of the child's life) has been frozen. The total credit is reduced by 37 pence for every £1 of income over £13,910 and the family element by 6.67 pence for every £1 over £50,000. This has the advantage of providing more help to those with the lower incomes but the disadvantage of enormously complicating the operation of the credit.

Although the extra resources have helped reduce child poverty, more is needed to meet the government's target of reducing child poverty by one half by 2010-11 (WPC, 2004, para 235). The greater support for the first child, given that the family element starts with one child but is not increased for more children, means that tax credits are not as successful in countering the higher vulnerability to poverty of large families. In addition, the interaction with Housing Benefit and other means-tested measures reduces the increase in net disposable income for many.

Box 7.4: Working Tax Credit

Working Tax Credit is payable to low-income households where at least one parent is in employment for 16 hours or more a week. For the first time, it also gives support to workers in low-paid jobs whether they have children or not. However, those without children have to be 25 or over and working at least 30 hours a week, not the 16 hours for parents (those with a disability or aged 50 or over and meeting specific conditions can qualify at 16 hours with supplements). WTC is phased out from a much lower level than CTC, being reduced by 37 pence for every £1 over £5,220.

In contrast to the replaced WFTC, CTC does not discriminate between children who have a parent in work and those who do not. However, the addition of WTC brings more income in total from tax credits where a parent is working on low wages.

The Treasury sees WTC as a major labour market measure working with the National Minimum Wage "to deliver a more flexible labour market, while ensuring that workers are protected against falls in income" (HM Treasury, 2005, p 4). How far the New Deal and tax credits have increased employment or have acted to get people into low-paid jobs and keep them there by subsidising poor-paying employers is not yet clear. The National Minimum Wage does provide a floor and there could be positive effects from the credits. However, problems of low-paid and poor-quality jobs with high turnover need to be tackled given their family-unfriendly impact (Toynbee, 2003, illustrating the impact, and EC 2003, ch 4, indicating particular problems in the UK). In addition, "the disincentives inherent in the scheme mean that WTC is more likely to reduce the number of workless households than encourage potential second earners in couples" (Bennett, 2005, p ix).

The arguments continue as to whether the new tax credits are part of the tax system or a 'modernised' form of means test delivered by Revenue and Customs (Adler, 2004). CTC has been presented as 'seamless and transparent', but there have been considerable operational problems. Fifty-five per cent of tax credit awards in 2004-05 had to be readjusted as income or other factors had changed during the tax year – 40% being overpaid and 15% underpaid (NAO, 2005, para 2.10). More than half the overpayments were to those on the lowest incomes who had least funds to pay them back.

The credits differ from other tax welfare in their need for yearly re-application separate from the annual tax return. This has important consequences for the rate of take-up currently estimated to be around 80%. In addition, tax credits are based on joint income just as means-tested benefits, while income tax switched to individual taxation in 1990: joint assessment has in effect returned for many couples.

Tax credits differ from benefits because they do not appear fully in the public accounts, and this has implications for policy review and debate. Through the two new tax credits, some £13.8 billion was transferred in 2004-05 (NAO, 2005, p R1). However, the figure in the Revenue and Customs' table on tax expenditures is only £4.4 billion (HMRC, 2006, Table 1.5 revised). The reason is that direct payment to the individual is counted as public spending, while reduction of income tax liability is not. In consequence, most of the spending on tax credits is shown in the public expenditure statistics but the rest is not: and that is part of its political attractiveness.

The innovation of tax credits for most children and for low-paid workers has been an important departure from the traditional link of the social division of welfare with the social division of labour. For the first time, tax welfare has been redistributive downwards and not regressive. Only the best-off do not qualify for CTC, although WTC is confined to the poorest. The new tax credits also mean a transfer of resources, often significant, from men to women. Lone parents, predominantly women, have particularly benefited.

Tax welfare for retirement

Major reforms have also been introduced in the use of the tax system to support people in their retirement. The system replaced went back more than 80 years with major changes in the 1950s (Hannah, 1986; Titmuss, 1958, ch 3). No taxes were collected on contributions to pensions made by both employee and employer, although there was a limit on what the employee could put in tax-free. The investment income arising was largely exempt from tax. Finally, lump sums payable on retirement were tax-free, usually up to one and a half times annual earnings with a generous ceiling. The pension paid out after that was taxable (for more detail, see Sinfield, 2000, p 144).

Comparative analyses by the Bank of England identified "*taxation*" as the first of "the main determinants of the scale of benefits and advantages of pension funds as means of saving" (Davis, 1991, p 381, emphasis in original). The generous tax reliefs, especially for senior managers, and corporation tax efficiencies have been the main reasons for the growth of company pensions (Pensions Commission, 2004, p 120).

The scale of pensions funds benefiting is immense, some £1,250 billion (Inland Revenue, 2004, para 26). Yet there has been astonishingly little research into how effective tax reliefs are in stimulating private provision for retirement and how far that leads to savings and economic growth (Hughes, 2000; Minns, 2001).

Despite the lack of evidence for their effectiveness, the tax reliefs are considerable. "One-fifth of all contributions to private pensions (occupational and personal pensions) come from tax relief" (Curry and O'Connell, 2004, p 19). The government estimates the net cost of tax relief on non-state pensions for 2005-06 at £13.7 billion (HMRC, 2006, Table 1.5 revised). This is much more than all means-tested assistance to the poorest older people before pension credit began. (Confusingly, pension credit, as family credit in the past, is not a tax credit, but a social security benefit delivered by the Department for Work and Pensions.)

The need to take account of the substantial scale of tax relief is made even stronger by its very uneven distribution. At least half the tax subsidy on contributions alone went to the top 10% of taxpayers, with a quarter going to the top 2.5%. This "strongly regressive pattern" left the bottom 10% of taxpayers with just 1% of the tax benefit (Agulnik and Le Grand, 1998, p 410). This is an outstanding example of the upside-down effect and the reverse of the targeting of pension credit in public policy.

In 2004-05, 60% of the tax reliefs on employees' contributions to pensions went to those paying the higher rate of tax or who would have been without this tax relief (*Hansard*, 2005) – one in eight of all taxpayers receiving that relief, and only one in 10 of all taxpayers below state pension age. Income tax is later due on the pension received but not on the lump sum. The value of the tax benefit is even greater to those paying higher-rate tax in working life but a lower rate in retirement.

The full extent of the indirect subsidies assisting the growth of inequality in retirement is contested and probably understated (Sinfield, 2000). £7.4 billion was lost to the revenue in 2005-06 by not levying employers' National Insurance contributions on their payments to occupational pensions in the same way as on other employee benefits such as cars and concessionary loans (HMRC, 2006, Table 1.5 revised). Through 'contracting-out', another £9.6 billion National Insurance contributions were transferred to non-state pensions.

Overall, the Pensions Policy Institute calculated "the net annual cost to the taxpayer" at "more than £19 billion" and equivalent to 1.8% of gross domestic product (Curry and O'Connell, 2004, p 9). According to OECD studies, the United Kingdom provides the greatest tax subsidies to pensions (for example, Adema, 2001).

The changes

It might be expected that governments concerned with value for money would act to reduce these subsidies. There have been some restraints: from the late 1980s, a limit – an 'earnings cap' – restricted the contributions and tax-free lump sum for the most highly-paid. In 1997, a particularly generous relief effectively giving extra subsidy to the growth of funds was ended, although critics argued that this was a 'raid' on the funds (Emmerson and Tanner, 2000, p 67).

In 2002, after reviews of the savings and investment structures stressed weaknesses in pension taxation, the Labour government consulted on a "radical simplification" of the tax treatment of pensions to persuade people to save more in individual or company pensions (HM Treasury and Inland Revenue, 2002 p 3; DWP, 2002). This was presented as a major element in bringing about the 1998 strategy for changing the mixed economy of welfare in retirement: the long-term goal was to shift pension provision from 60% public:40% private to 40% public:60% private (DSS, 1998).

The complex system of eight different regimes was replaced by two ceilings in April 2006 – see **Box 7.5**. "In practical terms this will mean that most people can make pension contributions with tax relief, up to whatever they can afford" (Inland Revenue, 2004, para 17).

Box 7.5: The new tax regime for non-state pensions, April 2006

A 'single lifetime limit' on the total amount of tax-free pension saving is complemented by a 'light touch' compliance regime with an 'annual limit' on the value of inflows to each person's pension savings that can gain tax relief. After the consultations the initial lifetime limit was raised from a proposed £1.4 million to £1.5 million, rising to £1.8 million by 2010; the annual limit from £200,000 to £215,000, to £255,000 by 2010 with five-yearly reviews after that.

The reform was presented very differently from any social policy change within public spending departments. Neither of the two consultative documents provided any evidence at all on the cost of the new arrangements for tax reliefs, nor on who would benefit and by how much. This neglect was all the more remarkable in view of explicit recognition in the taxation consultation paper that proposals need to be "considered in a broad social and economic context" (HM Treasury and Inland Revenue, 2002, para ii); constant concern about 'fiscal sustainability'; and particular emphasis in both consultation papers on 'fairness in retirement'. The introduction by two Ministers to the tax paper began: "This Government is committed to enabling all pensioners to share fairly in the rising prosperity of the nation" (HM Treasury and Inland Revenue, 2002, Foreword).

Yet, "in recent decades inequality in pensioners' incomes has widened dramatically" (DWP, 2002, p 109). The proportion of pensioners with any private pension income has risen to two thirds, but many get only a small amount little boosted by tax welfare. The very unequal opportunities that exist for people to contribute to a non-state pension are a major cause of being 'under-pensioned' (Curry, 2003). Well below half of the working-age population (42%) have been contributing to a non-state pension of any type, nearly nine out of 10 contributing at the top but only one in four at the bottom of the income scale (UK, 2002, paras 36-7). This largely reflects workers' economic bargaining power in the labour market, especially in the private sector.

The tax proposals paid no attention to a major and persistent shortcoming in the pension system – its treatment of women and particularly mothers (Ginn et al, 2001). The two thirds of pensioners who were women had a median income in retirement little more than half men's (EOC, 2005). Despite the Department for Work and Pensions consultation paper devoting its final chapter to the serious problems of women pensioners, especially in the older age groups, and specifically recognising that inadequate pensions explained their much greater risk of poverty (DWP, 2002, ch 7), there was no recognition that tax reliefs contributed to widening the gender inequality and no sign of 'joined-up policy making' by it, the Treasury or the Inland Revenue.

The most frequent consultation response was opposition to 'the punitive low level' of the proposed £1.4 million lifetime limit. The lobbying was considerable and very vigorous, with powerful bodies led by the Confederation of British Industry arguing that there should be no ceiling at all on the already 'very powerful' subsidy to pensions, in the words of the Treasury. The limit has been raised and the tax privileges of current 'pension pots' protected. The resultant publicity may have raised awareness of how much pensions tax welfare has benefited management and directors whose final-salary defined-benefit schemes have generally survived when workers were being switched to defined contributions with much reduced contributions. An analysis from the Trades Union Congress of boardroom pensions in the top 100 companies showed wide inequalities, with much higher rates of contribution building up to a full pension twice as fast as for other workers (TUC, 2005a, 2005b).

How the official cost estimates of the new tax regime will be made has not yet been decided. The consultation outcome helped the 'marzipan layer' while restricting the 'icing', the very highest earners. The fact that the official estimate of the additional cost of the change is no more than £130 million on top of an existing £13 billion (HM Treasury and Inland Revenue, 2004) indicates the considerable tax benefits that must have been going to the small number at the very top, even more than critics estimated.

"Two nations in old age"

Who really benefits from this form of tax welfare – the contributors, the employers or the pensions and insurance industry? In *The Irresponsible Society* in 1959, Richard Titmuss asked, "Who behind the 'decorous drapery of political democracy' (in Professor Tawney's phrase) has power?", and went on to argue that insurance and pension interests "increasingly become the arbiters of welfare and amenity" (Titmuss, cited in Alcock et al, 2001, p 141). Only rarely have their activities become public: "the most astonishing lobbying campaign of my entire political career" was Nigel Lawson's description of the well-orchestrated reaction to the rumour that, as Chancellor of the Exchequer in Margaret Thatcher's government, he might tax the pension lump sum (Lawson, 1992, p 369).

In developing the 2006 pensions tax reform, the government appeared more concerned to win over the pension industry and to keep the goodwill of employers wavering over their final salary schemes than to tackle the broader social and economic problem of creating a level playing field in retirement to replace the existing bias towards those already better-off and more secure. The Inland Revenue Review team that proposed the changes contained representatives from the pension industry and employers but none from the trade unions or any pensioner groups, and it is not evident that they will gain much from the change.

Effectively, the Inland Revenue, the pensions industry and the employers have been developing the mixed economy of welfare in relation to retirement, although this has received little recognition, either in the social policy literature or in broader policy making. These are the 'subterranean' processes of policy making revealed in an American study of *The Divided Welfare State* (Hacker, 2002). With the subtitle *The Battle over Public and Private Social Benefits in the United States*, Jacob Hacker analysed how tax privileges in pensions and health have been gained and defended: "subterranean politics ... allow policies to pass that would not survive if subjected to the bright light of political scrutiny or the cold calculations of accurate budgeting" (Hacker, 2002, pp 43-4). The mixed economy of American welfare has been shaped by the various interest groups, particularly pensions and insurance industries and employers, exercising considerable influence on the development of tax welfare (Howard, 1997; Hacker, 2002).

In the United Kingdom the distributive impact of tax welfare's support of occupational welfare was brought out clearly by Richard Titmuss half a century ago: "The outlines of a dangerous social schism are clear, and they are enlarging.... Already it is possible to see two nations in old age; greater inequalities in living standards after work than in work; two contrasting social services for distinct groups based on different principles, and operating in isolation of each other as separate, autonomous, social instruments of change" (Titmuss, [1955] 1958, pp 73-4).

Today the government is not only shifting the responsibility for supporting retirement even more towards the individual, but doing so by increasing tax support for the great majority of those who can save in order to advance this privatisation of pensions at the expense of the rest. The effect of increasing tax reliefs on government accounts is probably little different to increasing state pensions, but it is hard to believe that a 'radical' change would be proposed for the public programme without more precise costing than the simple assurance that "the impact will be affordable" (HM Treasury and Inland Revenue, 2002, para 4.30).

Recently, this tax welfare has received more public attention. The TUC has spoken out on the "expensive, ineffective and unequal" impact of tax incentives (TUC, 2005b). Having lost internal battles with the Treasury, Work and Pensions Ministers have openly referred, for example, to "a uniquely generous tax regime" where "pensions are so tax-privileged that the [pension] pot rose far faster courtesy of the taxpayer ... than any other savings vehicle" (*Lords Hansard*, 2004, cols GC 158 and 161).

Tax welfare and the welfare state

This chapter has focused on the two areas of tax welfare that affect most people and cost the most, but they are not the only ones, as **Table 7.1** shows.

Unlike pension tax reliefs, the age tax allowance is unusual in that it is phased out as taxable income rises so that there is no benefit at all above £19,500. More upside-down is the special tax exemption for the first £30,000 of payments on termination of employment, often used by management to get rid of senior staff with a taxpayer subsidy. Despite the limit being frozen at £30,000 since 1988, its cost is still 80% more than the contribution-based element of Jobseeker's Allowance. In contrast to social security benefits, there are fewer detailed requirements for its receipt and no statistics available on the number of recipients, let alone their characteristics, or the value of benefits actually received.

Tax welfare is not an extended part of the welfare state as some suggest. Tax credits are replacing or extending social security benefits but the many differences have been indicated. Other forms such as tax support to pensions are operated even more differently outside the control of spending departments. Not included in public expenditure, they are not subject to the routine monitoring of the activities of government departments by, for example, select committees and audit reviews.

The implementation of tax welfare has also attracted relatively little attention until the many problems associated with the tax credits. One claimed advantage for tax benefits has been that they require less administration than direct provision, making them more attractive to governments intent on reducing the role of the state, but there have been few studies compared to the constant, detailed examinations of social security. The shock of the Maxwell pension scandal helped generate action on many problems that had been allowed to lie dormant. "Significant overfunding of insured schemes and arrangements has until now been commonplace" with excessive tax-free lump sums (Eccleshall, 1995, p 5; see also Inland Revenue Pension Schemes Office, 1994, para 5). Yet these illegal activities were not made subject to any penalty until 1994, despite barely veiled calls by tax officials for sanctions for many years. The tolerance of 'non-compliance' in tax welfare contrasts sharply with the much greater pursuit of 'fraud' in the social security system (Cook, 1989).

Tax welfare in comparative perspective

Tax welfare is common in many countries, although it is not possible to build up a detailed comparative picture (OECD, 1984, 1996; McDaniel and Surrey, 1985; Greve, 1994; Kvist and Sinfield, 1997). The largest tax welfare is usually for pensions and may be increasing in many countries (Hughes and Sinfield, 2004). In many countries the management of tax-privileged pension funds has had both economic and social impact: Minns argues that privatisation of pension funds is not about better pensions for more people but "*about reducing the role of the state and expanding the role of stock markets, which is altogether a different proposition*" (Minns, 2001, pp xiv-xv, emphasis in the original; see also Hannah, 1988, ch 1; Blackburn, 2002).

The second largest reliefs are often those promoting owner-occupation – as in the UK until their abolition. In the United States, tax exemptions on employer contributions for medical insurance premiums and medical care come second in cost, indicating the importance of that occupational welfare there.

EU financial accounting conventions do not help to make tax welfare visible and so more open to analysis and accountability. Direct governmental contribution to welfare has to be shown in the public accounts but not the indirect use of tax benefits. Their use to encourage privatisation is likely to undermine European Social Model policies to promote solidarity and social inclusion as any redistribution through tax benefits with the exception of targeted tax credits is upwards. This reinforces the social division of welfare – and economic and political divisions too.

Conclusion

Tax welfare in the United Kingdom is changing. The introduction of tax credits to lift lower incomes and help families is an important break through what seemed to be a fixed pattern reinforcing existing inequalities. However, most elements of tax welfare continue to work to widen inequalities – and do so relatively invisibly, insulated from the democratic process.

That is a very compelling reason to take a broader framework for social policy analysis than 'the welfare state', particularly in the growing but fitful discussion of poverty and inequality. The government's first major review of pension tax relief in half a century failed to restrain in any major way the largest upside-down benefit in the tax welfare state. While both consultation documents headline a fair sharing in retirement (DWP, 2002; HM Treasury and Inland Revenue, 2002) and Ministers continue to emphasise that help is being 'targeted' on the poorest pensioners, the joined-up reality of disconnected reforms to income tax and pension credit is a reinforcement of inequality.

The impact, economic, political and social, of the largely hidden tax benefits in reinforcing inequality is generally neglected. What studies there are focus on the barest economics of tax welfare – how much does it cost; to a much lesser extent, who gets what; and only occasionally, who pays. The wider impact in "nurturing privilege" (Titmuss, 1958, p 52; in Alcock et al, 2001, p 69) and "naturalising inequality" (Platt, 2005, p 24) has rarely been discussed.

Even with the current tax credits, choice in policy debates is still presented in terms of universal benefits to all including 'those who do not need them' versus 'more efficient, better targeted' selective benefits to 'those who really need them', often with a filtering out of the 'undeserving poor'. In reality, means-tested conditionality for the worse-off who are seen as unable to compete in the market is often accompanied by concealed public subsidies through the tax system that help others, and particularly the better-off, to purchase their own private protection more easily in the market. There is little evidence that there are problems with take-up for these tax-targeted measures.

The closing off of universalistic and solidaristic policies is supported by a reframing of the concept of fairness – no longer the collective sharing of risks so that social costs do not fall unfairly, but a fairness based on an individualistic calculus where you get out what you put in, and even that can be distorted by the tax subsidies to the higher-paid. Nothing becomes 'wasted' in redistribution or prevention in this "individualisation of the social" (Ferge, 1997).

> All the main issues of selectivity versus universality, residual versus institutional models, vertical versus horizontal redistribution of resources, increasing or decreasing inequality, will look different if we employ a broader definition of the welfare system which includes fiscal [tax] and occupational welfare. (Ascoli, 1987, p 134).

Summary

- As well as collecting revenue for public expenditure, tax and National Insurance systems can, and do, increase the resources and welfare of specific groups and individuals.
- Tax welfare acts to reinforce and widen inequalities.
- Its subterranean workings conceal the scale and effects of this, so reducing its political visibility and democratic accountability.
- Through tax credits, tax welfare now also helps reduce poverty and the extent of low-paid work, although its operation has to be improved.
- Tax welfare deserves greater attention in analyses of the mixed economy of welfare, given that its use by governments to build up alternatives to state provision helps to shape and develop the mixed economy.
- Better understanding of the workings and the full cost of tax welfare would raise important questions of current policy making.

Questions for discussion

- Who are the main beneficiaries and losers from tax welfare?
- What are the main ways in which tax welfare has affected the development of the mixed economy of welfare?
- Why has tax welfare received little attention?

• Will the fact that Child Tax Credits are now available to the majority of families change the overall approach and impact of tax welfare?

Further reading

See Titmuss's original discussion of fiscal (tax) welfare (1958, pp 44-50; pp 65-7 in **Alcock et al, 2001**): the broader context and interaction across the social division of welfare are important.

For tax welfare and support for families and children: **Brewer and Adam (2004)**; **HM Treasury (2006)**; **Millar (2003)**; **Ridge (2003)**.

For analysis of tax benefits in pensions: **Curry and O'Connell (2004)**; **TUC (2005b)**; **Agulnik and Le Grand (1998)**; **Sinfield (2000)**.

For policy and practice on tax and benefit fraud: **Cook (1989, 1997)**.

I would strongly recommend **Hacker (2002)** and **Howard (1997)** for their detailed historical studies of the politics and policy making of tax welfare in the US as no comparable study is available here.

For limited comparative work on pensions, see: **Hughes and Sinfield (2004)**; and **Kvist and Sinfield (1997)**, comparing Denmark and the UK.

International reviews so far have made a point of not making direct comparisons across countries: **OECD (1996)** is the latest. Willem Adema and colleagues there have been examining what they call 'social-fisted measures' and TBSPS, 'tax breaks for social purposes' (for latest, **Adema and Ladaique, 2005**). Unfortunately, they do not include those which are not recognised as such by individual governments and thus omit some of the largest, such as tax benefits on pensions, from their main calculations. However, their analyses deserve much more attention than I have given them here.

Electronic resources

The extent of evidence on tax spendiing remains very limited. Detailed data are often published deep in official reports, in obscure appendices and generally for only one or two years at a time. The statistics usually appear with little discussion, and that is often confined to the introduction or revision of a relief. Many countries provide no data at all despite making considerable use of what other countries call tax expenditures.

The UK estimates appear in the same list in two places. The yearly pre-Budget report, usually in early December, includes data for two years at a time in table 7 of an 'associated paper' called 'Tax ready reckoner and tax reliefs' (www.hm-treasury.gov.uk/pre_budget_report). At the end of the tax year this reappears on the HM Revenue and Customs website with usually small amendments as table 1.5 (www.hmrc.gov.uk.stats/taxexpenditures/menu.htm).

Subsequent years incorporate revisions of previous year estimates, but no time series has yet been published in contrast to public spending. Subsequent reworkings have occured but have not been published. Some additional tables provide evidence on smaller reliefs.

Acknowledgement

Thanks to Dorothy Sinfield, Paul Dornan, Gerry Hughes and Sue Ward for their help and valuable advice.

References

Adema, W. (2001) *Net Social Expenditure: Second Edition*, Labour Market and Social Policy Occasional Paper no 52, Paris: Organisation for Economic Cooperation and Development.

Adema, W. and Ladaique, M. (2005) *Net Social Expenditure: 2005 Edition*, Employment and Migration Working Paper no 29, Paris: Organisation for Economic Cooperation and Development.

Adler, M. (2004) 'Combining welfare-to-work measures with tax credits: a new hybrid approach to social security in the United Kingdom', *International Social Security Review*, vol 57, no 2, pp 87-106.

Agulnik, P. and Le Grand, J. (1998) 'Tax relief and partnership pensions', *Fiscal Studies*, vol 19, no 4, pp 403-28.

Alcock, P., Glennerster, G., Oakley, A. and Sinfield, A. (eds) (2001) *Welfare and Wellbeing: Richard Titmuss's contribution to Social Policy*, Bristol: The Policy Press.

Ascoli, U. (1987) 'The Italian welfare state: between incrementalism and rationalism', in R.R. Friedmann, N. Gilbert and M. Sherer (eds) *Modern Welfare States: A Comparative View of Trends and Prospects*, Brighton: Harvester Wheatsheaf, pp 110-50.

Battle, K., Millar, M., Mendelson, M., Meyer, D. and Whiteford, P. (2000) *Benefits for Children: A Four-Country Study*, Ottawa: Caledon Institute.

Bennett, F. (2005) *Gender and Benefits*, London: Equal Opportunities Commission.

Blackburn, R. (2002) *Banking on Death – or Investing in Life: The History and Future of Pensions*, London: Verso.

Brewer, M. and Adam, S. (2004) *Supporting Families: The Financial Costs and Benefits of Children Since 1975*, Bristol: The Policy Press.

Cook, D. (1989) *Rich Law Poor Law*, Milton Keynes: Open University Press.

Cook, D. (1997) 'Social divisions of welfare: tax and social security fraud', in A. Robertson (ed) *Unemployment, Social Security and the Social Division of Welfare*, New Waverley Paper 13, Edinburgh: University of Edinburgh, pp 17-29.

Curry, C. (2003) *The Under-pensioned*, London: Pensions Policy Institute.

Curry, C. and O'Connell, A. (2004) *Tax Relief and Incentives for Pension Saving*, London: Pensions Policy Institute.

Davis, E.B. (1991) 'The development of pension funds – an international comparison', *Bank of England Quarterly Bulletin*, vol 31, no 3, pp 380-90.

Deakin, N. and Parry, R. (2000) *The Treasury and Social Policy: The Contest for Control of Welfare Strategy*, Basingstoke: Palgrave Macmillan.

DSS (Department of Social Security) (1998) *A New Contract for Welfare: Partnership in Pensions*, Consultation paper, London: DSS.

DWP (Department for Work and Pensions) (2002) *Simplicity, Security and Choice*, Cm 5677, London: The Stationery Office (www.dwp.gov.uk).

EC (European Commission) (2003) *Employment in Europe 2003*, Brussels: EC.

Eccleshall, R. (1995) 'PSO compliance audits, past and future', Paper presented at National Association of Pension Funds Regional Meeting, London, 25 May.

Emmerson, C. and Tanner, S. (2000) 'A note on the tax treatment of private pensions and Individual Savings Accounts', *Fiscal Studies*, vol 21, no 1, pp 65-74.

EOC (Equal Opportunities Commission) (2005) *Women and Pensions*, Briefing, London: EOC.

Ferge, Z. (1997) 'The changed welfare paradigm: the individualisation of the social', *Social Policy and Administration*, vol 31, no 1, pp 20-44.

Ginn, J., Street, D. and Arber, S. (eds) (2001) *Women, Work and Pensions: International Issues and Prospects*, Buckingham: Open University Press.

Greve, B. (1994) 'The hidden welfare state: tax expenditure and social policy', *Scandinavian Journal of Social Welfare*, vol 3, no 4, pp 203-11.

Hacker, J.S. (2002) *The Divided Welfare State: The Battle over Public and Private Social Benefits in the United States*, Cambridge: Cambridge University Press.

Hannah, L. (1986) *Inventing Retirement: The Development of Occupational Pensions in Britain*, Cambridge: Cambridge University Press.

Hannah, L. (ed) (1988) *Pension Asset Management: An International Perspective*, Homewood: Richard D Irwin.

Hansard (2005) Written Answer to PQ from Chris Huhne, 24 October, col 52W.

HMRC (HM Revenue and Customs) (2006) *Revenue and Customs Statistics* (www.hmrc.gov.uk/stats/).

HM Treasury (1995) *Tax Ready Reckoner and Tax Reliefs*, London: HM Treasury.

HM Treasury (1998) *The Modernization of Britain's Tax and Benefit System Number 2: Work Incentives: A Report by Martin Taylor*, London: HM Treasury.

HM Treasury (2005) *Budget 2005 Summary*, London: HM Treasury.

HM Treasury (2006) 'Building a fairer society', *Budget Report 2006*, London: The Stationery Office, pp 97-126.

HM Treasury and Inland Revenue (2002) *Simplifying the Taxation of Pensions: Increasing Choice and Flexibility for All*, London: The Stationery Office.

HM Treasury and Inland Revenue (2004) *Simplifying the Taxation of Pensions: The Government's Proposals – Partial Regulatory Impact Assessment*, London: The Stationery Office (www.hm-treasury.gov.uk).

Howard, C. (1997) *The Hidden Welfare State: Tax Expenditures and Social Policy in the United States*, Princeton, NJ: Princeton University Press.

Hughes, G. (2000) 'Pension financing, the substitution effect and national savings', in G. Hughes and J. Stewart (eds) *Pensions in the European Union*, Dordrecht: Kluwer, pp 45-61.

Hughes, G. and Sinfield, A. (2004) 'Financing pensions by stealth', in G. Hughes and J. Stewart (eds) *Reforming Pensions in Europe: Evolution of Pension Financing and Sources of Retirement Income*, Cheltenham: Edward Elgar, pp163-92.

Inland Revenue (2004) *Simplifying the Taxation of Pensions: Regulatory Impact Assessment*, London: Inland Revenue.

Inland Revenue Pension Schemes Office (1994) *Compliance Audits: The Findings so Far, Memorandum no 120*, Surrey: Inland Revenue Pension Schemes Office.

Kvist, J. and Sinfield, A. (1997) 'Comparing tax welfare states', in M. May, E. Brunsdon and G. Craig (eds) *Social Policy Review 9*, London: Social Policy Association, pp 249-75.

Lawson, N. (1992) *The View from No. 11*, London: Bantam.

Lords Hansard (2004) Baroness Hollis of Heigham, HL Deb, vol 665, 18 October, cols GC 158 and 161.

McDaniel, P.R. and Surrey, S.S. (eds) (1985) *International Aspects of Tax Expenditures: A Comparative Study*, Deventer: Kluwer.

Millar, J. (2003) 'From wage replacement to wage supplement: benefits and tax credits', in J. Millar (ed) *Understanding Social Security*, Bristol: The Policy Press, pp 123-43.

Minns, R. (2001) *The Cold War on Welfare: Stock Markets versus Pensions*, London: Verso.

NAO (National Audit Office) (2005) *Comptroller and Auditor General's Standard Report on the Accounts of the Inland Revenue 2004-05*, London: The Stationery Office.

OECD (Organisation for Economic Cooperation and Development) (1984) *Tax Expenditures: A Review*, Paris: OECD.

OECD (1996) *Tax Expenditures: Recent Experiences*, Paris: OECD.

Pensions Commission (2004) *Pensions: Challenges and Choices: The First Report of the Pensions Commission*, London: The Stationery Office.

Platt, L. (2005) *Discovering Child Poverty: The Creation of a Policy Agenda from 1800 to the Present*, Bristol: The Policy Press.

Ridge, T. (2003) 'Benefiting children? The challenge of social security support for children', in J. Millar (ed) *Understanding Social Security*, Bristol: The Policy Press, pp 167-88.

Sinfield, A. (2000) 'Tax benefits in non-state pensions', *European Journal of Social Security*, vol 2, no 3, pp 137-67.

Surrey, S.S. (1973) *Pathways to Tax Reform*, Cambridge, MA, Harvard University Press.

Titmuss, R.M. (1958) *Essays on 'The Welfare State'*, London: Allen and Unwin.

Toynbee, P. (2003) *Hard Work: Life in Low-pay Britain*, London: Bloomsbury.

TUC (Trades Union Congress) (2005a) *Pensionswatch2005: An Analysis of Director and Staff Pensions*, London: TUC (www.tuc.org.uk/pensions/tuc-10503-f0.cfm).

TUC (2005b) *Expensive, Ineffective and Unequal – Why the Incentives aren't the Answer to the Pensions Crisis*, London: TUC (www.tuc.org.uk/extras/incentivesreport.doc).

UK (2002) *National Strategy Report on the Future of Pensions Systems*, London, September.

WPC (Work and Pensions Committee) (2004) *Child Poverty in the UK*, Second Report of Session 2003-2004, HC 85-I, London: The Stationery Office.

eight

Occupational welfare

Edward Brunsdon and Margaret May

Overview

Occupational welfare is a significant but neglected dimension of the mixed economy of welfare and one subject to considerable change since the emergence of 'New Labour'. This chapter seeks to outline the main features of this form of welfare, review key recent developments through two case studies and consider the place of occupational provision in the UK's welfare nexus.

Key concepts

'Occupational welfare' • occupational social security • pay substitutes • pay supplements • work–life balance • defined benefit and defined contribution pensions • contracting out • national pension scheme • occupational healthcare • wellness initiatives • voluntarism

Introduction

This chapter addresses an important but neglected component of Britain's welfare order, namely, the non-wage benefits and services provided by employers for their staff. This provision, traditionally entitled 'occupational' or 'workplace' welfare[1], constitutes one of the three strands in the social division of welfare (see Chapter One). It has gained increasing significance over the past decade as employers have developed new schemes and the government has extended its welfare responsibilities. The value of employer support has also increased considerably in recent years, making a substantial contribution to recipients' standards of living and their overall quality of life (Torrington et al, 2005).

In spite of this importance, the nature and implications of occupational welfare have received only sporadic attention from social policy analysts. In part, this is a matter of preference, with the statutory and voluntary sectors providing more favoured research areas. But it is also due to several other factors. These include: an ambiguous intellectual division of labour that treats employment practices as the subject matter of several disciplines; the many difficulties of accessing appropriate data (May and Brunsdon, 1994; Brunsdon and May, 2002); and, not least, the conceptual conflation that when it is considered at all, occupational welfare is often subsumed within an undifferentiated notion of 'private' or 'market' welfare. This not only sidelines a key policy arena, it also obscures the complexity of the relations between statutory and non-statutory agencies and thereby conceals the different ways in which this type of welfare is traded, the parties and calculations involved and the outcomes.

Unravelling this complexity involves recognising the multi-sectoral nature of the trading. Employers from the statutory, voluntary, not-for-profit and commercial sectors offer welfare schemes for their employees. These may be provided in-house or purchased from external agencies. Suppliers may be from the commercial, voluntary or, in certain instances, the statutory sector. The workplace measures provided are highly variable; some forms of assistance and benefits are mandatory, but most are the product of employer choice. They range from different types of financial assistance, through health and social care services, education and training, housing and housing benefits to travel, concierge and leisure services (see **Table 8.1**). For employers, the calculations involve assessing which services and benefits meet their business needs. For governments, it is an agenda of both enhancing organisational and overall economic performance and shifting the costs and/or responsibility of welfare delivery away from the state.

The aim of this chapter is to examine the nature of occupational welfare in the UK and, through two case studies, consider the wide array of factors influencing its development and the policy concerns it raises. It starts by looking more closely at the concept itself and the range of welfare interventions it embraces before addressing recent changes and their outcomes.

What is occupational welfare?

Current conceptions of employer-sponsored provision stem from Titmuss's seminal treatise on the social division of welfare (see Chapters One, Three and Seven). In an attempt to counter attacks on what was then the newly established welfare state, he highlighted ways in which publicly funded and delivered welfare measures were paralleled by employer schemes (Titmuss, 1958a). These benefits and services he depicted through an inventory (see **Box 8.1**).

> **Box 8.1:** Titmuss' inventory of occupational welfare
>
> Occupational welfare "... include[s] pensions for employees, wives and dependants, child allowances; death benefits; health and welfare services; personal expenses for travel, entertainment, dress and equipment; meal vouchers; motor cars and season tickets; residential accommodation; holiday expenses; children's school fees; sickness benefits; medical expenses; education and training grants; cheap meals; unemployment benefit; medical bills and an incalculable variety of benefits in kind ranging from 'obvious forms of realizable goods to the most intangible form of amenity' (Royal Commission on Taxation, 1955)" (Titmuss, 1958a, pp 50-1).

While this provided a good indication of what he meant by occupational welfare, it nonetheless contained ambiguities, was a non-exhaustive listing and was time-bound. Attempts to tidy up this characterisation through a definition have led several analysts (including the current authors) to the human resources management field of 'employee reward'. Here, occupational welfare is considered a type of remuneration that is distinguished from base and incentive pay to form the 'above-wage' or 'non-pay' element of employee reward[2]. In an early formulation, Murlis describes it as "over and above basic remuneration which increases the well-being of employees at some cost to the employer" (1974, p 1) and, more explicitly, some 14 years later, as: "Items in the total package offered [directly] to employees over and above salary which increase their wealth and well-being at some expense to the employer" (Armstrong and Murlis, 1988, cited in Wright, 2004, p 181). What these general or broad-based definitions attempt to do is capture the rich array of non-wage options that employers have utilised in 'total reward' packages, allowing empirical research to detail what has been provided, when and by which organisations.

They have not, however, existed without criticism. In the human resources management literature, Wright suggests that such definitions are not selective enough, thus: "The potential list of what might be included stretches to [incorporate] sometimes quirky low-cost provisions that are not in the same ballpark as pensions, cars and holidays – either in terms of their cost to the employer or in relation to the value to their employees" (2004, p 181). In social policy, Farnsworth (2004a, 2004b) has taken a different tack, questioning whether all the benefits and services embraced by such definitions are relevant to welfare analysis. In his terms, a definition that includes the "full gamut" of employee benefits, placing sports-club membership and company cars alongside pensions and health screening, "go[es] beyond any useful conception of social policy" (2004a, p 151).

Whereas Wright's rhetorical argument seeks to narrow the definition on 'monetary' or 'value' grounds, Farnsworth attempts to do so on grounds of pertinence. He wants to separate "work-based social provision" that meets welfare needs from "forms of occupation 'fringe benefits'" (2004b, p 438) that he considers are primarily for business purposes. His attempt at demarcation consists of invoking Beveridge's "five giant social risks" and asking whether the benefits and services of occupational welfare eliminate or help to reduce these risks. Those workplace benefits that contribute to the reduction of ignorance, idleness, disease, squalor and want (2004a, p 151) become the subject matter of social policy, those that do not remain matters of business interest.

The first sign of problems with this division comes with his illustrations. Abandoning the assurance of assertion, he describes examples of work-based social provision in the following way: "[c]hildcare provision and family-friendly policies *may* help reduce the risk of unemployment; occupational pensions and sickness benefits *may* help to tackle want; and ... occupational healthcare *may* help to tackle disease and ill-health" (2004a, p 151, emphasis added). But if there is such tentativeness about their effects, should there not also be a tentativeness about their categorisation? After all, in his terms, they should not be part of 'workplace social provision' if they do not have the perceived effects. Equally, if there is a tentativeness about these effects, how can he be certain that those he excludes as business fringe benefits do not have direct or indirect welfare consequences? Why, for example, can sports-club membership or company cars not be preventive health measures maintaining fitness in the one instance and alleviating the stress of travelling in the other?

What this probing is suggesting is that Farnsworth's division is not a helpful analytical tool. As Titmuss himself recognised, whatever their source or designated purpose, all employee benefits and services have multiple and overlapping functions and welfare consequences. Many schemes that might initially be construed as 'business-oriented' have welfare effects. It may be an indirect outcome, but it is no less pertinent to social policy analysis. For these reasons, this chapter retains the broad-based definition of occupational welfare presented by Armstrong and Murlis (1988, cited in Wright, 2004, p 181) in its characterisation of current employer provision.

Current forms of occupational welfare

This definition permits the stratification of contemporary occupational welfare into nine main types of mandatory and voluntary benefits and services: occupational social security; education and training; social care; healthcare; concierge; housing; transport; leisure and community services. While some of these schemes are confined to employees, others also provide for spouses or partners (including civil partners under the 2004 Civil Partnership Act) and children. Some are offered on a flexible or cafeteria basis, allowing staff to choose the most suitable for their personal requirements, while others are matters of specific provision (CIPD, 2005a; IDS, 2005a). Space denies a detailed exposition but the main constituents of each type can be sketched in a general overview and table (**Table 8.1**), with two case studies (occupational pensions and healthcare) pursued in more detail. What needs to be borne in mind in the consideration of both the overview and the case studies is the numerous permutations of mandatory and voluntary employer provision that exist and the degree to which particular organisations, especially those in the non-statutory sectors, can fluctuate dramatically in terms of what they choose to offer and how they opt to deliver it. This kaleidoscope of provision, combined with the varying forms and degrees of state intervention and trading configurations, can lead to quite intricate accounts of the non–uniform ways these different types of welfare provision evolve.

General overview

Of the range of benefits and services listed in **Table 8.1**, perhaps the most widely recognised is *occupational social security*. This type of financial assistance exists as both mandatory and voluntary provision (Watson Wyatt, 2006). The former consists of pay substitutions, such as sickness benefit; maternity, paternity and adoption leave; and redundancy pay, while the latter includes above-statutory pay substitutions, such as occupational pensions; enhanced sick pay; maternity, paternity and adoption leave; birth and adoption grants; life and personal accident insurance; death–in–service benefits; enhanced redundancy pay; and pay supplements such as professional indemnity insurance, affinity benefits, interest-free loans and legal expenses.

Education and training benefits and services incorporate work-specific training as well as outsourced educational programmes and their financial support. Apart from paid time off for 16- to 18-year-olds for specified study or training, the major mandatory obligation concerns health and safety provision, which varies with industry-specific standards established by the Health and Safety Executive (HSE). Voluntary provision ranges from extra-mandatory health and safety training to an array of on- and off-site courses. These are usually vocational in nature, although some employers are also prepared to sponsor recreational

Table 8.1: Mandatory and voluntary forms of occupational welfare

Types of occupational welfare	Mandatory	Voluntary
1. Occupational social security		Occupational pensions (retirement; survivors; ill-health retirement)
		Life insurance/death-in-service benefits
		Personal accident insurance
	Statutory sick pay	Occupational sick pay
	Statutory maternity pay	Occupational maternity pay
	Statutory adoption pay	Occupational paternity pay
		Birth/adoption grants
	Redundancy pay	Enhanced redundancy pay
		Professional indemnity insurance
		Affinity benefits (for example, discounts for employee purchases)
		Interest-free loans

Table 8.1: (cont)

Types of occupational welfare	Mandatory	Voluntary
2. Education and training	*Health and safety legislation establishing training requirements* *Paid time off for 16- to 18- year-olds for specified study or training*	Health and safety (plus) Training/staff development schemes Study support: tuition/exam fees, equipment, books, subsistence, travel Study leave Subscription to professional bodies Personal development leave (sabbaticals, career breaks) Children's educational assistance (fees, subsidies, grants, loans)
3. Healthcare	*Health and safety legislation establishing healthcare responsibilities* *Antenatal care leave*	Occupational health services Wellness services Extended antenatal care leave Fertility treatment leave Leave/time off for appointments/treatment (medical/dental/ophthalmic) Private medical insurance Permanent health insurance/ long-term disability pay Health cash plans Critical illness insurance

Table 8.1: (cont)

Types of occupational welfare	Mandatory	Voluntary
4. Social care (including family-friendly and work–life balance provisions)		
General leave	*Paid holiday leave*	Extended (paid) holiday leave
	Civic duties	Extended civic duties leave
		Leave for religious festivals
		Leave for personal reasons
		Marriage and civil partnership leave
'Family'-related leave	*Maternity leave*	Extended maternity leave
	Paternity leave	Extended paternity leave
	Adoption leave	Extended adoption leave
	Parental leave	Extended (paid) parental leave
	Dependant emergency care leave	Extended (paid) dependant care leave
		Foster parent leave
		Grandparent leave
	Carers leave	Extended (paid) carers leave
		(Paid) bereavement leave
		(Paid) compassionate leave

Table 8.1: (cont)

Types of occupational welfare	Mandatory	Voluntary
4. Social care (continued)		
Flexible working arrangements	Other employees	Information services
	Right to request: parents of under-sixes and disabled children up to 18	Advice and counselling services (employee assistance programmes, stress management)
		Enhanced leave
Support services		
Redundancy	*Time off for job search/retraining*	Outplacement services (counselling, information/ advice, career planning, assistance with job-search/ application skills, placement services)
Pre-retirement services		Information and advice schemes
Post-retirement services		Befriending/visiting schemes
		Respite care
		Information and referral services
		Advice/parentcraft services
		Provisions for employees with disabled children
		Workplace nurseries
		Subsidy/voucher schemes
		(Salary sacrifice schemes)
Childcare services		Information, referral/advice services
		Workplace daycare
		Subsidy/voucher schemes

Table 8.1: (cont)

Types of occupational welfare	Mandatory	Voluntary
5. Housing		Company housing
		Relocation assistance
		Bridging loans
		Mortgage assistance/ subsidies
		Buildings/contents insurance
6. Transport		Company cars
		Car tax/fuel/insurance
		Car allowances
		Driving lessons
		Season ticket vouchers/ loans
		Free parking
		Travel insurance
7. Leisure		Sports/social/recreational facilities
		Subsidised sports/ recreational club membership
		Information/referral services
8. Concierge services		Subsidised cafeterias; meal allowances/vouchers
		Housework/laundry/shopping
		Employee secondments
9. Community schemes		Employee mentoring schemes
		Employee volunteering schemes
		Employee fundraising schemes

learning. In addition to financing these courses, they may offer study support in the form of fees for examinations and financial assistance for the purchase of books, equipment, travel and subsistence as well as study leave and personal development time (sabbaticals and career breaks). In some large commercial organisations, fee subsidies, grants and loans are extended to support the education of employees' children.

Occupational healthcare traditionally focused on reducing the risk of workplace injuries and, where they occurred, on their treatment (IPD, 1995). In the past decade, however, this type of provision has begun to be replaced by a broader approach that promotes healthy living and encompasses the whole workforce. Illustrated in the emergence of a host of 'wellness' initiatives (see **Box 8.3**), it signifies a new conception of proactive employee healthcare and an extension of employers' responsibilities. Where medical care is needed, funding usually occurs through different forms of sponsored insurance (IDS, 2003). Private medical insurance (PMI) is the most frequently used to pay for diagnoses and treatment costs and typically covers consultation, day surgery, hospitalisation, physiotherapy, radiology and other elective treatments. From the employers' perspective, it enables early medical assessment and treatment at convenient times as well as prompt surgical and rehabilitation services. Approximately 10% of employees (and in some instances their spouses, partners and dependent children) are covered by PMI, most of whom are in key positions (CIPD, 2005b). Recent changes in NHS services have, however, led a number of employers to look beyond PMI in order to finance additional forms of healthcare. Many, for instance, now offer healthcare cash plans to purchase dental, ophthalmic and chiropody services as well as medical treatment.

Social care provision, like healthcare, is also changing (IDS, 2002). Employers are turning away from traditional industrial social work to support and fund an array of personal counselling services (see **Table 8.1**). These services vary in terms of their provenance, modes of delivery and types of support. Their primary aim is to offer advice and assistance to employees with 'personal problems', stemming either from relational issues in the workplace or from their 'non-work' circumstances. In the employers' eyes, the service is particularly valuable where problems are considered to affect employee work performance and where counselling can provide a cost-effective way forward. Who supplies the service is subject to marked variation. In large businesses, it is likely to be an in-house or externally contracted specialist either from a voluntary or commercial provider. In small and medium-sized enterprises, the role of counsellor is more likely to be taken by line managers (Kiefer and Briner, 2003).

Workplace counselling is often combined with services aimed at enhancing employee welfare through a better balance between work and other interests and responsibilities. Collectively termed 'work–life balance (WLB) services', they are geared to employees with changing work, caring and/or personal development needs. Utilising time as a major welfare resource, they offer more flexible leave, career, location, working- and learning-time arrangements and other lifestyle benefits (Woodland et al, 2003). Provision here has primarily been driven by EU and UK legislation on working time, holiday and parental leave as well as flexible working arrangements. But the government has also invested in a number of measures to persuade employers to move beyond the statutory minima. In particular, it has actively promoted the business case for a range of WLB schemes, sponsoring research, building up a supportive evidence base and showcasing examples in national and regional campaigns.

Housing, transport, leisure and concierge benefits and services are all forms of provision that are specifically at the behest of employers and therefore subject to quite wide variation (Employee Benefits, 2005). Housing options range from the supply of company accommodation to various forms of financial assistance used to provide: relocation allowances; cheap mortgages or mortgage subsidies; bridging loans; and the means to purchase buildings and contents insurance. Financial help with transport includes the purchase of company cars, car insurance, travel insurance, road tax and fuel, loans or subsidies for bus/rail season tickets and payments for driving lessons. In the case of leisure, employers either supply facilities for sports, social and recreational activities and/or sponsor a range of options (for example, gym membership, attendance at particular sports or social events, concerts or other forms of entertainment). Concierge services can involve employers offering general information or referral services; providing subsidised cafeterias, meal allowances or vouchers; and supplying someone to undertake housework, shopping and/or laundry.

Community participation schemes constitute another expanding realm of occupational welfare (IDS, 2001). Linked, in some instances, to the growth of corporate social responsibility, these particular schemes offer staff the opportunity to engage in civic or voluntary work in the community (for example, as school governors or trustees) fundraising for local or national projects, mentoring, or more formal volunteering and citizenship schemes. Beyond verbal endorsements, employer support can take the form of secondments, financial contributions or paid leave for employees.

This section of the chapter has sought to illustrate the breadth of current mandatory and voluntary occupational welfare. The two case studies that follow consider two particular forms of provision in much greater depth. They have been chosen not simply because of the contrasting nature of their provision, their current status, types of voluntary initiative and forms of state intervention, but also because of the intricate, and differing, combinations of factors required to explain their development. They illustrate, in microcosm, the 'explanatory tariff,' or analytical demands made on those seeking to understand employer welfare's changing formations. Occupational pensions is a form of employer welfare that has recently been scaled back in response to a range of changing political, social and economic circumstances. In contrast, employer-sponsored healthcare is an expanding form of provision, which, while responding to NHS changes and government pressure, has also grown through a number of voluntary employer initiatives that are tailored to meet organisational needs.

Case studies in current occupational welfare

Case study 1: occupational pensions

As indicated in **Table 8.1**, the social security provided by employers encompasses a wide range of benefits. Of these, the most valuable for staff and the most expensive for employers is retirement pensions. As a form of occupational welfare, these date back to the 19th century, although the main period of growth occurred between the 1950s and 1980s, during which time coverage rose from less than 20% to approximately 50% of the workforce (Government Actuary, 1994). Contrasting clusters of factors in different work sectors drove this expansion. Among commercial organisations, for instance, occupational pensions were used as an enticement to recruit and retain staff at a time of low unemployment, strong union representation and tight labour markets. More potently, they were employed in reward management negotiations to defer or limit wage increases, thereby enabling firms to both expand and meet the demands of the UK's investment markets for short-term dividends. For public sector employers – including the newly nationalised industries – the calculations were quite different. While faced with a highly unionised workforce, many were committed to the notion that the state should operate as a 'model' employer and providing occupational pensions was a way of setting an example for others to emulate (Farnham, 1999). More pragmatically, they also presented a way around constrained budgets and a means of counterbalancing otherwise comparatively low wage levels. A similar mix of conditions also encouraged organisations in the voluntary sector, although resource constraints meant coverage here was more limited.

Developments across the sectors were prompted by two further factors: the promotion of a larger range of pension products and services by insurance companies (May and Brunsdon, 1999) and the continued support for occupational pensions by successive post-war governments (Lynes, 1997). What the insurance companies saw as market opportunities, the governments saw as alleviating some of their concerns about the funding of the state pension system. The Conservative endorsement was typically laced with an antipathy towards collectivism. For Labour, it amounted to an uneasy compromise between a commitment to state pensions and a recognition of their costs. The outcome was a distinctive pensions mix, with "one of the least generous state systems in the developed world" paralleled by "the most developed" voluntary-funded arrangements (Pensions Commission, 2004, p x).

The pattern had been set by Labour's cautious reform of the pre-war state insurance system. In following Beveridge's flat-rate formula, it sanctioned the notion of a basic state pension 'topped up' by other savings. Further, by setting rates lower than Beveridge advised and maintaining pre-war tax concessions, it opened the way for an expansion of employers' earnings-related measures. Subsequent Conservative governments extended fiscal relief and added a more direct inducement for organisations in 1961 when they introduced a 'graduated' (earnings-related) state pension and with it 'contracting out' arrangements for employers. Though Labour upgraded the state system and tightened prudential regulation in the 1970s, faced with a surge in workplace schemes, it retained this framework of mixed provision. It stipulated, however, that employer pensions should be at least equivalent to the state earnings-related system, re-enforcing this by agreeing measures to enhance public sector pension schemes.

The accommodation was not without its critics (Blackburn, 2002). Neo-liberal thinkers maintained that though preferable to state intervention, occupational pensions restricted individual choice and the development of a free pensions market. Socialist critics, borrowing from Titmuss (1958a, 1958b, 1963), attacked their uneven coverage, regressive distributional effects and the way they undermined support for state welfare. Their targets were obvious. Provision varied by sector, organisational size, occupational group and status, with the most generous pensions accruing to the mainly male incumbents of full-time, senior, managerial and professional posts. Pension fund managers lacked accountability, there was little protection for employee contributors if their firms collapsed, and some critics questioned employer willingness to sustain provision in a less favourable financial climate.

Occupational initiatives resulted in a wide variety of schemes that included 'gold-plated' executive pension schemes as well as those involving employer and employee contributions. Unlike the state's 'pay-as-you-go' system, the overwhelming majority of these were 'funded,' that is, contributions were paid into funds that were set aside in order to meet future pensions. They were held by trustees or financial bodies that were legally separate from the employer and primarily invested in equities (Hannah, 1986). The schemes were usually either 'defined benefit' (DB) or 'defined contribution schemes' (DC) and had differing implications for organisations and staff (**Box 8.2**).

Box 8.2: Main types of occupational pension

Scheme type	Provisions
Defined benefit schemes	These provide a guaranteed pension based on an employee's salary. There are two main types: (a) *final salary schemes* – based on the number of years of pensionable service, the accrual rate and final earnings; and, (b) *average salary schemes* – based on a percentage of the salary earned in each year of service.
Defined contribution/ money purchase schemes	Here the pension is based on the contributions made and investment return generated. Employers pay a defined percentage of earnings with the sum accumulated converted into an annuity on retirement.

Historically, public sector organisations offered DB schemes as did most private sector employers, especially in manufacturing. For employees, these secured a predictable retirement income. However, DB plans proved to be costly and unpredictable for employers that had to make up any shortfall in the fund arising from poor investments. DC schemes in contrast transferred the financial risk to employees as organisations guaranteed a contribution, not a benefit, level. Here the income received was contingent on the sum invested, the performance of the fund and annuity rates at the time of retirement.

Because of these risks, contracting out was initially confined to DB schemes. It was extended to DC plans under the 1986 Social Security Act as part of the broader Thatcherite attempt to promote individual choice and create a pensions market. To these ends, the government also enabled individuals to opt directly out of the state earnings-related scheme into a personal pension and removed compulsory membership of occupational programmes. These moves prompted a slowdown in occupational provision, a shift away from final salary plans by private sector employers and a decision to opt out by many new work entrants. The implications of these developments were masked by the buoyancy of pension fund investments in the 1980s and early 1990s, which gave new retirees historically high pensions and enabled many employers to take contribution 'holidays'.

When Labour came to power in 1997, the UK appeared to have an effective occupational pensions tier, so much so that it was hailed as 'a welfare success story' (DSS, 1998). In accordance with this assessment, the government factored workplace measures into a further remodelling of the UK's pension regime based on its 'third way' precepts (Powell, 2003). Contrary to earlier Labour policy, this centred on reducing state funding (to 40% rather than 60%) and expanding private saving. For employers, it entailed a new stakeholder pension scheme that extended provision to low-paid workers and small organisations, and introduced a tighter regulatory regime. New accountancy measures designed to bring the UK into line with Europe were also implemented and, more controversially, Labour increased taxation on pension funds.

In the years that followed, however, it became clear that government and employers had made "irrationally exuberant assumptions" (Pensions Commission, 2005, p 123) that led them to underestimate the pressures on provision. Labour had overlooked the 'retreat' from occupational pensions inherited from its predecessors and, mesmerised by unusually high equity returns, it, along with employers, had ignored the factors making for a rise in occupational pension costs. Foremost among these were rising life expectancies, an ageing population, falling birth rates and, consequently, a rapid rise in the dependency ratio. The government's new pension regulations and EU-derived gender equalities legislation were also adding to the costs.

The effects were realised at the turn of the millennium, when falling share prices led to widespread shortfalls in pension funds and the closure of a number of businesses. Many contributing employees were left without a pension and numerous private sector firms closed their DB schemes to new entrants, replacing them with DC or group personal schemes. The legal requirement to publish pension liabilities accentuated the crisis by alerting shareholders to the scale of pension fund deficits. To restore public confidence, the government in 2004 introduced a new regulatory body (the Pensions Regulator), a levy on employers to finance a Pension Protection Fund for employees affected by future business closures, and established an independent Pensions Commission.

The Commission, headed by Lord Turner, was charged with reviewing long-term savings and assessing whether there was a case for moving beyond the voluntarism of personal and occupational pensions. Its report, published in three phases (Pensions Commission, 2004, 2005, 2006), stimulated widespread debate and a raft of conflicting proposals. The Commission's recommendations were based on a detailed assessment of the options and a sophisticated analysis of the implications of demographic change and the inadequacies of all current forms of provision.

It advocated a more generous basic state pension, raising the state pension age to 68 to help fund it, and a new state-sponsored, earnings-related occupational system. These proposals were widely contested both inside and outside of government and on somewhat predictable grounds. After extensive negotiation and numerous redrafts (Wintour, 2006), a White Paper outlining the government's response was published in the spring of 2006 (DWP, 2006a). This followed Turner's blueprint for recasting the UK's mixed pension economy and proposed:

- relinking the basic state pension to earnings;
- a phased increase in the state retirement age to 68 by 2046;
- improved support for women; and,
- a new pensions savings system for all employees over the age of 22 entailing automatic enrolment (from 2012) in either:
  › a national scheme of personal accounts to be funded by compulsory contributions (consisting of 4% of earnings with 1% tax relief) from employees and matching contributions (3%) from employers;

or
  › an approved occupational scheme.

The overall implications are, at this point, difficult to ascertain. Approval criteria for the occupational schemes have yet to be determined, the funding and administrative costs arising from the new national scheme can only be estimated and the planned regulatory environment remains unclear. The initial responses from employers offer a mixed set of reactions. A significant proportion of commercial organisations may well choose to phase out their own pension provision in favour of the national scheme. Others may well make a business case for enhancing or 'topping up' the contributions to that scheme or, as a third option, retain their own. Further complications arise from uncertainties over plans for public sector pensions, where pre-White Paper agreements with trades unions have preserved lower retirement ages than in many commercial organisations.

Case study 2: occupational healthcare

Prior to the Second World War, occupational healthcare in the UK was primarily concerned with minimising the risk of workplace injuries and, where they occurred, with providing an initial form of treatment. Compared with what is available today, it was a very narrow basis of provision. Two sets of drivers explain its post-war growth: the steady development of UK and, more recently, EU health and safety legislation, and the recent rapid rise in employer healthcare initiatives. In the case of the former, expansion has occurred through a gradual accumulation of new laws with ever-widening powers and scope implemented and monitored by the Health and Safety Commission and the HSE. With the latter, change has been sporadic, voluntaristic and relatively recent – not emerging as a serious option for many organisations until the late 1980s.

The post-war health and safety legislation increased the preventive healthcare responsibilities of employers across an ever-widening number of work environments. It established minimum standards of cleanliness; revised specifications for workspace, working temperature, lighting and ventilation; washroom facilities; and protective guards for dangerous machinery. While health and safety laws reached the statute book on a regular basis throughout the forties, fifties and sixties, it was not until the 1974 Act that all types of workplace were subject to its governance[3]. The Act became the framework for subsequent legislation that saw the implementation of a number of new regulations responding to changing working hazards, technologies and work processes and that refined employers' and staff responsibilities for safety procedures, conduct and the management of equipment. The 1989 EU Framework Directives provided the next major legislative watershed. They also combined general principles of health and safety management with the concept of shared responsibility, adding to employer and employee responsibilities, and specifying six key areas (for example, manual handling and the use of VDU screens) for improvement. Running in tandem with the changes wrought by these directives was a further family of influential regulations emanating from the 1993 EU Working Time Directive. This saw the employers' management of working time as an essential element of staff health and safety. It introduced a maximum weekly working time, a minimum number of weeks' paid holiday, a minimum rest period for each working day and a maximum number of hours that could be worked each night.

Until the first Blair government, employer healthcare initiatives largely operated independently of health and safety. Those undertaken in the early post-war period were confined to supporting staff with known medical problems and to dealing with workplace absence. Whether undertaken in-house or 'bought in,' the services consisted of providing medical assessments, counselling, referral and rehabilitation support (CIPD, 2005c; IDS, 2005b). During the 1990s, companies began to expand their rehabilitation services and refocus their approach, extending services to the promotion of health for the whole workforce (CIPD, 2000). Known collectively by the name 'wellness services', they consisted of screening and diagnostic services, health counselling and education, preventive healthcare and specialist substance abuse services (see **Box 8.3** for examples of each of these types of service).

Box 8.3: The main wellness services offered by UK employers

Service	Illustrations
Screening and diagnostic services	Regular single-factor screening (for example, blood pressure, cholesterol, cardiac risk assessments, body weight, chest X-rays, hearing, sight, glaucoma, dental checks); personal profiling and risk assessments/feedback; specialist tests (for example, cancer screening); general wellness tests (for example, lifestyle audits).
Health counselling	Diet/lifestyle strategies; exercise/stress management/sleeping/ referrals.
Health education/promotion	Healthy lifestyles/hearts/eating/ageing/fitness campaigns; smoking cessation/alcohol care campaigns; mental health awareness campaigns ('special events/weeks'; health fairs; workplace healthcare 'champions/ambassadors'; workshops; courses; leaflets; posters; advice material in in-house journals; electronic bulletins; desk drops).
Preventive healthcare	Healthy catering/vending machines; 'free fruit' days; nutritional events; workplace smoking/alcohol policies; fitness/vitality facilities/programmes (on-/off-site sports facilities/gyms; personal fitness trainers/coaches/exercise classes; 'activities' events/competitions; 'walk/cycle more' campaigns/sponsorships; 'stair prompts'/free pedometers); complementary medicine facilities (on-/off-site: aromatherapy, reflexology; massage, yoga, pilates); lifestyle coaching (stress management/emotional health workshops/courses).
Specialist services	Alcohol/substance abuse counselling/support/referral services.

Recent estimates suggest around a third of employers offer some health promotion and/or other wellness services (Silcox, 2005). Few operate the full range and provision is dominated by large (statutory and non-statutory) organisations. It is nonetheless becoming increasingly significant as an employer-sponsored welfare option. Companies are being urged to increase their wellness services by leading firms from the corporate sector actively canvassing through pressure groups such as the European Health and Performance Management Community, Business Action on Health and London's Wellness Index for Business. Banks such as the RBS and Barclays, for instance, have recently added 'health and wellbeing managers' to their human resource directorates and have also invested heavily in extensive healthy living and working programmes. Organisations across the work sectors such as Unilever, Trent Water, Goldman Sachs, the BBC and Accenture have wellness programmes that include health risk assessments, advice on fitness, nutrition and emotional health, counselling for staff and their families, stress management, alternative therapies and rehabilitation schemes (Crabb, 2004; Overell, 2005: Paton, 2005).

This spread of provision is partly attributable to the cascading encouraged by the corporate pressure groups but also results from the continued competition to recruit and retain staff, and the cost-effectiveness of wellness services as a way of managing absenteeism and illness and as a way of counterbalancing potential claims of work-related stress (CBI/AXA, 2005). For employers, however, its main investment value rests with its promise to enhance productivity (IoD, 2002). The business case for preventive workplace health services is straightforward. They are cheaper than many more traditional benefits such as occupational pensions, they are a more visible and more immediate form of assistance for more of the workforce, and increase productivity both by creating a healthier, happier workforce and by cutting absenteeism.

When Labour came to power in the late 1990s, it was not slow to recognise the significance of these initiatives. It saw an opportunity to integrate the preventive healthcare provision involved in health and safety with these employer initiatives and within a strategy that saw the workplace as a key feature rather an adjunct of *public* health policy. The government's 'third way' had long harboured interests in a Scandanavian-style national occupational health system in which employers worked in a partnership with government and a restructured NHS in the provision of healthcare in the UK.

The main pillars of the government's approach were set out in the HSE's *Revitalising Health and Safety Strategy* (DETR, 2000a) and in the White Paper, *Health, Work and Well-Being*, in 2005 (DWP/DH/HSE, 2005)[4]. The first posited a new approach to occupational health based on three main goals:

- the use of the workplace as an environment to enable individuals to maintain and enhance their health;
- a significant reduction in the incidence of work-related ill-health; and,
- a parallel reduction in the numbers absent from work due to illness or disability.

To attain these, it set targets for improving health and safety practices and developing workplace healthcare. These focused on reducing:

- the incidence of fatal and major accidents by 10% by 2010;
- the numbers of working days lost per 100,000 workers from work-related injury and ill health by 30% by 2010;
- the incidence of cases of work-related ill health by 20% by 2010; and
- achieving half these targets by 2004 (most of which it has met – www.hse.gov.uk/statistics/index.htm, accessed 22 May 2006).

The 2005 White Paper expanded this framework. It detailed a 'new, innovative and far-reaching strategy' to revamp public health 'around work' and expand employer healthcare (DWP/DH/HSE 2005, p 8). At its core were measures for:

- the establishment of a National Director of Occupational Health;
- the establishment of a Charter for Health, Work and Wellbeing;
- the establishment of a Framework for Vocational Rehabilitation;
- the establishment of a National Stakeholder Council, Network and Summit;
- the establishment of local stakeholder councils;
- the development of an Investors in People 'healthy business assessment and health standard';
- the establishment of a national workplace health award system;
- encouragement for companies to report occupational health and safety as part of their business performance reports;
- the establishment of NHS Plus (enabling NHS occupational health support and advice for external employers);
- the establishment of Workplace Health Connect (an advisory service for small and medium-sized enterprises [SMEs]);
- training for GPs and other health professionals in occupational health;
- encouragement for government organisations to set an example to other employers.

What the government is seeking is a confluence of state and employer-sponsored provision in a work-based welfare system. At its core is the belief in paid employment as both the most effective antidote to social exclusion and the guarantor of individual welfare. It maintains that high productivity involves more than easing benefit claimants and other 'non-workers' into work; it requires workplace measures to tackle the ill-health absenteeism (that often precipitates individuals into benefit dependency) and, more generally, the maintenance of a healthy workforce (DWP, 2006b). Such measures, it is argued, will lift the UK from a 'low' to a 'high road' economy based on new, high performance organisations (Porter and Ketels, 2003).

Conscious of the problems encountered in its attempt to expand occupational pensions, the government has relied on 'soft' policy instruments rather than direct legislation, regulation or fiscal support to effect this strategy. Exhorting employers to expand their healthcare provision on business grounds, it has developed:

- Compact arrangements with employers;
- 'best-practice' guidance and examples;
- advice centres;
- awareness-raising campaigns;
- benchmarking schemes;
- recognition and 'league table' systems 'for high performers', and
- an evidence base for the effectiveness of workplace healthcare.

By early 2006, the government had appointed the UK's first national director for health and work and held the first of the planned summits to promote workplace healthcare. This saw the launch of a charter committing signatory employers and other agencies to 'delivering a healthier future for working people'. Workplace Health Connect is now operational and, through the DTI's Business Link, HSE and the Advisory, Conciliation and Arbitration Service (Acas), it provides a wealth of healthcare advice, particularly for small organisations. Acas (2006) promotes 'healthy living' in its 'model workplace' guidance for SMEs, as does the DTI's Fit for the Future campaign (DTI, 2001). The government can also point to new proactive wellness services in Whitehall, the prison service, local government and police authorities (Cabinet Office, 2004, 2005) and in the NHS through its Improving Working Lives Standard (DH, 2000).

The government has some grounds for optimism, with spending on occupational healthcare set to grow and the emergence of a new market involving suppliers from the public (NHS Plus), voluntary (for example, British Heart Foundation) and commercial sectors (BUPA Wellness, Nuffield and HSA) (Tulip, 2005). The demand from non-corporate employers, however, has been uneven and it is becoming clear that without a strong legislative steer and financial incentives, the comprehensive occupational healthcare provision that the government seeks is unlikely to develop (Coates and Max, 2005).

Conclusion

What emerges from the descriptive overview and the more detailed case study analyses is a highly complex picture of diverse and changing provision. Each type of occupational welfare has its own history and formation, makes its own analytical demands, and has its own permutations with different forms of statutory provision. In consequence, each type may well play a distinct role in the mixed economy and have differing impacts on the social division of welfare. Occupational welfare can enhance the security, quality of life and disposable incomes of those who receive it. But as it largely consists of discretionary rewards linked to labour market positions (Smith, 2000; Taylor, 2002, 2003; White et al, 2004; Kersley et al, 2005), it is unlikely to deliver the equities expected of state benefits and services.

Notes

[1] Space pre-empts consideration of the workplace welfare provided by bodies such as trade unions and professional organisations.

[2] Incentive pay includes bonuses, share schemes and other forms of performance-related pay.

[3] Among the last to be included were hospitals and educational institutions.

[4] These built on a raft of government publications from a range of departments (DH, 1998, 1999, 2000, 2004; Wanless Report, 2002; Cabinet Office, 2004, 2005; DETR, 2000b).

Summary

- Occupational provision is a neglected but significant element in the mixed economy of welfare.
- It can most usefully be defined as the non-wage mandatory and voluntary benefits and services provided by employers for their employees (and in some instances their spouses/partners and children).
- The past decade has seen a substantial reshaping of employer-sponsored welfare.
- Each type of occupational welfare has its own history and formation, and makes its own analytical demands.
- The nature of government intervention varies with the different types of provision.
- Occupational welfare can enhance the security, quality of life and disposable incomes of those who receive it.
- As a largely discretionary benefit, it is unlikely to deliver the equities expected of state benefits and services.

Questions for discussion

- How would you account for recent developments in occupational pension provision?
- On what grounds might you support the pension reforms set out in the 2006 Pensions White Paper?
- Why are employers beginning to invest in wellness services?
- How effective is the government's occupational health policy likely to be?
- How can the differences between occupational welfare provisions in public sector and other organisations be explained?

Further reading

There are few general studies of occupational provision in the UK; accounts of the different benefits and services offered by employers are scattered in company reports, business surveys and human resources management publications and journals. The most accessible are the various studies conducted by the Chartered Institute of Personnel Development (CIPD), Income Data Services (IDS) and Industrial Relations Service (IRS) and the journals *People Management* and *Personnel Today*. There is, however, a wealth of often highly technical writing on pensions, the best synopsis of which are the three Turner reports **(Pensions Commission, 2004, 2005, 2006)**. Broader 'starter' accounts can be found in **Farnsworth (2004a, 2004b)** and our earlier explorations of this area **(May and Brunsdon, 1999; Brunsdon and May, 2002)**. Though somewhat dated, **Shalev (1996)** provides a stimulating introduction to the comparative study of occupational welfare.

Electronic resources

To keep up to date with government policy on occupational provision (and the responses to consultation documents), the following are particularly useful: www.dwp.gov.uk (the Department of Work and Pensions website, which has links to the Pension Commission reports and consultations); www.dti.gov.uk (the Department of Trade and Industry website, with links to Business Link and other advisory agencies); www.doh.gov.uk (the Department of Health website, which covers workforce as well as policy issues); www.hse.gov.uk (the Health and Safety Executive website).

Differing perspectives on government policy and on the development of employer-sponsored welfare can be found at: www.cipd.co.uk (the Chartered Institute of Personnel and Development website, which offers a wealth of material including fact sheets designed for students); www.bitc.org.uk (Business in the Community, with links to Business Action on Health and other employer groups); and www.tuc.org.uk (the Trades Union Congress website).

The European Foundation for Living and Working Conditions (www.eurofound.eu) provides access to a wealth of comparative material.

References

Acas (Advisory, Conciliation and Arbitration Service) (2006) *The Model Workplace*, London: ACAS.

Blackburn, R. (2002) *Banking on Death or Investing in Life: The History and Future of Pensions*, London: Verso.

Brunsdon, E. and May, M. (2002) 'Evaluating New Labour's approach to independent welfare', in M. Powell (ed) *Evaluating New Labour's Welfare Reforms*, Bristol: The Policy Press, pp 61-84.

Cabinet Office (2004) *Managing Sickness Absence in the Public Sector*, London: Cabinet Office.

Cabinet Office (2005) *Ministerial Taskforce on Health, Safety and Productivity One Year On Report*, London: Cabinet Office.

CBI (Confederation of British Industry)/AXA (2005) *Absence and Labour Turnover Study*, London: CBI.

CIPD (Chartered Institute of Personnel and Development) (2000) *Occupational Health and Organisational Effectiveness*, London: CIPD.

CIPD (2005a) *Flexible Benefits*, London: CIPD

CIPD (2005b) *Absence Management: A Survey of Policy and Practice*, London: CIPD.

CIPD (2005c) *Training*, London: CIPD.

Coates, D. and Max, C. (2005) *Healthy Work: Productive Workplaces*, London: The Work Foundation.

Crabb, S. (2004) *The PM Guide to Wellness at Work*, London: People Management.

DETR (Department for Environment, Transport and the Regions) (2000a) *Revitalising Health and Safety*, London: DETR.

DETR (2000b) *Securing Health Together*, London: DETR.

DH (Department of Health) (1998) *Our Healthier Nation: A Contract for Health*, London: The Stationery Office.

DH (1999) *Saving Lives: Our Healthier Nation*, London: The Stationery Office.

DH (2000) *The NHS Plan: A Plan for Investment, A Plan For Reform*, London: The Stationery Office.

DH (2004) *Choosing Health: Making Healthier Choices Easy*, Public Health White Paper, London: DH.

DSS (Department of Social Security) (1998) *New Ambitions for Our Country: A New Contract for Welfare*, London: HMSO.

DTI (Department of Trade and Industry) (2001) *People and Performance: Unlocking Employee Potential*, London: DTI.

DWP (2006a) *Security in Retirement: Towards a New Pension Settlement*, London: DWP.

DWP (2006b) *A New Deal for Welfare: Empowering People to Work*, London: DWP.

DWP/DH/HSE (Department of Work and Pensions/Department of Health/Health and Safety Executive) (2005) *Health, Work and Well-being – Caring for Our Future*, London: The Stationery Office.

Employee Benefits (2005) *Benefits Book 2005*, London: Employee Benefits.

Farnham, D. (1999) 'Human resource management and employment relations', in S. Horton and D.Farnham (eds) *Public Management in Britain*, Basingstoke: Macmillan, pp 107-27.

Farnsworth, K. (2004a) *Corporate Power and Social Policy in a Global Economy*, Bristol: The Policy Press.

Farnsworth, K. (2004b) 'Welfare through work: an audit of occupational social provision at the turn of the new century', *Social Policy & Administration*, vol 38, no 5, pp 437-45.

Government Actuary (1994) *Occupational Pension Schemes 1991: Eighth Survey by the Government Actuary*, London: HMSO.

Hannah, L. (1986) *Inventing Retirement*, Cambridge: Cambridge University Press.

IDS (2001) *Secondments and Volunteering*, IDS Study 704, London: IDS.

IDS (2002) *Employee Assistance Programmes*, IDS Study Plus, Winter, London: IDS.

IDS (2003) *Private Medical Insurance*, IDS Study 745, March, London: IDS.

IDS (2005a) *Flexible Benefits*, IDS HR Study Plus 811, December, London: IDS.

IDS (2005b) *Absence Management*, IDS HR Study 810, November, London: IDS.

IoD (Institute of Directors) (2002) *Health and Wellbeing in the Workplace: A Director's Guide*, London: IoD.

IPD (Institute of Personnel Development) (1995) *Managing Occupational Health*, London: IPD.

Kersley, B., Alpin, C., Forth, J., Bryson, A., Bewley, H., Dix, G. and Oxenbridge, S. (2005) *Inside the Workplace: Findings from the 2004 Workplace Employment Relations Survey*, London: DTI.

Kiefer, T. and Briner, R. (2003) 'Handle with care', *People Management*, 23 October, pp 48-50.

Lynes, T. (1997) 'The British case', in M. Rein and E. Wadensjo (eds) *Enterprise in the Welfare State*, Cheltenham: Edward Elgar, pp 309-51.

May, M. and Brunsdon, E. (1994) 'Workplace care in the mixed economy of welfare', in R.M. Page and J. Baldock (eds) *Social Policy Review 6*, Canterbury: SPA, pp 146-69.

May, M. and Brunsdon, E. (1999) 'Commercial and occupational welfare', in R.M. Page and R. Silburn (eds) *British Social Welfare in the Twentieth Century*, Houndmills: Macmillan, pp 271-98.

Murlis, H. (1974) *Employee Benefits Today*, London: British Institute of Management.

Overell, S. (2005) 'Where do you stand on health?', *Personnel Today*, 25 October, pp 33-6.

Paton, N. (2005) 'The health of nations', *Personnel Today*, 25 October, pp 30-1.

Pensions Commission (2004) *Pensions: Challenges and Choices: The First Report of the Pensions Commission*, London: The Stationery Office.

Pensions Commission (2005) *A New Pensions Settlement for the Twenty First Century, The Second Report of the Pensions Commission*, London: The Stationery Office.

Pensions Commission (2006) *Implementing an Integrated Package of Pension Reforms: The Final Report of the Pensions Commission*, London: The Stationery Office.

Porter, M.E. and Ketels, C.H.M. (2003) *UK Competitiveness: Moving to the Next Stage*, DTI Economics Paper 3, London: Department of Trade and Industry/ Economic and Social Research Council.

Powell, M. (2003) 'The third way', in P. Alcock, A. Erskine and M. May (eds) *The Student's Companion to Social Policy* (2nd edn), Oxford: Blackwell, pp 100-6.

Shalev, M. (ed) (1996) *The Privatization of Social Policy? Occupational Welfare and the Welfare State in America, Scandinavia and Japan*, Basingstoke: Macmillan.

Silcox, S. (2005) 'Health promotion works', *IRS Employment Review 828*, July, pp 22-5.

Smith, I. (2000) 'Benefits', in G. White and J. Drucker (eds) *Reward Management: A Critical Text*, London: Routledge, pp 152-77.

Taylor, R. (2002) *Britain's World of Work – Myths and Realities*, Swindon: Economic and Social Research Council.

Taylor, R. (2003) *Managing Workplace Change*, Swindon: Economic and Social Research Council.

Titmuss, R.M. (1958a) 'The social division of welfare', in R.M. Titmuss *Essays on the Welfare State*, London: Allen and Unwin.

Titmuss, R.M (1958b) 'The irresponsible society', in R.M. Titmuss *Essays on the Welfare State*, London: Allen and Unwin.

Titmuss, R.M (1963) *Income Distribution and Social Change*, London: Allen and Unwin.

Torrington, D., Hall, L. and Taylor, S. (2005) *Human Resource Management* (6th edn), Harlow: Prentice Hall/Financial Times.

Tulip, S. (2005) 'Market review: healthcare', *People Management*, 21 April, pp 46-7.

Wanless, D. (2002) *Securing Our Future Health: Taking a Long Term View, Final Report*, London: HM Treasury.

Watson Wyatt Data Services (2006) *Benefit Report Europe 2006*, London: Watson Wyatt Data Services.

White, M., Hill, S., Mills, C. and Smeaton, D. (2004) *Managing to Change? British Workplaces and the Future of Work*, Houndmills: Palgrave Macmillan.

Wintour, P. (2006) 'Firms face £2.6bn bill for extra staff pension contributions in government white paper', *The Guardian*, 22 May.

Woodland, S., Simmonds, N., Thornby, M., Fitzgerald, R. and McGee, A. (2003) *The Second Work–Life Balance Study*, London: Department of Trade and Industry.

Wright, A. (2004) *Reward Management in Context*, London: Chartered Institute for Personnel and Development.

nine

The mixed economy of welfare: a comparative perspective

Michael Hill

Overview

This chapter will start by exploring the extent to which mainstream comparative work deals with the mixed economy of welfare. It will then go on to look at ways in which mixed economy issues are considered in relation to social security, healthcare and education. It will end by exploring issues about social care, where broader concerns about the mixed economy are more in evidence.

Key concepts

Regime theory • bringing issues about the family into comparative theory • regulatory models • limited comparative work on the voluntary sector • complexity of provision/delivery relationships

Introduction

In many respects, issues about the extent to which countries have a mixed economy of welfare are becoming a central preoccupation of comparative studies. In that sense, there is a need here to give attention to the dominant perspectives in this field. On the other hand, few such studies concern themselves with the mixed economy as a whole. Originally, the comparative concern was almost exclusively with issues about the relationship between the state and the market. More recently, issues about the family have been explored comparatively. But issues about the role of the community and the voluntary sector get little attention. In addition, to some extent as a consequence of data limitations, comparative studies tend to focus upon inputs, particularly the funding of social policy, giving little attention to the more complex aspects of policy delivery, in respect of which the mixed economy is more in evidence. These points will be explored first through a brief examination of comparative theory and then by means of an exploration of specific policy areas.

Comparative theory and the mixed economy

Early comparative analysis, where it was not simply atheoretical, tended to be concerned with explaining levels of state expenditure. It worked with a view of the 'welfare state' that either saw welfare as essentially something provided by the state, or with a notion that development entailed the replacement of other sources of welfare by state welfare. The earliest systematic comparative studies of welfare states followed a largely determinist line (for example, Wilensky and Lebaux, 1965), contributing a view that social policy development was a largely one-dimensional growth in which rising gross domestic product (GDP) would inevitably bring with it growing state expenditure on social policy. Later, this approach was challenged by scholars who felt dissatisfied with the high level of generality in these studies, emphasising broad trends and paying little attention to variation in policy content (Higgins, 1981; Jones, 1985). However, the dominant approach to explaining variation still (a) saw welfare as something coming from the state, and (b) looked to political variation to explain differences. Walker and Wong criticise the ethnocentric bias embodied in the concern with the welfare *state*, seeing it as "a capitalist institution ... embodied in a democratic (that is parliamentary) institutional structure" (2004, p 119). In the same way, Gough and Wood see the analysis of "Western social policy [as] ... associated with particular sets of means (the state) towards the ends of ensuring security of welfare" (2004, p 4). In this sense, social policy is seen as a central aspect of Polanyi's 'great transformation' of capitalism (1944) or in terms of a social democratic 'truce' between capital and labour secured through action by the latter to influence the state.

Concern with this notion of influences on different forms and levels of state intervention was a key element in the development of what has become the dominant modern approach to comparative social policy, Esping-Andersen's regime theory (1990). While Esping-Andersen's theory represents a crucial move away from the unitary developmental approach that saw states as on a general evolutionary path in which, with economic development or democracy, there would be an inevitable growth in state welfare, its emphasis on 'welfare regimes' still puts the state at the very centre of the analysis. However, it also brings out very clearly issues about the state–economy relationship. This is particularly embodied in Esping-Andersen's use of the notion of 'decommodification' (the extent to which access to benefits and services are detached from determination by the market). His explanation of the extent to which decommodification occurs is, of course, then based on an analysis of politics, with the strength of social democratic parties the crucial variable. However, there is nothing implicit in regime theory that has to link it in this way. One may contrast regime types without at the same time accepting Esping-Andersen's original explanation of how they arise.

Esping-Andersen's regime model involves the postulation of three regime types:

- the social democratic regime, the most decommodified type, characteristic of the Nordic countries;
- the liberal, the least decommodified, characteristic of the United States, the United Kingdom, Australia and New Zealand;
- an intermediate type, which tends to be rather confusingly labelled as either conservative or corporatist, characteristic of much of continental Europe (and particularly controversially, Japan), where social benefits are extensive but very much determined by labour market status.

The model has attracted both considerable criticism and a range of attempts to improve on it (see Arts and Gelissen, 2002, for a review). The conservative/corporatist category has been seen to involve a rather large 'bag' of diverse societies, so some writers (particularly Ferrara, 1996), have identified a separate southern European variant. It has been pointed out that in devising it, Esping-Andersen used data about cash benefits, therefore not taking into account the whole range of social policies, and it has been argued that issues about systems and issues about their redistributive effects are often not satisfactorily teased out (Bonoli, 1997). This issue about the policy area chosen is important (see Powell and Barrientos, 2004). But with respect to the mixed economy of welfare, the most important challenge to the original approach has come from scholars interested in the issues around gender and welfare. Their approach has stressed the issues around families, neglected in the original concern to explore state–market relationships (Lewis, 1992, 1993, 1997; Sainsbury, 1994, 1996; O'Connor, 1996).

Since Sainsbury (1996), comparative contrasts between state, market and family roles have been quite widely made, although little has been done to tie issues concerning the role of the voluntary sector into comparative analysis. Voluntary sector actors are certainly more salient in some societies than others. There are grounds for expecting this to be particularly the case in societies where there has been a strong cultural commitment to the delegation of care tasks to local organisations, and particularly to faith-based organisations, as embodied in Catholic social theory. This characterises some of Esping-Andersen's conservative societies. The strong state tradition in Scandinavia has been conversely seen as inhibiting voluntary action. However, there is evidence from Sweden refuting that hypothesis (Lundström and Svedberg, 2003); the social democratic tradition involves high participatory norms. Many of the liberal societies also have strong voluntary organisation traditions (not least the United States). Studies by Anheier and Salamon (2001) explore these issues, but face difficulties about how exactly to identify a strong voluntary sector (in terms of levels of volunteering or in terms of the incidence of voluntary organisations). Volunteering is shown to be high in much of northern Europe and in the United States but low in southern Europe and Japan. Perhaps therefore the key distinction here is in terms of the strength of family care traditions rather than evidence that variations in voluntary organisation vigour across societies follow the lines of the Esping-Andersen model.

So far, this discussion of the roles of the various sectors has given no attention to the way social policy is delivered, to its regulation or to the way in which payment may be separated from provision. These, too, are topics for which it is difficult to put together data that facilitate comparative analysis. A possible approach to analysing alternative regulatory regimes comes in Hall and Soskice's classification of varieties of capitalism (2001). They distinguish between 'liberal market economies' and 'coordinated market economies'. In the former:

> … firms coordinate their activities primarily via hierarchies and competitive market arrangements…. Market relationships are characterized by the arm's-length exchange of goods or services in a context of competition and formal contracting. In response to the price signals generated by such markets, the actors adjust their willingness to supply and demand goods or services, often on the basis of the marginal calculations stressed by neoclassical economics. (Hall and Soskice, 2001, p 8)

In the 'coordinated market economies' by contrast:

> … firms depend more heavily on non-market relationships to coordinate their endeavors with other actors and to construct their

core competencies. These non-market modes of coordination generally entail more extensive relational or incomplete contracting, network monitoring based on the exchange of private information inside networks, and more reliance on collaborative, as opposed to competitive, relationships to build the competencies of the firm … economies are more often the result of strategic interaction among firms and other actors. (Hall and Soskice, 2001, p 8)

The state is crucially a more active partner, linking with a range of interest groups.

Hall and Soskice suggest that these alternative ways of organising economic institutions will have implications for social policy, with a much stronger emphasis on minimising interference with market processes in the liberal economy. Hence, they make a specific connection between their classification and Esping-Andersen's work (Hall and Soskice, 2001, pp 50-1). However, interestingly, Hall and Soskice identify six nations in 'more ambiguous positions' (France, Italy, Spain, Portugal, Greece and Turkey). They suggest there may there be another 'Mediterranean' type of capitalism marked by a mixture of coordinated arrangements with "more liberal arrangements in the sphere of industrial relations" (Hall and Soskice, 2001, p 21).

It may be questioned whether this work – explicitly concerned with relationships between the state and economic institutions – advances our understanding of regulatory relationship in social policy beyond Esping-Andersen's regime theory, except in areas where social policy and employment issues converge. Here other variations have emerged, notably Lødemel and Trickey's classification of the UK 'New Deals' (2001) as, along with those in Denmark and the Netherlands, involving an 'emergent' hybrid approach to linking economy management and active approaches to labour supply issues.

Social security

Esping-Andersen's original comparative work (1990) is almost totally preoccupied with distinctions between nations in respect of social security expenditure. But even in this area of social policy arrangements are complicated in ways this theory does not bring out. Powell's introduction in this volume has, of course, stressed the need to relate 'social divisions' issues to mixed economy issues, and, as Sinfield's contribution shows, relationships between cash benefits and taxation are important (see Chapters One and Seven). In the social security field, there are therefore areas for comparison between countries not merely in terms of levels and types of expenditure but also in terms of the ways in which expenditure is funded. Considerations here are (a) the relationship between tax funding and contribution funding, (b) the role played by employers as opposed to employees in relation to the latter and (c) the extent to which social security provision is private but may then be mandated or regulated by the state.

Table 9.1 provides evidence on how state social transfers are funded. There is a large group of nations where social insurance contributions are a very significant source of social transfer funds. In a number of cases – France, Spain, Japan, Ireland and Korea – social transfers are hardly a charge on any other form of taxation at all. At the other extreme, there are two nations without any form of social insurance contribution (Australia and New Zealand) and the curious case of Denmark, where a very generous social insurance system is nevertheless only marginally funded by contributions.

Social security contributions often come from employers as well as employees. In the European Union (EU), employers' contributions range from a low of

Table 9.1: *Social security funding through social insurance contributions*

Country	% of social security expenditure funded by contributions
Spain	98
Ireland	94
Japan	94
France	91
South Korea	90
Belgium	89
Sweden	87
Hungary	85
Netherlands	83
Italy	82
Canada	82
Austria	80
Czech Republic	77
Germany	75
Finland	74
Switzerland	71
Portugal	70
Norway	60
United States	59
Poland	58
United Kingdom	47
Denmark	13
New Zealand	0
Australia	0

Source: OECD (2003) data on social contributions

about 9% of expenditure in Denmark to a high of about 52% in Spain, with an average across the 15 nations of the pre-2004 Union of about 38% (European Commission, 2004). Exceptionally, employers may be the sole contributors to the costs of some part of the social security scheme (unemployment insurance in the United States, family allowances in France and Belgium). Looking at employers' contributions across the EU countries, we find that they exceed employees' contributions in all the countries except Denmark and the Netherlands and are more than double the latter in Belgium, Finland and Italy (European Commission, 2004).

Where social security is contributory, other institutions are often involved in service delivery. A particular feature of the social insurance schemes of continental Europe has been arrangements for management in which employers' and employees' organisations have been involved. However, the massive impact of these schemes on public expenditure, and the need for special state subsidies for groups outside the mainstream employment fields, have led to very extensive state control.

But social security may also involve private payments, often mandated or regulated by governments. In the UK, such mandation applies, for example, to most provision for income replacement during short-term sickness, while, in the area of pensions, regulation of private arrangements is increasing and mandation is on the agenda. **Table 9.2** shows how varied is the extent of private pension investment. What is significant here is the massive pension markets in a number of countries at the top of the table but their almost complete absence in some other large welfare states (notably France and Germany). The presence of most of the countries at the top of that table can be predicted from Esping-Andersen's regime theory, but not Switzerland, the Netherlands and Denmark. These contrasts secure increasing attention in the comparative literature in the light of the efforts by the World Bank (1994) and others to promote private funding of pensions, and the resistance to this in favour of more egalitarian state systems (see Myles, 2002; Bonoli and Shinkawa, 2005).

A related issue here is the extent to which these large pensions investments are subsidised by tax relief (see Chapter Seven).

Healthcare

Table 9.3 highlights variations between countries in the extent of public financing of health expenditure.

We do not seem to have here a division of nations closely corresponding to Esping-Andersen's regimes. Apart from the United States, all the nations in the 'liberal' group have systems dominated by the public sector, with the UK particularly high in this respect. While two 'social democratic' nations head the list, the difference between them and nations in the 'conservative' group is

Table 9.2: *Private pension investment, 2003, as share of GDP*

Country	Private pension investment as % of GDP
Switzerland	126
Netherlands	94
United Kingdom	66
United States	66
Australia	56
Canada	52
Denmark	28
Japan	13
Portugal	12
Finland	8
Spain	7
New Zealand	6
France	5
Hungary	5
Austria, Belgium, Czech Republic, Germany, Italy, Korea, Norway	All 4 or below

Source: OECD Global Pensions Statistics Project reported in OECD (2005). There are no data for Ireland, where the figure may well be large.

quite slight. One nation from the 'conservative' group, Switzerland, seems to have quite a lot in common with the United States. The other consideration that might be brought in here concerns the presence or absence of social insurance. Yet here the nations without social insurance are scattered throughout **Table 9.3**.

Bambra's work (2005a, 2005b) supports this view. She explicitly 'tests' Esping-Andersen's theory by looking at health policy for the dates he used in his work (1990) in terms of three measures:

- private health expenditure as a percentage of GDP;
- private hospital beds as a percentage of total bed stock;
- the percentage of the population covered by the state health system.

Table 9.3: *Public sector health spend as a percentage of total health spend, 2002**

Country	Public spend as a % of total spend
Czech Republic	92
Sweden	86
Norway	85
Denmark	83
United Kingdom	83
Japan	82
Germany	79
New Zealand	78
France	76
Finland	75
Ireland	75
Italy	75
Poland	72
Belgium	71
Hungary	71
Spain	71
Austria	70
Canada	70
Portugal	70
Australia	68
Switzerland	58
Korea	54
United States	45

Source: calculated from data in OECD (2004b).

* 2001 in cases of Australia, Japan and Korea; data for the Netherlands are missing from the source.

She arrives at three 'groups', as set out in **Table 9.4**.

However, there is a need to go beyond the simple dichotomy between public and private funding. In relation to healthcare, mixed economy issues can be brought out more clearly. There are a number of roles the state may play in relation to healthcare. These are as:

- regulator;
- funder/purchaser;
- provider/planner.

Table 9.4: Bambra's healthcare 'regime' typology

Group 1 ('liberal' equivalents)
Australia
United States
Group 2 ('conservative' equivalents)
Austria
Belgium
France
Germany
Ireland
Italy
Japan
Netherlands
Switzerland
Group 3 ('social democratic' equivalents)
Canada
Denmark
Finland
New Zealand
Norway
Sweden
United Kingdom

Any specific system is likely to involve a combination of all or most of these roles. While logically there is no reason why the state cannot be involved in planning and providing without funding, in practice the three are likely to be mixed together, although the state may be only be a part-funder.

The relationship between the role of the state as funder and the role of the state as provider can logically take any of four forms – funder and provider, neither funder nor provider, a funder but not a provider, or a provider but not a funder. The history of health provision in Britain has involved the development, with the coming of the NHS, of a system where the state was both funder and provider, though, more recently, there has been some evolution towards relinquishing part of the provider role. Saltman and von Otter (1992, see also Saltman, 1998) have demonstrated similar complexities in the Swedish system, where local authorities are the key units in the system and recent developments have also involved the evolution of mixed provider systems. Social insurance-funded systems, such as those in France, Germany and the Netherlands, often allow for payments to private providers, as well as supplementation from private funds. All the cases where funding and provision are not unified require quite complex arrangements to deal with issues such as:

- the making, variation and termination of contracts;
- the determination of the amounts and forms of reimbursement for services;
- the ways in which public and privately funded activities may be mixed;
- the monitoring of standards and the determination of needs for new services.

Education

In the field of education policy, there are (apart from the obvious absence of social insurance) many similar features in the public/private mix. **Table 9.5** provides similar data to those in **Table 9.3** but for education.

Here, apart from the fact that the United States again sits near the bottom of the table, we have a very different public–private breakdown than that for health. A 'liberal' nation, New Zealand, is at the top of the table together with

Table 9.5: *Public sector spend as a percentage of total spend on education, 2000*

Country	Public spend as a % of total spend
New Zealand	100
Poland	100
Finland	98
Norway	98
Portugal	98
Denmark	97
Sweden	97
Austria	95
Belgium	93
France	93
Switzerland	93
Italy	92
Czech Republic	91
Netherlands	91
Ireland	89
Spain	88
Hungary	86
United Kingdom	85
Canada	81
Germany	81
Japan	74
Australia	74
United States	69
Korea	61

Source: calculated from data in OECD (2004c).

one of the former Soviet bloc countries, closely followed by a group of 'social democratic' states together with a southern European one. There is no pattern here that can be straightforwardly predicted from regime theory.

Most of the governments in the OECD (Organisation for Economic Cooperation and Development) group of nations spend most of their money in the public sector. There are two striking exceptions to this: the Netherlands, where only around 20% is spent on the direct support of the public sector, and Belgium, where the figure is a little less than 50% (OECD, 2004a). These providers seem likely to be voluntary bodies. The main source of this sector has been religious groups, many of which were pioneers of education. In the Netherlands, the phenomenon of 'pillarisation' (Lijphart, 1975), under which divisions between Protestants and Catholics in that country were handled through the acceptance of separate institutions, seems likely to have been important.

A more detailed examination might reveal significant differences between the school sector and the higher education sector, contrasting countries with a strongly statist approach to university education (the Netherlands and Germany) and countries with strong private sectors (like the United States, Japan and Korea). More complex questions might be explored about the quasi-autonomy given to universities, as in the UK, and the impact of state funding patterns on this.

But to return to the question about the evidence for 'regimes', posed in the discussion of Bambra's work on healthcare, the introduction of a variable identifying publicly supported private systems would do little more than highlight the special characteristics of the Low Countries.

The comparisons in this section, for education, and in the previous one, for health policy, are obviously very crude ones, but they do suggest that in looking at these policies one might want to start somewhere very different from regime theory (except inasmuch as the Scandinavians tend come at the top and the United States at the bottom of the public proportion leagues, though that is hardly the basis for a universalisable theory). Consideration of these policy areas obviously neglects some aspects of the mixed economy. The family role in health and education is obviously important but hard to quantify, let alone compare. The role of the voluntary sector is in principle traceable through exploration of the role of non-state organisations, particularly churches, in health and particularly education. The next section, on social care, extends the discussion of these issues further and necessarily picks up some aspects of the healthcare picture, given the extent to which formal healthcare needs to be supplemented by informal social care.

Social care

Social care policy will be given rather fuller attention as an area where the mixed economy is rather more evident, both in respect of inputs from all sectors and in respect of complex delivery arrangements.

Table 9.6 sets out an approach to a typology for social care, which has been derived from, but goes beyond, Esping-Andersen's original three regimes (1990), developing his 1999 rethink on family roles, though still not integrating issues about the voluntary sector. This owes much to the work of Siaroff (1994) and Ferrara (1996).

Table 9.6: *A typology of systems highlighting alternative approaches to care*

	Individual	**Family**
State	1. Rights to care	2. Support of family care efforts
Market	3. Purchase of care	4. Family on its own

In this new classification, category 1 can be equated with the Nordic social democratic welfare states, 2 with the conservative regimes of northern Europe, 3 with the liberal regimes and 4 with the conservative southern European regimes (plus Japan) regimes. This last type is alternatively to be seen either as more 'protective' of the housewife outside the labour market or as increasing her 'dependency' within the family.

What is at stake here is an issue about the way in which three alternatives for care – family, market and state – are combined in various societies. Hence, there are six alternatives as set out in **Table 9.7**.

This could, of course, be further complicated by the addition of the fourth alternative, the community, but that would complicate the analysis considerably. In the absence of comparative data, it has been left out.

In any real-world situation, as has been stressed, there are likely to be elements of family, state and market; the issues that deserve attention concern the extent

Table 9.7: *Logical alternative care patterns*

Family alone
Market alone
State alone
Family plus market
Family plus state
State plus market
All three

to which any particular variant is dominant. **Table 9.8** examines data on European countries to explore this. The analysis is confined to European nations because of data availability, and the list is limited to larger nations, all of which have relatively similar demographic profiles.

Table 9.8 offers some basis for sorting countries according to the schema in **Table 9.6**, albeit with some data that only partly tell the story. Two clear categories can be identified:

- Countries where family care is clearly predominant (Italy and Spain). Interestingly, these are two nations in Esping-Andersen's 'conservative' category that some of his critics prefer to reassign to a southern European type.
- Countries where state care is much more salient than elsewhere (Sweden and Denmark).

In the second case, the deduction about the dominance of state over market is assumed from the high public spend, which can then be expected to account for a considerable part of the high overall spend on formal care. An alternative deduction may be made in the case of the Netherlands, where the levels of family care and public expenditure are low but the level of formal care is high. That is the nearest that can be found in this group of nations to a clear market

Table 9.8: *Contrasting care patterns within Europe*

Country	Public spend on aged care as % of GDP	% of over-65s getting formal care (public and private)	% of over-65s living with others (excluding spouses)
Sweden	3.8	19.9	2
Denmark	3.1	27.3	2
Finland	1.6	20.5 (est.)	14
France	0.7	12.6	6
Germany	0.7	16.4	5
United Kingdom	0.6	10.6	8
Austria	0.5	28.9	17
Netherlands	0.4	20.8	3
Belgium	0.4	11.9	14
Italy	0.2	6.7	14
Spain	0.3	4.5	18

Source: for the first two data columns, Casey et al (2003, table 19); for the third, European Commission (2004, p 180). The figure from Finland is marked 'est.' because the table included a range and the mid-point has been selected. Note that the figure on households is a prediction for 2010 based on 1995 data.

type. Had countries outside Europe been included, it seems almost certain that the United States would have fallen into this category.

The Netherlands stands alone in this classification of European nations in a category to which Esping-Andersen's theory would expect the UK to belong as well. The UK instead seems to be remarkably like two continental European nations, France and Germany, in a category of nations in which strong state and market elements are present together.

That leaves three nations. In Austria and Belgium, there seem to be quite strong market and family elements. Finland is interesting in that the data suggest both a high state and a high family contribution to care.

Overall, then, here is a way of looking comparatively at the care of elderly people (a look at the care of children, which tends to have been a concern of many of the studies of families and welfare, might well have produced rather different results). The rudimentary typology developed has similarities to those of others, particularly Esping-Andersen's, but diverges in interesting ways. It is interesting to note that Bettio and Plantenga's comparison of European care regimes (2004), which also includes consideration of the care of children, arrives at the following categorisation:

- Countries that appear to delegate all the management of care to the family (Italy, Greece and Spain) with two 'outlier' cases – Portugal, where there is high female labour market participation and Ireland, lying between this group and the next one.
- Countries with high dependence on informal care, but where this is much more salient in respect of childcare than of care for elderly people (UK and the Netherlands).
- Countries with 'publicly facilitated, private care' (Austria and Germany).
- Countries with quite well-developed formal care strategies (Belgium and France).
- Countries with moderate to high levels of formal care (Denmark, Finland, Sweden).

Obviously, the inclusion of childcare introduces modifications, but it also suggests that there are processes of change going on that imply that once the two extremes are identified (the 'Nordic' and the 'southern'), the position of the nations in between will be heavily influenced by the indices chosen.

Had East Asian nations been included, they would probably have fallen into the predominantly family category – certainly, OECD data on Japan point that way. In the case of East Asia, the interesting questions concern their future evolution in this area.

Some writers remain uneasy about efforts to force distinctions between care systems into a regime typology. It has been argued that care services cannot be typologised so easily. Anttonen and colleagues (2003), who studied care for both children and elderly people in Finland, Germany, Japan, the UK and the US, had hoped to apply a version of the regime typology to care but concluded that this was not feasible. They point out two key complications: first, social care is seldom standardised and, second, countries do not have 'coherent patterns' of service delivery:

> A country may simultaneously provide or support care services that are universal and appear to confer genuine citizenship rights alongside others that are selective and sharply rationed. Equally, there is ... a considerable variety of delivery mechanisms. In some aspects of a nation's care services, direct public provision may be the rule, in others contracting out to the private or voluntary sectors, the use of tax credits or payments for care may be the dominant method. (Anttonen et al, 2003, p 168)

However, it is too early to abandon the quest for a systematic approach to this subject. What is being explored here is only tendencies, which (as has been shown) cannot be equated with regimes in any rigid way.

As far as care for adults, particularly elderly adults, is concerned, even in the most broadly encompassing state welfare systems rights to care are qualified in various ways. In Sweden, Denmark and Finland, care for elderly people is subject to the application of means tests and there is therefore also the private purchase of care. At the other extreme, in the systems where marketisation is most evident, the provision of state care for the elderly poor in exceptional circumstances has a history as old as the Poor Law. The issue, then, is of drawing lines within what is in many respects a shared approach throughout all nations between care as something widely subsidised from the public purse and something only exceptionally supported in this way. The United Kingdom sits interestingly in the middle, with a very mixed – often, indeed, illogically mixed – system, with free healthcare, means-tested residential care and domiciliary services limited by complex rationing and charging systems.

On the family side of the equation, the interesting issue is about the extent to which there are cash benefits available that reduce the burden of family care. The interesting development here is the emergence of care insurance in Germany and Japan. These offer an alternative to the straight choice between state and markets suggested earlier as likely as family care declines, since cash benefits can be used to subsidise family care. Again, the UK is interesting as an in-between case, inasmuch as there are various cash benefits available offering partial support of care that may be used to enhance family income or contribute to the purchase of care. In the UK and elsewhere, there is also increasing interest in the use of 'direct payments' to enable individuals to purchase their own care (Leece and Bornat, 2006 – note the comparative essays in chapters 4 and 15).

Purchase and provision

The examination of the issue of care particularly highlights the issues surrounding the distinction between purchase and provision, also evident in the health sector in many countries and in the education sector in rather fewer. The second aspect of Anttonen and colleagues' (2003) objection to typologisation stresses the wide range of ways in which care is provided as opposed to paid for. The discussion above has been primarily concerned with who carries the costs; there is a need now to give a little more attention to the purchase–provision relationship, given the range of possible providers and the even greater range of ways in which purchase and provision may be related to each other. Much of the mixed economy of welfare literature in the UK is about this separation.

As Anttonen and colleagues recognise, the link between the state as payer and the arrangements for provision may be complex. Various efforts have been made to specify the options. For example, a complicated matrix to delineate purchaser–provider relationships in the UK in Wistow et al (1994, p 37, figure 3.1) delineates, on one dimension, the public, voluntary and private sectors and, on the other, the following:

- coerced collective demand;
- voluntary collective demand;
- corporate demand;
- uncompensated individual consumption;
- compensated individual consumption;
- individual donation.

On the provider side, three sectors roughly define the alternatives to direct provision by the state: the private sector, the voluntary sectors, and informal care (meaning in most cases the extended family). A negative stance on the feasibility of typology development seems justified by difficulty in finding comparative work that helps us to identify differences in choice between the provider options when the state is the payer. There are three questions here about possible differences between states in respect of:

- propensities to use the private sector;
- willingness to subsidise families;
- propensities to use the voluntary sector.

The logic of the Esping-Andersen model suggests that, where the public sector does fund care, interest in drawing in the private sector might be expected to be strongest in the 'liberal' regimes and weakest in the 'social democratic' ones.

But efforts to draw the private sector in as providers seem to have been as widespread in Scandinavia as in the UK and the US. This issue has been examined a little in an article by Bahle (2003), which compares the UK with France and Germany, indicating the importance of the trend towards the privatisation of provision, but suggests significant institutional influences on how this has developed. Comments at the beginning of this chapter indicated the difficulties in trying to explore this issue further with respect to the voluntary sector, given the limited comparative data and the way it has been analysed by scholars not interested in relating it to mainstream comparative social policy theory.

Issues surrounding the subsidy of families are complicated by the diversity of ways in which this may occur. This has been given more comparative attention than the levels of subsidy per se. A particular concern of analyses of the role of women in welfare has been the implications of alternative ways of providing state support for care. One amplification of that is to recognise an important difference between paying the cared-for (leaving them choices about where to purchase, including, of course, the possibility of using the money within the family) and paying the carer (in which case a much more prescriptive stance may be taken on who is to do the caring). But Ungerson (1995) and more recently Daly (2002) have also identified that subsidy to carers may come in a variety of ways: cash payments, opportunities to secure subsidised leave from work, credits for social security, and relief from taxation. There is scope for comparative work that takes this part of the analysis of care systems further.

Conclusion

This chapter has explored the way in which the mixed economy of welfare is handled in comparative studies. Any typology imposes a rough framework on reality; consequently, many people shy away from typologies, seeing their creation as a game that contributes nothing to our understanding. The defence of typologies is that even a rough framework can bring key issues to light and help us to explore comparisons in a more sophisticated way. And anything more than a rough framework gets hopelessly over-elaborate in this respect. We can end up, in the words of Esping-Andersen, in a situation in which "the desired parsimony ... [is] sacrificed and we might as well return to individual comparison" (1999, p 88).

The mixed economy of welfare is particularly hard to handle comparatively, the essence of the mixed economy of welfare proposition being that systems are 'mixed' in often complex ways.

What has been done here has been merely to suggest that the 'mixes' may differ significantly sometimes. Understanding those differences just a little may help to understand (a) processes of change in individual societies and (b) prospects for policy interventions (particularly policy borrowings). However, it is difficult to be specific about comparisons relating to some of the key dimensions – particularly variations in voluntary sector provision and variations in regulation. In many respects, in relation to a topic like this, comparison between a very limited number of nations that can focus on the richness of variation may often be more appropriate.

Summary

- Mainstream comparative theory deals with some aspects of the mixed economy, but its approach stems from a preoccupation with the relationship between state and market.
- Issues about family differences have been introduced with some success into comparative theory, but wider considerations about communities and the role of the voluntary sector have been given little attention.
- An examination of policy differences in respect of social security, health and social care amplify the main comparative concerns and suggest some important issues about alternative relationships between social policy provision and delivery.
- An examination of social care enables a broader examination of the complexity of the mixed economy, posing difficult choices between simple modelling of differences and the capture of wider complexities through case studies.

Questions for discussion

- To what extent is it possible to develop a systematic approach to national comparisons that gets beyond the state–market dichotomy?
- Do comparative studies throw any light on the validity of the view that choice implies marketisation?

Further reading

As indicated in the text, this topic has been explored rather little in the comparative literature. **Esping-Andersen's (1999)** revision of his regime theory touches on the issues, while the source with the best overall analysis – the book by **Anttonen and colleagues (2003)** – is wary of generalisation. **Daly's (2002)** article offers a useful alternative approach to this topic.

References

Anheier, H.K. and Salamon, H.K. (2001) *Volunteering in Cross-national Perspective: Initial Comparisons*, Civil Society Working Paper 10, London: London School of Economics.

Anttonen, A., Baldock, J. and Sipilä, J. (eds) (2003) *The Young, the Old and the State: Social Care Systems in Five Industrial Nations*, Cheltenham: Edward Elgar.

Arts, W. and Gelissen, J. (2002) 'Three worlds of welfare capitalism or more?', *Journal of European Social Policy*, vol 12, no 2, pp 137-58.

Bahle, T. (2003) 'The changing institutionalisation of social services in England and Wales, France and Germany: is the welfare state on retreat?', *Journal of European Social Policy*, vol 13, no 1, pp 5-20.

Bambra, C. (2005a) 'Worlds of welfare and the health care discrepancy', *Social Policy and Society*, vol 4, no 1, pp 31-41.

Bambra, C. (2005b) 'Cash versus services: "worlds of welfare" and the decommodification of cash benefits and health care services', *Journal of Social Policy*, vol 34, no 2, pp 195-214.

Bettio, F. and Plantenga, J. (2004) 'Comparing care regimes in Europe', *Feminist Economics*, vol 10, no 1, pp 85-113.

Bonoli, G. (1997) 'Classifying welfare states: a two-dimensional approach', *Journal of Social Policy*, vol 26, no 3, pp 351-72.

Bonoli, G. and Shinkawa, T. (eds) (2005) *Ageing and Pension Reform Around the World*, Cheltenham: Edward Elgar.

Casey, B., Oxley, H., Whitehouse, E., Antolin, P., Duval, R. and Leibfritz, W. (2003) *Policies for an Ageing Society: Recent Measures and Areas for Further Reform*, Economics Department Working Paper 369, Paris: Organisation for Economic Cooperation and Development.

Daly, M. (2002) 'Care as a good for social policy', *Journal of Social Policy*, vol 31, no 2, pp 251-70.

Esping-Andersen, G. (1990) *Three Worlds of Welfare Capitalism*, Cambridge: Polity Press.

Esping-Andersen, G. (1999) *Social Foundations of Post-industrial Economies*, Oxford: Oxford University Press.

European Commission (2004) *The Social Situation in the European Union 2004*, Luxembourg: European Commission.

Ferrara, M. (1996) 'The "southern model" of welfare in social Europe', *Journal of European Social Policy*, vol 6, no 1, pp 17-37.

Gough, I. and Wood, G. (2004) *Insecurity and Welfare Regimes in Asia, Africa and Latin America: Social Policy in Development Contexts*, Cambridge: Cambridge University Press.

Hall, P.A. and Soskice, D. (2001) *Varieties of Capitalism: The Institutional Foundations of Comparative Advantage*, Oxford: Oxford University Press.

Higgins, J. (1981) *States of Welfare*, Oxford: Blackwell.

Jones, C. (1985) *Patterns of Social Policy: An Introduction to Comparative Analysis*, London: Tavistock.

Leece, J. and Bornat, J. (eds) (2006) *Developments in Direct Payments*, Bristol: The Policy Press.

Lewis, J. (1992) 'Gender and the development of welfare regimes', *Journal of European Social Policy*, vol 2, no 3, pp 159-73.

Lewis, J. (ed) (1993) *Women and Social Policies in Europe: Work, Family and the State*, Aldershot: Edward Elgar.

Lewis, J. (ed) (1997) *Lone Mothers in European Welfare Regimes*, London: Jessica Kingsley.

Lijphart, A. (1975) *The Politics of Accommodation: Pluralism and Democracy in the Netherlands*, Berkeley, CA: University of California Press.

Lødemel, I. and Trickey, H. (eds) (2001) *An Offer You Can't Refuse: Workfare in International Perspective*, Bristol: The Policy Press.

Lundström, T. and Svedberg, L. (2003) 'The voluntary sector in a social democratic welfare state – the case of Sweden', *Journal of Social Policy*, vol 32 , no 2, pp 217-38.

Myles, J. (2002) 'A new social contract for the elderly?', in G. Esping-Andersen (ed) *Why we need a New Welfare State*, Oxford: Oxford University Press, pp 130-72.

O'Connor, J. (1996) 'From women in the welfare state to gendering welfare state regimes', Special issues of *Current Sociology*, 44/2.

OECD (Organisation for Economic Cooperation and Development) (2003) *Revenue Statistics 1965-2001*, Paris: OECD.

OECD (2004a) *Education at a Glance*, Paris: OECD.

OECD (2004b) *Health Data 2004*, Paris: OECD.

OECD (2004c) *OECD in Figures 2004*, Paris: OECD.

OECD (2005) *Pension Markets in Focus*, Paris: OECD.

Polanyi, K. (1944) *The Great Transformation*, New York, NY: Rinehart.

Powell, M. and Barrientos, A. (2004) 'Welfare regimes and the welfare mix', *European Journal of Political Research*, vol 43, no 1, pp 83-105.

Sainsbury, D. (ed) (1994) *Gendering Welfare States*, London: Sage Publications.

Sainsbury, D. (1996) *Gender Equality and Welfare States*, Cambridge: Cambridge University Press.

Saltman, R. (1998) 'Health reform in Sweden: the road beyond cost containment', in Ranade, W. (ed) *Markets and Health Care*, London: Longman, pp 101-21.

Saltman, R.B. and von Otter, C. (1992) *Planned Markets and Public Competition*, Buckingham: Open University Press.

Siaroff, A. (1994) 'Work, welfare and gender equality: a new typology', in D. Sainsbury (ed) *Gendering Welfare States*, London: Sage Publications, pp 82-100.

Ungerson C. (1995) 'Gender, cash and informal care: European perspectives and dilemmas', *Journal of Social Policy*, vol 24, no 1, pp 31-52.

Walker, A. and Wong, C.-K. (2004) 'The ethnocentric construction of the welfare state', in P. Kennett (ed) *A Handbook of Comparative Social Welfare*, Cheltenham: Edward Elgar, pp 116-30.

Wilensky, H.L. and Lebaux, C.N. (1965) *Industrial Society and Social Welfare*, Glencoe, IL: Free Press.

Wistow, G., Knapp, M., Hardy, B. and Allen, C. (1994) *Social Care in a Mixed Economy*, Buckingham: Open University Press.

World Bank (1994) *Averting the Old Age Crisis*, Oxford: Oxford University Press.

ten

The global and supra-national dimensions of the welfare mix

Nicola Yeates

Overview

The importance of attending to the global context in which social policy is formulated and implemented is now established. Relating this context to the mixed economy and social divisions of welfare concepts, this chapter examines the involvement of international organisations (IOs) in social policy formation in respect of provision, finance and regulation of welfare services. It then focuses on the various processes by which IOs' policies may shape the welfare mix, both in 'developed' and 'developing' countries. It concludes by considering the relationship between supra-national and national organisations in the development of the mixed economy of welfare through a case study of pensions.

Key concepts

International governmental organisations • international non-governmental organisations • global social policy • supranationalism

Introduction

No study of social policy is nowadays complete without an appreciation of the global dimensions of welfare state development. At one level, this translates into sensitivity to the wide diversity of ways that welfare is provided, funded and regulated in different countries around the world. This is the terrain of cross-national comparative social policy and was the subject of Chapter Nine in this volume. At another level, attention to the global context of social policy entails attending to the movement of capital, goods, services, people and ideas between countries and the social and economic policies and practices of international governmental and non-governmental organisations and their intersection with countries' histories, traditions, trends, institutions and policies. These processes and entanglements are essentially the terrain of global social policy.

This chapter examines the global and supra-national dimensions to the mixed economy of welfare (MEW) and the social division of welfare (SDW) through a focus on the social policy dimensions and impacts of international organisations (IOs). Our focus lies primarily with international governmental organisations (IGOs), in particular the United Nations (UN), the World Bank, the International Monetary Fund (IMF), the Organisation for Economic Cooperation and Development (OECD) and the European Union (EU), but we also draw attention to international non-governmental organisations (INGOs) as appropriate. The discussion is organised around three main questions. First, what are the contributions of these IOs to debates about the appropriate balance between different sectors in the provision, funding and regulation of welfare? Second, to what extent do IOs influence national social policy formation? Third, how do these influences occur, and through which processes and mechanisms are they channelled? The discussion is broadly internationalist in orientation and the experiences of Britain are situated in the context of a variety of countries of different levels of 'development', geo-political position and welfare mix.

The chapter is organised in the following way. It begins by reviewing the scale and scope of involvement of IOs in social policy formation generally, giving some examples of the ways in which they intersect with welfare provision, finance and regulation (section one). The discussion develops in section two through an examination of the conceptual, theoretical and methodological issues associated with analysing these organisations' involvement in, and influence on, social policy. Following this, we explore the contributions of different IGOs to social policy formation in section three and examine the influence of IGOs on MEW and SDW in section four; here we review some of the research literature as well as some recent developments in pensions policy. The chapter ends with a brief review of the principal points of discussion and reflects on the supra-national dimensions of MEW and SDW in the light of broader debates about the influence of IOs on social policy reform.

The scale and scope of IOs' involvement in social policy

International cooperation and action in matters of social policy are by no means a recent affair (Yeates, forthcoming: 2007) but over the course of the 20th century this cooperation has expanded substantially. Thousands of IOs are now involved in numerous international agreements, treaties, regulations and accords. International organisations come in many shapes and sizes (**Table 10.1**). One distinction is between international *governmental* organisations (IGOs) and international *non-governmental* organisations (INGOs). IGOs are essentially international fora through which sovereign governments collaborate, while INGOs are international fora through which non-governmental organisations – voluntary and charitable organisations, trade union organisations, industry associations and business groups – collaborate. Another distinction is between IOs that operate on a global scale (for example, World Bank, World Social Forum) and those that do so on a sub-global, or world-regional, scale (EU, European Social Forum); regional formations often enter into trans-regional cooperative alliances with each other (for example, EU-Caricom, EU-Mercosur) as well as working closely with IGOs. In fact, many governments and non-governmental organisations are simultaneously members of global and regional IOs.

IOs vary considerably in terms of resources. Some IGOs are little more than political alliances or clubs comprising a minority of the world's governments (OECD, G8, G24). Some have no independent legal force or permanent secretariat (for example, G8); others have the force of international law behind them (World Trade Organization [WTO], EU, UN) and/or substantial bureaucracies (International Labour Organization [ILO], World Bank). Some INGO secretariats have greater numbers of staff than some IGOs (compare, for example, the WTO's 630 staff with Oxfam's 2,800 staff) and command significant budgets.

Compared with national governments, IGOs' involvement in social policy is quite limited. However, substantial, routine cooperation exists in a variety of social policy domains: employment; migration; social security; pensions; education; healthcare; social services; food security; population control; and humanitarian aid and relief. Of all such institutions, including other regional formations, the EU has the most extensive involvement through labour and social law, the structural funds and various social programmes. However, there have been important attempts at regulation through standard-setting efforts at the international level in the UN and its satellite agencies, such as the ILO and the World Health Organization (WHO), and some recent experimentation in

Table 10.1: Examples of global and regional IGOs and INGOs

International governmental organisations	International non-governmental organisations
Global	
World Bank	World Economic Forum
International Monetary Fund	World Social Forum
United Nations	International Confederation of Free
UN agencies, for example,	Trade Unions
International Labour Organization,	International Planned Parenthood
World Health Organization,	Federation
Unicef	OXFAM, War on Want
World Trade Organization	International Chamber of Commerce
Organisation for Economic	International Pharmaceutical
Cooperation and Development	Industries Association
G8, G77, G24, and so on	
Regional	
European Union	European Services Forum
North American Free Trade	European Trade Union
Agreement	Confederation
South Asian Area for Regional	European Social Forum
Cooperation	Asian Social Forum
Mercado Común del Sur	Focus on Global South
(Southern Core Common Market,	
or Mercosur)	
Caribbean Community and	
Common Market (Caricom)	
Southern African Development	
Community	

international financing for welfare services (ILO's Global Social Trust, WHO's global health partnerships). The World Bank is also tangibly engaged in social provision through the loans it makes to countries; these loans are used to finance programmes of aid and relief and health, social welfare and population programmes that are often delivered in partnership with national and international NGOs. Finally, the WTO has emerged as a key actor in global social regulation over the past decade with the inclusion of health and social care, education and social security in its General Agreement on Trade in Services (GATS). The involvement of IGOs in the regulation, financing and provision of the health and welfare services is, then, substantial (**Table 10.2**).

Table 10.2: Examples of IGO involvement in provision, finance and regulation

	Provision	Finance	Regulation
Global	Humanitarian relief, population programmes, social development projects, special global (health, social) funds delivered through IGOs and INGOs	Revenue raised from appeals, donations and Overseas Development Assistance channelled into ad hoc humanitarian relief, special global funds, debt relief and differential pricing (drugs)	International labour and social standards through ILO, OECD Conventions; human rights through UN; social, health and education regulation in international trade law, economic fora
Regional (EU)	Human resources/ social funds, regional development funds	Revenues raised from customs and government donations distributed through agricultural and structural funds	Labour and social standards through regulations, directives and agreements

Source: adapted from Deacon (2003)

Understanding the influence of IOs on social policy

The study of IOs' influence on social policy and the welfare mix raises a number of conceptual, theoretical and methodological issues. At the conceptual level, it is helpful to distinguish between different kinds of processes through which IOs may impact upon social policy. Extending the work of Leibfried and Pierson (1996), we can identify four such processes in the global context:

1. Measures to construct uniform social standards at world-regional or global levels. Regional-level examples of social regulation are the EU's Social Charter/Protocol and its equality and health and safety initiatives, and Caricom's health initiatives. Global-level examples include the ILO's Labour Conventions, the WHO's Health Conventions, the OECD's Guidelines for Multinational Enterprises and the UN's Global Compact.

2. Regulatory reform aiming to promote market integration. Examples here include the EU's and Mercosur's labour mobility and social security measures to promote freedom of movement, and various measures by a wide range of regional formations and global agencies such as the WTO to promote international trade in goods and services.

3. Indirect pressures of economic integration that encourage restructuring of national welfare states. Examples include the feared spectre of 'social dumping' and 'race to the bottom' scenarios prompted by, for instance, the creation of regional or global markets through trade and investment liberalisation measures or monetary union. This also includes the more direct effects on national welfare systems of attempts to create international markets in health, education and financial services. IOs come into the equation here insofar as they are both a political expression, and a driving force, of market integration processes that impact on domestic social policy reforms.

4. IOs contribute to framing knowledge, generating ideas and developing policy options. Much of what many IGOs 'do' is to provide a forum for mutual education, analysis and debate. While this may not directly produce formal agreements or common policy agendas, it can be important to promoting shared analyses, beliefs and concerns that may provide a platform for future collaboration and/or that may find their way back into national institutional arenas and inform policy reforms taking place there.

The extent and nature of IOs' influence on national social policy and welfare mixes can be missed if we only focus on the first process, that is, the range and number of IOs' 'positive integration' measures. While this is the most obvious one to focus on (and is often the primary or only subject of many early studies of supranational social policy), it needs to be supplemented by attention to the other processes and mechanisms. This raises a more general point, namely that it is not always possible to clearly demarcate between global, world-regional, national and sub-national spheres. Governments, social movements, trades unions, professional associations and trade associations routinely work through world-regional and global fora, while IOs enjoy institutionalised access to and authority over national policy formation and decision-making procedures, albeit to various extents. Indeed, much of what passes for 'domestic' policy may simply be implementing international obligations (for example, 'British' equality, human rights and health and safety legislation implements EU and UN law), while international law can enshrine national interests and sensitivities by allowing exemptions and differential implementation periods (many EU and WTO agreements and regulations do this). This carries into the NGO arena: 'national' voluntary and charitable organisations may be supported by and work closely with IGOs as well as governments. Much of the World Bank's development assistance and the European Commission's European Social Funds are channelled through national NGOs, and NGOs are essential to the policy development and implementation work of many international organisations and governments (Yeates, 2001).

Although 'national' welfare states seem to be the primary institutional sites of social policy, they are shaped by and operate within a highly complex multi-tiered, 'polycentric' polity. This both constrains social policy formation and provides additional avenues and opportunities through which policy development occurs. Thus, national social policies and welfare states cannot be regarded as the outcome of domestic forces working to achieve their goals only in domestic arenas, nor can the influences at work be regarded as uni-directional (from supra-national 'down' to national levels). Instead, 'national' and 'supra-national' are better thought of as different elements of a multi-faceted governance structure whose different levels or 'tiers' are mutually constitutive and through which influence 'travels' multi-directionally. It is therefore as appropriate to ask questions about the ways in, and extent to, which actors located in domestic arenas influence the formation of supra-national policy as it is to ask questions about the ways in which supra-national agencies and actors shape the course of national social policy.

The study of influence also necessitates engaging with theoretical and methodological issues relating to causality. Even if we accept that welfare states are complex systems embedded in an overall system in which all parts affect each other, we still need to ask questions about how policies create an event such as changes to the role of the state in welfare provision, regulation and funding. Equally, we need to examine why policies do not create the kinds of change intended – why there is continuity in arrangements. This requires articulating theoretical ideas of what the causal relationships may be (for example, direct, indirect, spurious or conditional effects; reciprocal and feedback processes) and an appropriate research methodology to collect the necessary evidence (Hage and Foley Meeker, 1988). In short, we need to carefully distinguish between different processes and effects before we can confidently pronounce that the action of an IO is responsible for a change in national social policy.

Thus, it is possible to accept that IOs attempt to influence the direction of social policy reform nationally and that (elements of) those preferences and prescriptions can be found in national reforms without necessarily attributing a simple causal influence in such a process exclusively to them (Pierson, 1998; Hay and Watson, 1999). National actors may develop solutions to problems quite independently of the arguments advanced by IOs, while an idea adopted by a government may be promoted by more than one IO. Tracing the influence of an IO on domestic policy reform may be further complicated by the possibility of significant time lag between the promulgation of the idea and actual policy changes. Its effects may be partially or wholly obscured or mediated by countervailing forces. Finally, attention to instances of influence and policy change also needs to be matched by attention to instances of non-influence in order to specify the various contingent factors and conditions impacting on policy reform. Armingeon and Beyeler's (2004) study of the 'ideational' impact of the OECD on member states clearly illustrates these issues, while also providing an important case study of the conditions under which an IO like the OECD influences domestic social policy reform (**Box 10.1**).

Box 10.1: The OECD and national policy reform

The OECD's Country Surveys (CSs) are a key method by which the OECD aims to advance its policy agenda among its member countries. Armingeon and Beyeler (2004) examined the effectiveness of this method by examining the degree of concordance between recommendations issued to 14 western European OECD states* in the period 1970-2000 and domestic policy reforms. The study aimed to test the OECD's own claims of the efficacy of its recommendations as well as the claims of critics complaining about the marketising effects of the OECD's social policy on domestic provisions.

The study found a high degree of consistency in the advice of the OECD to these countries but a low degree of efficacy overall. Although there was an apparent reasonable degree of concordance between recommendations and reforms (eight countries adhered to more than half of the CS recommendations, and policy changes in six others corresponded to its CS recommendations in 50% or less of the time), there was no clear evidence of direct causal links between recommendations and reforms. First, the authors argue, the 'fit' could be explained by supra-national institutions other than the OECD, in particular the EU. Second, policy changes introduced nationally had in some cases been under way before they were subsequently recommended by the OECD. Third, some policy changes result less from new insights offered by the OECD and more from changing domestic circumstances that provide conducive conditions for options to be adopted.

By also examining the instances of discordance, the study shed light on the conditions under which recommendations were accepted. Policy recommendations were rejected if they were perceived to be at odds with the following: the power of major actors; settlements and procedures of institutionalised and successful cooperation between social partners and government; the social values and attitudes or the accepted major role of the state held by the overwhelming majority of the citizens. The study showed that recommendations were referred to and adopted only if they fitted with the priorities of powerful political actors. The study also found considerable time lags between recommendations and reforms, while the policy reforms adopted often fell short of the extent of reform recommended by the OECD.

The main conclusion of the study was that "OECD proposals do not lead to far-reaching policy change" (p 238). This is attributed to the OECD's absence of regulatory and financial sanctions, and its consequent inability to force governments and parliaments to consider its proposals. Its influence is also tempered by the fact that its reports are presented in a way that reduces media and political usability. This is not to say the OECD is insignificant as a global policy actor, only that its influence may be more subtle. More positively (for the OECD, at least), it is an authoritative source of comparable statistical data widely used by national governments, and is extensively involved in developing ideas, analyses and descriptions that can broadly frame policy discussion: "As an epistemic community, the OECD helps align, sustain and stabilise beliefs in proper economic and social policy" (p 239).

* Denmark, Finland, Norway, Sweden, Belgium, France, The Netherlands, Germany, Switzerland, Greece, Italy, Spain, UK and Ireland.

Even when IGOs appear to successfully frame governments' policy choices and steer their decisions, these choices and aims can be mediated, diluted or thwarted by policy implementation and enforcement processes. Policy implementation is a weak area for IGOs because they neither control this part of the policy process, nor do they have a local presence or any strong powers of enforcement. Indeed, on the whole they rely on local actors to raise and pursue implementation issues with their government and/or the organisation concerned. This structural dependence of IGOs on national political and administrative systems inevitably leaves room for manoeuvre in the interpretation and application of those policy choices. (Yeates, 2001)

Moreover, most IGOs can apply only indirect and informal methods of coercion, although some can exert leverage through legal and financial mechanisms (**Table 10.3**). However, these powers are used relatively rarely and are most effective when supported by a strategy of engagement throughout the policy process. Indeed, the World Bank has been successful in getting its desired policy reforms implemented not only because it is able to exert leverage over governments by providing (or withholding) finance, but also because it has formed alliances with other similarly oriented global and domestic policy actors supporting the reforms. Indeed, the World Bank remains closely involved in the policy process following the enactment of reform legislation by providing continuing technical advice to fix legal and regulatory issues subsequently arising (Orenstein, 2005). In essence, an organisation's ability to apply legal and financial sanctions is not always in itself sufficient, and for a political authority to be truly authoritative and effective it must also engage with other actors and interests throughout the political and policy processes.

This general point is further illustrated by the ILO. ILO Conventions have

Table 10.3: *Surveillance and enforcement mechanisms of selected IGOs*

	Type	Means	Institutional mechanism
EU	Regulatory	Legal authority	Bureaucratic (EC)
	Financial	Fines	Legal (European
	Moral	Collective pressure	Court of Justice)
OECD	Moral	Collective pressure through regular peer review and moral suasion	Country surveys of the Economics and Development Review Committee
ILO	Moral	Collective pressure through regular peer review and moral suasion	Implementation reviews
WTO	Regulatory	Legal authority	Legal (disputes
	Moral	The offending government addresses the problem or makes reparations to the complainant government in the form of trade concessions	resolution process)
World Bank	Financial	Receipt of development funds conditional on following bank's policy prescriptions	Poverty Reduction Strategy Papers, debt relief programmes
	Moral		
IMF	Financial	Receipt of loans conditional on following IMF's policy prescriptions	
	Moral		

legal authority but the ILO does not possess powers of enforcement and relies on moral suasion to achieve its regulatory aims. To give an example, one measure of the influence of the ILO on national systems is the extent to which governments ratify ILO Conventions. In these terms, the ILO can be said to be reasonably influential, with over 6,000 ratifications of its Conventions by member countries. However, only 111 member countries (out of 178, 62%) have ratified all eight ILO Conventions pertaining to fundamental human rights[1]. Moreover, there is considerable variation between the Conventions in terms of the extent to which they are ratified. Thus, only 141 countries have ratified Convention 138 on the abolition of child labour and 168 members have ratified Convention 29 on the elimination of forced and compulsory labour. There is also considerable variation between member countries in terms of the number of Conventions ratified. Of note here is that (among long-standing members, the US and Myanmar have each only ratified two out of the eight Conventions, followed by Afghanistan and Somalia [three each] and Oman and Singapore [four each]). Of course, ratification is only a measure of statutory intent and says nothing about whether these intentions are carried out, so it is possible that governments that have ratified a Convention (and that appear to be influenced by the ILO) are not actually implementing it. Equally, those governments that have not ratified a Convention (and would not appear to be influenced by the ILO) may in practice be observing internationally accepted standards.

This issue of statutory intent versus delivery – and of the distinction between formal and informal regulatory mechanisms more broadly – is further illustrated by Dixon's (1999) study, which ranked 172 countries by how closely their social security systems adhere to a set of ILO standards[2]. The top-ranked countries could thus be said to be most influenced by the ILO, while the bottom-ranked countries are, in this approach, least influenced by the ILO[3]. Of note here is that some of the top-ranked countries (central and eastern Europe, Russia) are beset by financial and political crises that inhibit their ability to deliver on their statutory obligations. Finally, despite the apparent influence of ILO social security standards globally, it is worth noting that, although statutory social security coverage is almost complete in advanced industrialised countries, more than half the world's population remain excluded from any type of statutory scheme (van Ginneken, 1999; ILO, 2000).

IGOs' social policy prescriptions and impacts

The international institutional arena is a key battleground over which political struggle over the future of welfare capitalism is fought. The work of Deacon and his colleagues (Deacon and Hulse, 1996; Deacon, Hulse and Stubbs, 1997, 2003; Deacon, 2000, 2005a, 2005b, 2007) has been important in demonstrating the dimensions of this political contestation and the positions of principal IGOs within the debate. As **Table 10.4** shows, the range of welfare futures backed by these institutions is confined to variants of liberalism with its emphasis on individual responsibility and choice, a restricted role for the public sector in finance and provision and a substantial one for the private (commercial) sector, and minimum (and preferably informal) social, labour and health regulations. There is also a notable absence of any IGO advancing a social democratic or redistributive agenda. These ideological struggles take place between different sections within these organisations as well as between different organisations. Thus, while some sections of the OECD offer 'welfare as burden' discourses, others promote 'welfare as investment' discourses. The World Bank advances both 'welfare as social cohesion' as well as 'welfare as investment'

Table 10.4: *Global social policy discourse*

Orientation	Welfare world	Agency promulgating
Existing welfare as:		
Burden	Liberalism (for example, US, UK)	IMF, OECD, WTO
Social cohesion	Conservative, corporatist (for example, France, Germany)	EU, ILO, World Bank
Investment	South East Asia	OECD, World Bank
Redistributive commitment	Social democracy (for example, Nordic countries)	–
Emerging welfare as:		
Safety net	Social liberalism	World Bank, EU, WTO
Work-fare	Social liberalism	IMF
Citizenship entitlement	Futuristic	ILO, CoE
Redistribution	–	

Source: adapted from Deacon and Hulse (1996, p 52).

discourses, while also pursuing policies of privatisation and public sector retrenchment. Some parts of the IMF are discussing the desirability of universal primary education and healthcare, while other parts of it are promoting selectivism and privatisation in public welfare services (Deacon, 2000).

The World Trade Organization deserves specific mention here. For many it is the ultimate institutional manifestation of neo-liberal globalisation, equipped with legal powers to progress and enforce a 'free trade' agenda on signatory states. The WTO is a relatively 'young' international organisation (established in 1995) and is one that potentially has considerable effects on social policy. Indeed, for some, the inclusion of health, education, financial services and utilities (water, energy) in the General Agreement on Trade in Services (GATS) heralds a rapid and irreversible acceleration towards the end of public financing, provision and regulation of these services where this already exists and prevents public services from emerging where it does not. Some analysts fear that the agreement contains an in-built bias in favour of commercial provision generally, that it favours foreign service providers over domestic ones, that it permits only minimal public regulation that would not provide adequate consumer protection and that it will erode cross-class support necessary for the development of public welfare services (Pollock and Price, 1999; Deacon, 2000; Sexton, 2001). Some of these fears have been partially allayed by governments' own reluctance to make specific commitments in health and education under this agreement but the general concerns about the invidious long-term effects of GATS on public services remain (see Yeates, 2005 for a review of this debate). However, it is too early to tell what effects this particular agreement will have on social policy reform and its outcomes for the welfare mix. This is an under-researched international organisation compared with others of similar standing, in particular the EU, ILO and World Bank.

The global struggle that is occurring is essentially about the appropriate aims of public policy and the role of the state in social and economic development more broadly. It is a conflict between neo-liberal values of individual responsibility, 'choice', self-interest and enforceable contractual rights, and social democratic ones of collective responsibility, social cohesion, integration and equity (Dixon, 1999; Deacon, 2007). The conflict has been at its most intense in relation to social protection, particularly pensions, and has been played out in many regional and country contexts around the world. We now turn to review the dimensions of the debate and IGOs' involvement therein, together with some research evidence regarding the progress of pension reform and the implications for MEWs.

The ILO and World Bank represent the principal contrasting positions in this struggle. For most of the 20th century the ILO's position as premier global authority in matters of social protection was uncontested[4]. Emanating from northern European corporatist traditions of social protection, it advocated a major role for publicly funded (tax or insurance), regulated and provided schemes as the means for ensuring widespread access to a minimum standard of living. Commercial and informal schemes were to play a minor, supplementary role in this overall approach (**Table 10.5**). The ILO's approach gained broad international acceptance and influenced the shape of national social security and labour systems in numerous countries, especially among developing countries, as a growing number of newly independent states became members of the organisation (Otting, 1994; Kay, 2000).

During the mid-1990s, the World Bank openly challenged the ILO's approach, and its dominant position in the pensions arena. The World Bank's 1994 publication, *Averting the Old Age Crisis*, argued in favour of pared-down public schemes providing a subsistence income for the 'critically poor' and much greater reliance on informal, occupational and commercial schemes for everyone else (**Table 10.5**). Only this approach, it argued, would enable countries to become (or remain) fiscally sustainable and economically competitive, and permit them to address inconsistencies in statutory pension coverage and payment levels. Interestingly, this 'one-size-fits-all' model was

Table 10.5: World Bank and ILO approaches to pension reform

Feature	World Bank	ILO
Basic state pension	Means-tested (tax-based)	Universal (tax-based)
Second tier	Individualised, compulsory, defined-contribution pension, privately invested	Solidaristic, pay as you go, defined-benefit state pension
Third tier	Voluntary additional private savings/ investment	Voluntary additional private savings/ investment

Source: Deacon (2005a, p 163)

not carried over into the health and education domains. For instance, the World Bank argued that health services could not be handed over to the private sector because of substantial imperfections in the health market and that the appropriate welfare mix should be decided on a case-by-case basis (Deacon et al, 1997; Bhatia and Mossialos, 2004). However, as Mehrotra and Delamonica (2005) point out, the World Bank consistently and de facto encourages private sector involvement in social services.

Although the World Bank is not the only global actor advocating pension privatisation, there is no doubt that it has been instrumental in transforming pension privatisation into a mainstream policy idea. It joined an existing transnational coalition that began in Chile in the early 1980s involving economists embedded in a US-based movement to initiate radical reform in economic policy making. Through the advice of Chilean reformers to other governments, pension privatisation became a template for reform, particularly in Latin America and later also in central and eastern Europe (Holzmann et al, 2003; Orenstein, 2005). The World Bank facilitated this international diffusion by applying the model around the world, irrespective of country history, tradition or circumstance. It provided institutional, human and financial resources to assist governments to model pensions reforms and push through World Bank-preferred reforms. Many of these governments were from middle-income developing countries receiving advice and support from international development agencies and loans from the World Bank for development projects. The World Bank has been facilitated by other global policy actors. Thus, in various regions around the world, the World Bank and ILO have vied with each other to have countries adopt their particular approach and have been joined by other regional entities such as the EU, United States Agency for International Development (USAID) and IMF in central and eastern Europe; the IMF, Asian Development Bank, OECD and Asia-Pacific Economic

Cooperation in Asia; USAID, United Nations Development Programme, IMF and Inter-American Development Bank in Latin America (Deacon et al, 1997; Deacon, 2001; Holzmann et al, 2003; Müller, 2003; Whiteford, 2003; Orenstein, 2005). Many of these international organisations have their headquarters in Washington DC.

In terms of the actual impact on national reforms, however, the evidence appears to be more mixed. In Latin America, only Chile's pension system comes closest to the World Bank paradigm; Bolivia, El Salvador and Mexico fit the World Bank paradigm partially; and the remaining countries enacted reforms closer to the ILO paradigm than to that of the World Bank (Cruz-Saco and Mesa-Lago, 1998). Similarly, Fultz and Ruck (2001) show that most central and eastern European countries are reforming their public schemes without establishing a mandatory private pillar. The World Bank is also having a hard time persuading the Chinese government to adopt its pension model, as indicated by its continued criticism of Chinese policies (Whiteford, 2003). That said, even if the policy model is not followed to the letter, policies might be broadly consistent with the World Bank paradigm or adopt particular elements from it (Deacon, 2000; Cruz-Saco, 2002).

In more general terms, the general influence of neo-liberal thinking on this area of policy is evidenced by the fact that many governments have retreated from more redistributive, socially cohesive types of reform and embraced a greater role for the private sector in pensions provision. Few governments have fully privatised systems, but many have partially privatised systems or a private option within public systems (Ferrera et al, 1995) and they are displaying increasing comfort with the promotion of individual retirement savings for investment in the stock market/equity investment. The EU is notable in this respect, and a raft of pension reforms that follow this trend have been pushed through in recent years. The German government proposes tax breaks for voluntary private retirement savings from workers. In Britain, where private sector involvement in pension provision is already among the most advanced, the Labour government introduced new tax-financed pensions and saving vehicles (Stakeholder Pension, Individual Savings Account), and aims to increase the proportion of private:public retirement income from 40:60 to 60:40. The Swedish government has partially privatised its pension system by requiring workers to put 18.5% of their income aside for retirement, 2.5% of which can be invested in an individual account, while the remainder is used to fund a pay-as-you-go programme of notional individual accounts no longer based on work history but on lifetime income. In France, the government has set up an equity savings plan (*Plan d'Epargne en Actions*) and wants to allow workers to set aside as much as a quarter of their pay against which employers would make matching contributions up to a set annual limit. In Ireland, the government introduced individual investment accounts (Personal Retirement Saving Accounts) to facilitate increased individual savings, extend supplementary pensions coverage and widen the range of pension providers. The Italian government has introduced changes to the way 'severance pay' and private savings are managed; by putting the money into managed pension funds, it hopes to boost the domestic pension fund market.

Conclusion

The overall argument of this chapter has been that the character of national welfare states and processes of social policy formation cannot be understood without reference to the global and supra-national dimensions of the welfare mix. We focused on international organisations because they are a primary institutional manifestation of international cooperation. This review of the global dimensions and impacts of social policy proceeded through a specific focus on IGOs, at global and world-regional levels, and their relationship to national contexts. Although it is in practice difficult to clearly demarcate national from supra-national levels and spheres of policy formation, there is a clear supra-national dimension to social policy. We reviewed the various ways in which questions of social policy have been approached by international and regional governmental organisations. We have seen that questions about the appropriate balance between statutory, commercial, voluntary/charitable and informal arrangements in the provision, funding and regulation of health, education and welfare services are being discussed in these fora. We further noted that these debates address questions about the proper role of the state and non-state bodies in social and economic development, the place of individual versus collective responsibility, and the role of public policy in achieving social integration, opportunity and equity.

Three broad conclusions can be drawn from this discussion. First, IOs are tangibly involved in social policy formation but their involvement in the provision, funding and regulation of welfare services is not on the same scale as national governments. Moreover, the extent and nature of their involvement varies according to policy area (some IOs are more directly concerned with social security and labour than health or emergency relief) and the organisation concerned (the World Bank is involved in provision and funding of services through its development loans, whereas the WTO is only involved in regulation; only the EU is directly involved in all three aspects).

Second, it is important to distinguish between different types of regulation in accounting for the ways in which IGOs relate to, and impact on, national institutional and policy arenas. Thus, we noted the distinction between formal (legal authority, financial sanctions) and informal regulations (peer review, benchmarking) in this context, together with the importance of IGOs having enforcement as well as monitoring mechanisms available to them. However, we also saw that the use of these compliance mechanisms is not generally sufficient for an IGO wishing to influence the course of domestic policy reform and that to be most effective it also has to adopt a policy of engagement with national and local actors throughout the policy process.

Third, with regard to the question of the influence of supra-national organisations, there is little evidence to support the idea that IGOs have consistently direct and uniform impacts on the course of national social policy reform. Instead, their influence varies depending on the nature of the IO, and the policy area, policy issue and country in question, as well as other factors. Thus, contrary to 'apocalyptic' accounts of IOs as forces that are steering national policy reform, we find instead that IOs have moderate and often far more subtle effects: they are indeed contributing to the framing of policy debates and policy choices, but they are one of many forces informing policy reforms and their efficacy in shaping the character of welfare provision, funding and regulation is contingent. Thus, while states' grip over the policy process may have loosened in some respects, they remain key players and arbiters in social policy – working in alliance with IOs as well as being in conflict with them. This is not to deny inequalities of power within these fora or that some actors/ governments attempt to use their power to impose social standards on others, only to emphasise that international cooperation is, at the end of the day, the cooperation of sovereign states and that the power of national states to enforce the law, raise revenue and coordinate complex programmes of activity remains for the large part unrivalled.

Notes

[1] The eight Conventions cover matters of freedom of association and collective bargaining, the elimination of forced and compulsory labour, the elimination of employment and occupational discrimination, and the abolition of child labour.

[2] This study articulates a comprehensive set of 860 design and administration features for basic and supplementary social security schemes, on which ILO social security Conventions focus. These features incorporate financing, administration, coverage, eligibility and provision (for example, periodicity of payment; benefit generosity relative to prevailing living standards). Scores are assigned for each feature and countries ranked into 'league tables' (see Dixon, 1999, pp 199-205 for a full account of methodology and pp 207-64 for rankings).

[3] Note, in this regard, that the UK was ranked joint 37th with Brazil and the US was ranked joint 62nd with Ecuador.

[4] As of October 2005, the International Labour Code comprised 183 Conventions and 159 Recommendations; around one in five Conventions and one in 10

Recommendations deals exclusively or almost entirely with social security matters, mostly relating to public schemes.

Summary

- The character of national welfare states and processes of social policy formation cannot be understood without reference to the global and supra-national dimensions of the welfare mix.
- IOs in social policy are important agents, with implications for the provision, finance and regulation of welfare services, but the extent and nature of their involvement varies according to policy area and the organisation concerned.
- The balance of mechanisms varies between provision, finance and formal and informal regulation.
- IOs have moderate and subtle rather than direct and uniform impacts on the course of national social policy reform, with their influence varying depending on the nature of the IO, and the policy area, policy issue and country in question.

Questions for discussion

- Given the importance of international organisations in social policy is it possible to talk of mixed economies of welfare and social divisions of welfare as 'national' constructs?
- Drawing on this chapter and suggested further reading, outline points of similarity and difference between an international governmental organisation and a national government of your choice in respect to the provision, financing and regulation of social policy in the domain of social security, health or education.
- Draw up a list of the kinds of institutional characteristics and powers an IGO would need to have in order to achieve maximum effectiveness in pursuing its social policy aims. Now compare these to the actual characteristics of IOs such as the World Bank, WTO or the ILO. What kinds of changes to these organisations would be required to meet the requirements as set out in your first list?
- Drawing on your knowledge and understanding of the relationship between MEWs and SDW, discuss the implications for social (in)equalities of social policy prescriptions of organisations like the World Bank and WTO.

Further reading

In addition to following up the references cited in this chapter and the electronic resources, the following texts are recommended: **Yeates (2001)** and **George**

and Wilding (2002). Both of these discuss at length the implications of 'globalisation' processes for social policy and provision. For more information about social policy in developing countries, see **Hall and Midgley (2004)**. For further discussion of the themes and issues in the field of global social policy, the best summary overview is **Deacon (2003)**, while **Deacon (2007)** provides an updated review of policy debates and developments at global level. *Global Social Policy: Journal of Public Policy and Social Development* (Sage Publications) publishes a range of full-length and shorter articles on issues, debates and developments in global social policy. The *Journal of European Social Policy* focuses specifically on countries within the EU and the social policy dimensions and impacts of the EU institutions.

Electronic resources

There is an extensive range of online resources covering issues of globalisation and social policy. The following two websites are particularly useful in this regard. www.globalwelfare.net provides a range of learning and teaching resources for students, educators and researchers, including extensive links to a wide range of research and activist organisations and groups' websites that contain further information on the various issues discussed in this chapter. The site also provides a direct link to the e-Library for Global Welfare and ESDS International (the UK ESRC/JISC-funded Economic and Social Data Service), which makes available a range of international datasets in an accessible format.

www.elibraryforglobalwelfare.org is a searchable database of research and policy documents and statistical indicators relating to human welfare around the world. The database allows simple and advanced searches according to a range of criteria, including type of resources, geographical area of interest, policy area and institution.

References

Armingeon, K. and Beyeler, M. (eds) (2004) *The OECD and European Welfare States*, Aldershot: Edward Elgar.

Bhatia, M. and Mossialos, E. (2004) 'Health systems in developed countries', in A. Hall and J. Midgely (eds) *Social Policy For Development*, London: Sage Publications, pp 168-204.

Cruz-Saco, M.A. (2002) *Labour Markets and Social Security Coverage: The Latin American Experience*, Extension of Social Security Paper 2. Social Security Policy and Development Branch, ILO, Geneva: International Labour Organization.

Cruz-Saco, M.A. and Mesa-Lago, C. (1998) (eds) *The Reform of Pension and Health Care Systems in Latin America: Do Options Exist?* Pittsburgh, PA: University of Pittsburgh.

Deacon, B. (2000) *Globalisation and Social Policy: The Threat to Equitable Welfare*, Occasional Paper 5, Geneva: Unired Nations Research Institute for Social Development.

Deacon, B. (2003) 'Supranational agencies and social policy', in P. Alcock, A. Erskine and M. May (eds) *The Student's Companion to Social Policy* (2nd edn), Oxford: Blackwell, pp 241-9.

Deacon, B. (2005a) 'Global social policy: from neo-liberalism to social democracy', in B. Cantillon and I. Marx (eds) *International Cooperation in Social Security: How to Cope with Globalisation?*, Antwerp: Intersentia, pp 157-82.

Deacon, B. (2005b) 'From "safety nets" back to "universal social protection": is the global tide turning?', *Global Social Policy*, vol 5, no 1, pp 19-28.

Deacon, B. (2007) *Global Social Policy and Governance*, London: Sage Publications.

Deacon, B. and Hulse, M. (1996) *The Globalisation of Social Policy*, Leeds: Leeds Metropolitan University.

Deacon, B. with Hulse, M. and Stubbs, P. (1997) *Global Social Policy: International Organisations and the Future of Welfare*, London: Sage Publications.

Deacon, B., Ollila, E., Koivusalo, M. and Stubbs, P. (2003) *Global Social Governance: Themes and Prospects*, Helsinki: Globalism and Social Policy Programme.

Dixon, J. (1999) *Social Security in Global Perspective*, Westport: CT Praeger.

Ferrera, P., Goodman, J. and Matthews, M. (1995) *Private Alternatives to Social Security in Other Countries*, National Centre for Policy Analysis Policy Report 200 (www.ncpa.org).

Fultz, E. and Ruck, M. (2001) 'Pension reform in central and eastern Europe: emerging issues and patterns', *International Labour Review*, vol 140, no 1, pp 19-43.

George, V. and Wilding, P. (2002) *Globalization and Human Welfare*, Basingstoke: Palgrave.

Hage, J. and Foley Meeker, B. (1988) *Social Causality*, London: Unwin Hyman.

Hall, A. and Midgley, J. (2004) *Social Policy for Development*, London: Sage Publications.

Hay, C. and Watson, M. (1999) 'Globalisation: "sceptical" notes on the 1999 Reith Lectures', *Political Quarterly*, vol 70, no 4, pp 418-25.

Holzmann, R., Orenstein, M. and Rutowski, M. (eds) (2003) *Pension Reform in Europe: Process and Progress*, Washington DC, WA: World Bank.

ILO (International Labour Organization) (2000) *World Labour Report 2000 Income Security and Social Protection in a Changing World*, Geneva: ILO.

Kay, S. (2000) 'Recent changes in Latin American welfare states: is there social dumping?', *Journal of European Social Policy*, vol 10, no 2, pp 185-203.

Leibfried, S. and Pierson, P. (1996) 'Social policy', in H. Wallace and W. Wallace (eds) *Policy-Making in the European Union*, Oxford: Oxford University Press, pp 185-207.

Mehrotra, S. and Delamonica, E. (2005) 'The private sector and privatisation in social services: is the Washington consensus "dead"?', *Global Social Policy*, vol 5, no 2, pp 141-74.

Müller, K. (2003) *Privatising Old-Age Security: Latin America and Eastern Europe Compared*, Aldershot: Edward Elgar.

Orenstein, M. (2005) 'The new pension reform as global policy', *Global Social Policy*, vol 5, no 2, pp 175-202.

Otting, A. (1994) 'The International Labour Organization and its standard-setting activity in the area of social security', *Journal of European Social Policy*, vol 4, no 1, pp 51-7.

Pierson, P. (1998) 'Irresistible forces, immovable objects: post-industrial welfare states confront permanent austerity', *Journal of European Public Policy*, vol 5, no 4, pp 539-60.

Pollock, A. and Price, D. (1999) 'Rewriting the regulations', *The Lancet*, vol 356, 9 December, pp 1995-2000.

Sexton, S. (2001) *Trading Health Care Away? GATS, Public Services and Privatisation*, CornerHouse Briefing no 23, The Cornerhouse, Sturminster Newton, Devon (www.thecornerhouse.org.uk/briefing/index.shtml).

van Ginneken, W. (1999) *Social Security for the Excluded Majority Case Studies of Developing Countries*, Geneva: International Labour Organization.

Whiteford, P. (2003) 'From enterprise protection to social protection: pension reform in China', *Global Social Policy*, vol 31, no 1, pp 45-77.

World Bank (1994) *Averting the Old Age Crisis: Policies to Protect the Old and Promote Growth*, New York, NY: Oxford University Press.

Yeates, N. (2001) *Globalization and Social Policy*, London: Sage Publications.

Yeates, N. (2005) 'The General Agreement on Trade in Services: what's in it for social security?', *International Social Security Review*, vol 58, no 1, pp 3-22.

Yeates, N. (forthcoming: 2007) 'Globalisation and social policy', in J. Baldock, N. Manning and S. Vickerstaff (eds) *Social Policy* (3rd edn), Oxford: Oxford University Press.

eleven

Conclusion: analyses in the mixed economy of welfare and the social division of welfare

Martin Powell

Overview

This chapter draws together some of the main issues arising from the book. It gives a brief overview of the welfare mix over time and space. It then focuses on the changing welfare mix under New Labour, the forgotten dimensions of finance and regulation, the importance of a 'three-dimensional' MEW, the links between MEW and other debates, and the impact of MEW and SDW.

Key concepts

Changing welfare mix • New Labour • finance • regulation • the 'three-dimensional MEW' • impact of MEW and SDW

Introduction

The title of this chapter is derived from the pioneering account of Sinfield (1978). While 'analyses' may promise a little too much, this concluding chapter aims to reinforce the importance of MEW and SDW. Drawing on the material from earlier chapters, it examines the importance of MEW and SDW over time and space. MEW and SDW are important in an analytical rather than a descriptive sense. It is important to examine changes in the complex three-dimensional space of provision, finance and regulation rather than focusing on simple and misleading changes in one dimension such as provision. The chapter then examines how MEW and SDW are linked to important debates in social policy, and how they are associated with complex differential impacts on service users.

MEW and SDW over time and space

The mixed economy of welfare (MEW) and the social division of welfare (SDW) are vital, but relatively neglected, concepts in social policy. Mayo (1994, p 26) writes that "the MEW has been fundamental to the welfare state in Britain, although the mix has clearly varied between services and over time, just as the mix varies between Britain and the USA, for instance". John Stewart (Chapter Two) draws attention to the historical importance of MEW. While many authors claim that the mix changes over time, he points out that the components of MEW themselves change over time. For example, the 'voluntary sector' in the 19th century was not the same as the 'voluntary sector' today. Nevertheless, the different components of MEW in the UK follow a fairly broad trend – or 'moving frontier' – over time. In simple terms, private, voluntary and informal components of welfare were historically the dominant sources of welfare. From 1601, the most important role of (local) state welfare was located in the Poor Laws. For example, in the early 19th century, there were "only three ways of getting a state education: by being a cadet, a felon or a pauper" (Fraser, 2003, p 85). State intervention increased from about the mid-19th century onwards (Fraser, 2003; Harris, 2004). Collectivist solutions increased at the expense of individualist ones. Sidney Webb's view of the importance of 'socialism' is given in **Box 11.1**. However, it also serves to highlight the importance of state intervention. As Stewart shows, it is important in highlighting the rise of the state that the moves from local to central state are not forgotten (see also Brian Lund, Chapter Three); neither is it satisfactory simply to focus on the UK, as MEW is also likely to have varied between the nations of the UK.

Box 11.1: Sidney Webb's account of the importance of the state

The individualist town councillor will walk along the municipal pavement, lit by municipal gas and cleansed by municipal brooms with municipal water, and seeing by the municipal clock in the municipal market that he is too early to meet his children coming from the municipal school, hard by the county lunatic asylum and municipal hospital, will use the national telegraph system not to walk through the municipal park, but to come by the municipal tramway to meet him in the municipal reading-room by the municipal art gallery, museum and library where he intends to consult some of the national publications in order to prepare his next speech in the municipal town hall in favour of the nationalisation of canals and the increase of Government control over the railway system. "Socialism, Sir", he will say, "don't waste the time of a practical man by fantastic absurdities. Self-help, Sir, individual self-help, that's what made our city what it is". (Sidney Webb, 1889, cited in Fraser, 2003, pp 122-3)

Nevertheless, it is possible to construct an alternative view of the importance of non-state sources of welfare at that time (**Box 11.2**; see also Finlayson, 1994; Harris, 2004).

Box 11.2: Alternative account of the importance of non-state welfare

The collectivist town councillor passes the voluntary hospital, hard by the voluntary school and the voluntary housing, on his way to see the doctor from his Friendly Society. He later buys some goods at the Co-op, including some 'over-the-counter' medicine for his child (who is not covered by the Friendly Society scheme). He returns home, to thank the neighbour who will be looking after the child, while he goes to the council meeting to make a speech on the value of municipal welfare in the city.

It is generally accepted that the importance of state welfare increased during the twentieth century through the Liberal Reforms of 1906-14, culminating in the 'classic welfare state' introduced by the 1945 Labour government after the Second World War. The historian, A.J.P. Taylor (1970, p 25), opens his account of *English History 1914-1945* with the famous claim that: "Until August 1914 a sensible, law-abiding Englishman could pass through life and hardly notice the existence of the state, beyond the post office and the policeman".

Although it would be fair to say that the non-state elements assumed less importance after 1945, in some accounts they were almost completely neglected. However, there are clear differences between the largely state-provided health and education services and the greater pluralism found in housing and social care. Neither should it be forgotten that one of the most important parts of the classic welfare state was rooted in the regulation of employment levels through Keynesian demand management rather than by direct state employment. A number of commentators claim that, with the ending of the 'classic welfare state', there has been a change in the mix between state and non-state sources of welfare (to be discussed later). Stewart (Chapter Two) shows that many contemporary debates on topics such as the role of the state, the 'dependency culture', mutual solutions, cooperation and partnership, and civil society have clear historical echoes. The words widely attributed to Aneurin Bevan may be of some value for politicians and think-tanks grappling with what they falsely consider new problems: don't gaze in the crystal ball when you can read the bloody [history] book.

As well as varying over time, we saw that MEW also varies over space (see Chapter Nine) and that it is influenced by international organisations (Chapter Ten). Chapter Nine shows that that systems are mixed in often complex ways. The dominant modern approach to comparative social policy focused on state–market relationships, especially on the level of 'decommodification' (the extent to which state goods and services are detached from the market) (Esping-Andersen, 1990). In response to his feminist critics, Esping-Andersen (1999) also acknowledged the importance of 'defamilisation' (the extent to which women are detached from the gendered obligations of unpaid labour within the household). This still leaves a large gap on the role of the voluntary sector in the comparative MEW. While the welfare mix bears some broad relationships to 'welfare regimes' (Esping-Andersen 1990), there is considerable variation within regimes (such as the UK and US within the 'liberal' regime), between variations between services within one country (such as the NHS and housing within the UK), and between services in different countries (patterns of healthcare do not neatly map onto patterns of education or social care). Moreover, while the 'social democratic' or 'Scandinavian' regime relies heavily on the state, this does not mean that voluntary provision is totally lacking (Dahlberg, 2005). The picture is further complicated by our limited knowledge of the different patterns of provision, finance and regulation. It is clear that simply examining the welfare state tells us little about the other dimensions of MEW, as illustrated by **Table 9.2**, which shows that private pension investment as a share of GDP varies from 126% in Switzerland to about 4% in Norway.

Chapter Ten discusses the supra-national dimensions of MEW and SDW, particularly how the welfare mix is influenced by international organisations (IOs). These vary greatly in age, size, agenda, mechanisms and impact. The chapter brings out strongly the points that the impact of organisations cannot be simply associated with their size (for example, the World Trade Organization has only 630 staff) and or with ownership/provision. In particular, the influence of organisations such as the World Bank and the International Monetary Fund

(IMF) can be seen through conditions attached to finance (as the example of the IMF's role in the UK in the 1970s showed [Powell and Hewitt, 2002, p 95]). On the other hand, the influence of the International Labour Organization (ILO) and the European Union can be seen in regulation (see **Table 10.3**). Some fear that the continuing battle between the heavyweight World Bank and the middleweight ILO may lead to further privatisation of public pensions (see also Chapter Nine). As Chapter Ten concludes, questions about the appropriate balance between statutory, commercial, voluntary and informal arrangements in the provision, funding and regulation of health, education and welfare services are discussed by these organisations and that transnational and global social policy has a clear role in the international dimensions of MEW and SDW. Both of these chapters show that the comparative and global dimensions of MEW are far from fully understood. Even less is known about the international dimensions of SDW (but see Chapter Seven; Shalev, 1996; Howard, 1997; Peters, 2005).

MEW and SDW under New Labour

Chapter One introduced a three-dimensional approach to MEW (**Figure 1.2**), differentiating the dimensions of provision, finance and regulation. This differs from the work of Burchardt (1997), Burchardt et al (1999) and Hills (2004) in that their third dimension is choice rather than regulation. Smithies (2005) has updated the Burchardt typology, concluding that shifts in the composition of welfare activity have been relatively small and gradual. In the period from 1979-80 to 1999-2000, the pure public category fell from 52% to 49%, while the entirely private category increased from 24% to 29%. However, these figures were heavily influenced by housing, where the figures changed from 18% to 15% and 58% to 63%, respectively. This can be contrasted with the pure public category for social security, which increased from 57% to 64%, and for personal social services, which fell from 71% to 42%. Excluding the housing category, the total figures vary little, with moves from 62% to 61% for pure public and 15% to 17% for pure private. In other words, as Hills (2004) shows, only about half of welfare activity falls within this category of the 'Morrisonian welfare state' (public provision and finance).

While this analysis suggests that changes have been relatively minor, the contributors to this volume (Chapters Three to Eight) broadly claim that there have been many important changes in MEW and SDW under New Labour. Brian Lund (Chapter Three) points out that there are extensive debates in political philosophy about the role of the state. New Labour has extended the role of the state in terms of the traditional quantitative measure of state expenditure, but there have been possibly more important qualitative changes in other dimensions such as regulation. Lund reminds us that even the 'classic welfare state' did not consist solely of direct state provision (cell 1 in **Figure**

11.1), with only transfer payments of social security, and health and education provision largely in this category. Even in the NHS, there was considerable professional self-regulation, which made state 'command and control' hierarchical line management difficult. He also reminds us that discussions of 'the state' in MEW traditionally say little about local government, which has a major role in the provision, financing and regulation of services. He points to increasing diversity and pluralism under New Labour, and claims that social housing now appears to be the most pluralistic welfare sphere and a potential model for a more MEW in other welfare domains. He also signals the great potential importance of the Private Finance Initiative (PFI), reborn and renamed Public Private Partnerships (PPPs) under New Labour (see also Chapter Four).

Mark Drakeford (Chapter Four) argues that in an increasingly plural pattern of welfare provision, the commercial end of MEW has moved from the margin to the mainstream of government thinking. He makes the important differentiation between the transfer of assets and the reallocation of responsibilities, which focuses attention on the debate on whether ownership matters. He claims that rolling back the state has rolled forward a set of responsibilities, resulting in the privatisation of risk. The Blairite orthodoxy is that those on the receiving end are indifferent to the operation of MEW, but Drakeford points to cases that suggest that public opinion differs from that view. He goes on to highlight the importance of new forms of ownership such as 'semi-autonomous organisations' in a landscape of greater diversity and pluralism. He claims that Foundation (Hospital) Trusts were one of the defining features of the second Blair administration, with some supporters and many critics viewing their introduction as the end of the NHS as a nationalised industry. This new landscape also includes the introduction of new regulatory, audit and inspection bodies. It may be fair to claim these new bodies have not been an unqualified success as they keep changing their names (for example, NCSC to CSCI to HSCC; CHI to CHAI) at a rate that must please printing firms.

Pete Alcock and Duncan Scott (Chapter Five) illustrate the complexity and diversity of the 'loose and baggy monster' of the voluntary and community sector (VCS) by pointing to the debate about the best term for the sector. VCS, like informal welfare (Chapter Six) is located in 'civil society', which is generally regarded as being separate from state and market, but, as **Figure 5.1** shows, there is some degree of overlap between the sectors. Alcock and Scott write that it is difficult to underestimate the importance of the diversity within the sector. New Labour has set out a number of important policies that affect VCS, including those on civic renewal, social capital and volunteering. They focus on the shift towards the 'contract culture' where contracts tend to replace grants, and which highlights moves from support to regulation and control. This focuses on a tension in the New Labour agenda where it is unclear whether it desires a strong and independent VCS, or simply regards VCS as an agent of service delivery that is subject to greater central scrutiny.

Hilary Arksey and Caroline Glendinning (Chapter Six) show that the informal sector, like VCS, is diverse, including friends, families, neighbours, 'the community' and self-help groups, but is characterised by reciprocity, and is largely decommodified (unpaid) care. Although it is difficult to quantify this type of care in such an informal or 'hidden' economy, it is likely that this sector is an even more significant source of non-statutory welfare than VCS, to the extent that the state welfare system would not be able to cope without informal care. One estimate considered that the cost to the state of replacing the support provided by informal carers in the UK was roughly equivalent to the cost of the NHS. Arksey and Glendinning focus on family care, which is given by an estimated 6.8 million adults. This is a very diverse group, mostly of working age, but with some carers aged over 90, and others aged between five and seven. Although the gender of carers is not that different, those with large number of care hours are disproportionately female. New Labour policy is seen as broadly positive but of limited significance. While there may be large potential differences in some cases (for example, **Box 6.4**), local policy implementation remains patchy and piecemeal, with local authorities having additional responsibilities, but few additional resources. They point to the importance of devolution, especially long-term care in Scotland (cf Chapter Two). They also argue that direct payments – an example of greater consumerism – generally increases choice, control and flexibility over when, how, and from whom services are received.

Adrian Sinfield (Chapter Seven) points out that while tax welfare has generally been neglected in most social policy analysis, it has a longer history than the welfare state. Attention has recently increased with the moves to tax credits. While fiscal welfare has traditionally been regarded as regressive (or as providing 'upside-down benefits'), some advantages such as Mortgage Tax Relief have been ended; in his first Budget the Chancellor launched a poorly understood but controversial 'raid' on pension dividends, and tax credits have the potential to be progressive (when they are correctly calculated). On the other hand, the 'two nations in old age' (Titmuss, 1963) may be exacerbated by new rules on Self Invest Private Pension Schemes. As Sinfield comments, it is "puzzling that a tax relief likely to benefit only a rich minority should be introduced" by a Chancellor committed to 'social justice', resulting in a "uniquely generous tax regime".

Edward Brunsdon and Margaret May (Chapter Ten) examine occupational welfare, another important but neglected component of Britain's welfare order. This is a diverse and complex area (**Table 10.1**). It was introduced in the pioneering work of Titmuss (1963), but Brunsdon and May show that it is an area with many unanswered questions. They focus on two case studies. The first concerns the topical issue of pensions, bringing the story right up to May 2006. The recently established Pensions Commission (2004, p x) claims that

Britain has "one of the least generous state systems in the developed world" paralleled by "the most developed" voluntary-funded arrangements. This would not be entirely surprising to any student of the history of the welfare state, except that Beveridge would have preferred mutual rather than commercial providers (Hewitt and Powell, 1998). The second case concerns occupational healthcare or 'wellness'. This clearly fits the template of occupational welfare in that it is likely to be regressive. In other words, many senior executives receive more in 'fringe benefits' than many lower-paid staff receive in salary.

All this represents somewhat of a puzzle. The quantitative approach of Smithies (2005) (mentioned earlier) suggests little change, while the contributors here generally point to more far-reaching changes (see **Box 11.3**). There are a number of possible reasons for this. First, the quantitative data largely refer to the period up to 1999-2000, and it is possible that more recent data might show greater changes. Second, the contributors to this text examine changes to SDW as well as to MEW. Third, they largely focus on 'qualitative' policy changes and mechanisms rather than quantitative expenditure data. Fourth, changes to expenditure data may take some time as the results of policy changes 'kick in', while the contributors here point to changes that may in a 'thin-end-of-the-wedge' fashion lead to far-reaching changes in the future (such as PFI/PPP). Lastly, the quantitative data do not examine the dimension of regulation, in which some fundamental changes have occurred.

Box 11.3: The modern MEW

The New Labour politician at her surgery listens to her constituents' complaints about PFI hospitals; Foundation Hospitals; Independent Treatment Centres; being forced to 'go private' as a patient's dentist decided to leave the NHS; the poor performance of private pensions; schools being supported by raffles held by Parent Teacher Associations; being unable to find accommodation through the housing association that was formerly owned by the local authority; the Playgroup failing to get any funding from the National Lottery; the problems of spending direct payments; being forced to pay privately for acupuncture; considering selling the family house to pay for drugs that are not available on the NHS; being forced to sell a home to finance long-term residential care; receiving a letter demanding the repayment of over-paid tax credits; having a private pension that is not secure (unlike those of MPs); and having to pay for private security as the police are only interested in collecting the 'poll tax on wheels' of speeding fines: "if only the police collected money for each mugger they arrest!".

"What a lot we have done for the people", she thinks, "thank goodness the Tories are no longer in power."

The three-dimensional MEW

We saw in Chapter One (**Figure 1.2**) that a one-dimensional view of MEW is inadequate, in that it neglects the dimensions of finance and regulation. Much recent writing has focused on moves from state to market, such as privatisation, marketisation or commodification (for example, Morgan, 1995; Drakeford, 2000; Leys, 2001; Pollock, 2004). However, privatisation is an overloaded term, with limited analytical power (Le Grand and Robinson, 1994; Drakeford, 2000).

It is more fruitful to examine changes in MEW as movements from origin to destination cells. The most far-reaching moves would involve all three dimensions (for example, from 1a to 6b; from the core or heartland of the welfare state – public provision, finance and regulation – to private finance and provision with limited or no public regulation. It follows that 'privatisation' could involve the three-dimensional move described above (1a to 6b: P1), but might also cover *any* move down from the top row (for example, 1 to 5: P2; 2 to 10, and so on), *any* shift to the right from the first column (for example, 1 to 2: P3; 5 to 7, and so on) or *any* shift from high to low regulation (any a to b: P4). For example, Knapp (1989) discusses in more detail consumer charges (cell 5), contracting out (cell 2) and market allocations, "the quintessence of privatisation" (cell 6) (p 226). The 'private provision of public welfare' (Papadakis and Taylor-Gooby, 1987) strictly refers only to cell 2. In some ways, it might be preferable to differentiate destinations such as privatisation (towards column 2 or row 5), voluntarisation (towards column 3: V1 and row 9: V2), and informalisation (towards column 4: I1 and row 13: I2). This could be linked

Figure 11. 1: *Recent moves in MEW*

Provision					
Finance		**State**	**Market**	**Voluntary**	**Informal**
State		1a (high P3 regulation) P4	2a	3a V1	4a
		1b (low P1 regulation)	2b	3b	4b ►I1
Market	P2	5a 5b	6a 6b	7a 7b	8a 8b
Voluntary		9a 9b V2	10a 10b	11a 11b	12a 12b
Informal	I2	13a 13b	14a 14b	15a 15b	16a 16b

with dimensions such as deprovided, definanced and deregulated, but 'deregulated voluntarisation' or 'deprovided informalisation' are ugly terms.

There have been some recent changes in ownership/provision. For example, PPP/PFI schemes effectively transfer public assets such as schools and hospitals into private ownership (Chapters Three and Four). Similarly, some local authority (or 'council') housing has been transferred to social landlords.

In addition to changes in ownership/provision, other recent changes involve moves in finance and regulation. There have been some examples of privatising finance, or moving financial burdens from the state to the individual. Many schools and hospitals are increasingly reliant on charitable (including National Lottery) rather than state funding. Introducing or increasing user charges in state services (for example, increasing prescription charges) involves moves from cell 1 to cell 5. Many people now cannot find a dentist willing to treat them under the NHS (breaking Tony Blair's promise in 1999 that everyone would have an NHS dentist by 2001), and so are forced to 'go private', either paying directly or taking out a private subscription scheme. In some cases, people unable to afford private fees have resorted to 'DIY dentistry', involving the household toolbox or a piece of string attaching the tooth to a door. Despite a 1997 manifesto pledge, some elderly people in England still have to sell their houses to pay for private residential care. There have been cases of people selling their houses in order to finance operations or drugs privately. Students in England now have to pay 'top-up' tuition fees in higher education. New Labour abolished the Conservatives' means-tested Assisted Places Schemes, whereby parents got state financial support to enable them to send their children to private schools, but it has introduced a superficially similar 'choose-and-book' scheme in health, where patients in England can opt to be treated free at the point of use in private hospitals or Independent Diagnostic and Treatment Centres. It has also allowed a scheme of direct payments (Chapter Six), where users of social care services can pay for the services they would like.

Turning to regulation, as we saw in Chapter One, it is generally claimed that the importance of regulation has increased to form a 'regulatory state' or 'audit society', where governments 'steer rather than row', or indeed where government has moved to governance, with 'more control over less' (see **Box 11.4**; see also Chapters Four and Eight). In terms of **Figure 11.1**, this represents a broad move from b (low regulation) to a (high regulation). However, there are many instances of regulatory failure (see Powell and Hewitt, 2002), or what Moran (2003, p 171) terms the 'the age of fiasco'.

This three-dimensional account shows that it is misleading to look at one dimension, such as provision, in isolation. This means that a simple 'rolling back' (or 'rolling forward') of the state thesis fails to do justice to a complex situation. There have been moves backward and forward on all dimensions, and the overall balance may vary between sectors (cf Burchardt, 1997; Smithies, 2005): perhaps two steps forward and one back in one sector, but vice versa in another. It follows that it remains difficult to come to any clear judgement about state control (direct ownership and finance against indirect regulation) and any effects on distributional impact (see below).

Analysing MEW

It has been argued here that it is difficult to analyse complex situations with simplistic terms such as 'privatisation'. Privatisation has been used to cover many different strategies. However, there are many different 'routes to market' (Clarke, 2004), with different origins and destinations across different dimensions (**Figure 11.1**).

Moreover, some of the 'privatisation' debate has been limited and confusing. Deakin and Wright (1990, p 1) claim that instead of a drive for better public services, the right has launched a drive for fewer public services, relying on the Orwellian incantation of 'public bad, private good'. This claim is a little oversimplified, and it is possible to claim the converse, with some commentators assuming 'public good, private bad'.

It appears rather a sweeping assumption that the state is always better at everything under all circumstances. Indeed, some elements within the left have been highly critical of state services. As the London Edinburgh Weekend Return Group (1980, pp 9, 52) puts it, the claim that state services are better than private services is true, but only up to a point. Sometimes, state provision leaves a bad taste in our mouths, and "our experience belies the myth of the welfare state". From a consumer point of view, it is possible to contrast the more successful privatisation of telecoms with the tragedy or farce of water privatisation, while it may be difficult to choose between privatised rail services and the nationalised British Rail.

The debate is sometimes dogged by a poor grasp of history. Claims that the NHS is being 'privatised' forget that Aneurin Bevan's NHS since 1948 has allowed general practitioners to be independent contractors or 'small shopkeepers', consultants to work in the private sector, and private practice in NHS facilities. This means that, against the ideals of the Socialist Medical Association, Bevan built 'privatisation' into the very core of the NHS. Similarly, the 'Beveridge welfare state' was built on the concept of a voluntary or private 'superstructure' or 'extension ladder' on top of a state base. For example, Beveridge supported independent pensions *if* they supplemented an adequate national minimum (Powell and Hewitt, 1998). The debate is sometimes insular, in that any comparative examples are limited to private medicine in the US rather than apparently successful mixed systems in Europe.

In other cases, the debate is problematic because issues are confused or conflated. For example, Gabriel and Lang (2006, p 178) claim that privatisation makes public services contingent on the ability to pay, which confuses production and finance. Not all public services are free at point of use (for example, council houses, NHS prescriptions), and it is possible that privately owned but publicly funded services could be free at the point of use. The argument is often based on the 'thin-end-of-the-wedge' argument that privatisation leads to commodification. In other words, privatisation is the first stage in a process of charging for services (for example, Crouch, 2003; Pollock, 2004).

'The ghost at the feast': MEW's links to other debates

Although MEW and SDW have not featured strongly in recent debates in social policy, they may be seen as the 'ghost at the feast' in other recent debates (**Box 11.4**) that have clear links with MEW and SDW, but tend not to draw on them.

Box 11.4: Debates not linked to MEW

Citizenship and consumerism

A number of writers claim that consumerism has partially or wholly replaced citizenship, and that users of welfare services have become 'citizen-consumers' (for example, Crouch, 2003; Gabriel and Lang, 2006). Services have become privatised, marketised, commercialised or commodified (Leys, 2001; Pollock, 2004), and there is greater reliance on public–private partnerships, resulting in the decline of the public realm (Clarke, 2004; Marquand, 2004) and moves from 'political to economic man'; voice to exit, and voice to choice.

Civil society

Giddens (1998) writes that the 'Third Way' involves a renewal of civil society, and state and civil society acting in partnership. Similarly, the 'new mixed economy', which looks for a synergy between public and private sectors, utilising the dynamism of markets, but with the public interest in mind. Turning to 'positive welfare', "the state should step in only when those institutions [church, family and friends] don't fully live up to their obligations" (p 112). Giddens goes on to claim that "the theme that 'welfare state' should be replaced by the 'welfare society' has become a conventional one in recent literature on welfare issues" (p 117).

Governance

Rhodes (1997) regards governance as a broader term than government, where services are provided by any permutation of government and the private and voluntary sectors. However, the boundaries between public, private and voluntary

---

sectors have become shifting and opaque, and even meaningless. The government, or 'regulatory state', substituted regulation for ownership, and attempts to 'steer rather than row'.

New Public Management

Governments need no longer own all facilities, but can finance and regulate rather than provide ('the enabling state'). Osborne and Gaebler (1992) claim that governments should 'steer rather than row'. This means that they are concerned with performance and audit.

Risk

Beck (1992) and Giddens (1994) argue that we now live in a 'risk society'. The traditional welfare state managed risks collectively, but a consumer society has seen moves towards the individualisation or privatisation of risk of 'DIY social policy' (Klein and Millar, 1995; see Kemshall, 2002), with major problems if, for example, private or occupational pensions fail.

Partnership

Partnerships can involve relationships between two or more different sectors within a mixed economy of welfare, including public–public, public–voluntary, public–community and public–private partnerships. They have a long history, with some pre-dating the 'welfare state' (Powell and Glendinning, 2002, p 4).

Public service ethos

It is claimed that treatment is necessarily better in public institutions because the staff that work in them have a 'public service ethos'. In other words, a 'public' doctor is superior to a 'private' doctor. To use the language of Le Grand (2005), the former are 'knights' while the latter are 'knaves'. It follows that ownership matters: finance (paying for treatment in private facilities) and regulation are inferior to a state-owned facility. However, some question the existence of the public service ethos (see discussions in IPPR, 2001; Moran, 2003). Some staff, such as medical consultants, often work in both sectors: does that mean that they are transformed from knights to knaves when they enter the door of a private hospital? Public ownership did not prevent poor treatment in some cases, including major scandals over treatment of patients at some long-stay hospitals. Of course, it is difficult to see the counterfactual: whether conditions would have been worse in private facilities.

The brief overviews in **Box 11.4** necessarily oversimplify more complex debates, but they should be sufficient to indicate the potential links with MEW and SDW, and suggest that both debates might be improved by drawing on alternative perspectives.

The impact of MEW and SDW

As MEW and SDW vary over time and space, so their distributional impact also varies. We saw in Chapter One that Rose and Shiratori (1986) argue that 'total welfare' is the sum of state, market, voluntary and informal sources, but Mishra (1990, pp 110-14) claims that a focus on 'total welfare' is not simply the 'sum of the parts', as the components "cannot simply be regarded as functionally equivalents" as they are based on different principles and they differ in scope. In our wider terms, the debate is whether the total welfare is the additive sum of the components or a non-additive function of them. In short, the two possibilities are:

$$TW = S + P + I + V + O + F$$

or

$$TW = f\,(S, P, I, V, O, F)$$

where TW = total welfare; S = state; P = private; I = informal; V = voluntary; O = occupational; and F = fiscal.

The view here is that total welfare cannot be analysed in terms of simple additions, just as you cannot add apples and oranges to add to fruit. The different components are based on different entitlement rules, and will result in different distributional impacts. For example, a transfer from state to informal (read: female) care leads to increasing gender inequality, and ignores entitlement (citizenship) as no 'right' to charity exists.

Analysing recent distributional impacts is problematic as two distinct but related processes have occurred simultaneously. First, there are the changes in MEW and SDW that have been described above. Second, there have been changes in delivery mechanisms of 'choice and voice'. Putting the two together, there have been some moves from state to market, but also moves from voice to choice, or from citizenship to consumerism, within state services.

The traditional view tends to be that state services are associated with greater equity. In other words, in MEW, private, voluntary and informal sectors are more inequitable than the state, while in SDW, occupational and fiscal welfare is more inequitable than statutory welfare. All this suggests that any move away from the state will result in greater inequity. Drakeford (Chapter Three) considers that the greatest casualty of recent MEW changes has been one of the cardinal founding principles of the British welfare state, that of equality. However, Le Grand (1982) argues that state welfare may be regressive in that it gives more to rich than poor citizens (but see Powell, 1995). The political right has used the Le Grand thesis as ammunition that the welfare state has failed, and so should be privatised. The political right and some elements within the left have argued for the renewal of civil society (see **Box 11.4**). This favours decentralist, voluntarist, mutual or associational solutions over state ones (for example, Freedland, 1998; Burns et al, 1994; Hirst, 1994). New Labour argues that we should draw on a rich heritage of mutualism in order to reach 'real public ownership' to achieve 'power to the people', where communities are in control (for example, Blears, 2003). Similarly, it is generally argued that statutory provision is more progressive than fiscal or occupational provision (for example, Titmuss, 1963). However, while it is difficult to see how occupational welfare might be progressive (see Chapter Eight), it is possible that fiscal welfare (for example, tax credits) has the potential for progressive design (see Chapter Seven).

Turning to delivery mechanisms, Klein and Millar (1995, p 303) write that: "One of the most significant trends of recent decades has been the growing importance of do-it-yourself social policy: i.e. individuals constructing their own welfare mix both within the public sector and in private markets". The optimistic reading is that this allows the exercise of choice, and transforms passive clients into active citizen-consumers. Advocates of 'market socialism' such as Le Grand (2005) argue that choice systems can be progressive, giving examples such as differential vouchers and capitation formulas that favour poor people. The pessimistic argument is that like all DIY jobs, it can go disastrously wrong (Powell and Hewitt, 2002). Greater choice can easily result in the transfer and individualisation of risk (see **Box 11.4**), resulting in inequality between good and bad choosers. However, it is not a question of choice disrupting a situation of existing perfect equity. It is likely that both choice and voice are linked with inequality, and it is an empirical question of the levels of inequality associated with both forms, and whether different people will be affected. Neither is it wise to put one's full trust in the state: there are many cases of women retiring with inadequate pensions, partly due to poor or no advice about pension decisions during their working lives.

Conclusion

It is worth emphasising once again that MEW and SDW are important but neglected concepts in social policy. While a sole emphasis on state provision might have been inaccurate, although excusable, during the period of the 'classic welfare state' from about the mid–1940s to the 1970s, this would be very misleading for times before and after that period in the UK, and for many other countries in the world. In other words, a narrow focus on the welfare state misses out a great deal in social policy. As well as varying over time and space, the mix within MEW also varies by sector. For example, in the UK, healthcare remains largely provided, while the state has always been a much less important provider of housing. Finally, we have moves between the dimensions of MEW, or in the words of Drakeford (Chapter Four) a "shifting cocktail of ownership, funding and regulation".

All this means that it is necessary that any analysis of social policy must look beyond the state to the other elements of MEW – private, voluntary and informal – and beyond statutory services to the other components of SDW – occupational and fiscal. It follows that well-being does not depend solely on politicians, but also on individuals acting as purchasers or carers, voluntary organisations and employers. In many ways, people make their own social policies, but not in circumstances of their choosing. It is clear that the traditional concern of welfare state provision is an inadequate focus for the study of social policy that must also consider finance and regulation. Welfare is more than the welfare state, but, while welfare state provision is not the only way to provide social policies, there are continuing debates about the best way to provide them. However, in order to engage with these debates, we must break out of the cell (see **Figure 11.1**) of state provision in order to explore the wider worlds of MEW and SDW.

Summary

- The state element of the MEW has seen a broad rise and fall over time.
- The dimensions of finance and regulation have tended to be neglected, resulting in limited 'one-dimensional' analyses.
- Many recent debates in social policy have tended not to draw on the MEW.

Questions for discussion

- How can an understanding of the MEW inform other debates in social policy?
- Place recent moves in the MEW onto **Figure 11.1**.
- Is state welfare necessarily more progressive than the alternatives channels of the MEW and the SDW?

Further reading

It will have become clear by now that there is little recent material analysing the MEW and the SDW. In addition to the sources given for Chapter One, see **Cabinet Office (2006)**.

Electronic resources

See www.publications.parliament.uk/pa/cm/cmhansrd.htm for parliamentary debates.

Think-tanks from a variety of perspectives discuss material on public and private welfare. See for example (in alphabetical order):

Adam Smith Institute: www.adamsmith.org/

Catalyst: www.catalystforum.org.uk/

Centre for Policy Studies: www.cps.org.uk/

Civitas: www.civitas.org.uk/

Institute for Public Policy Research: www.ippr.org.uk/

For recent commentaries on social policy from an anti-statist position, see the website that accompanies James Bartholomew's book, *The Welfare State We're in* (www.thewelfarestatewerein.com/).

Some empirical work on public and private welfare is available at the London School of Economics CASE site, although it is now dated: http://sticerd.lse.ac.uk/dps/case/cp/Paper2.pdf (Burchardt); http://sticerd.lse.ac.uk/dps/case/cp/CASEpaper93.pdf (Smithies).

References

Beck, U. (1992) *Risk Society*, London: Sage Publications.

Blears, H. (2003) *Communities in Control*, London: Fabian Society.

Burchardt, T. (1997) *Boundaries between Public and Private Welfare*, CASEpaper 2, London: London School of Economics.

Burchardt. T., Hills, J. and Propper, C. (1999) *Private Welfare and Public Policy*, York: Joseph Rowntree Foundation.

Burns, D., Hambleton, R. and Hoggett, P. (1994) *The Politics of Decentralisation*, Basingstoke: Macmillan.

Cabinet Office (2006) *The UK Government's Approach to Public Service Reform*, London: Cabinet Office.

Clarke, J. (2004) 'Dissolving the public realm?', *Journal of Social Policy*, vol 33, no 1, pp 27-48.

Crouch, C. (2003) *Commercialisation or Citizenship. Education Policy and the Future of Public Services*, London: Fabian Society.

Dahlberg, L. (2005) 'Voluntary and statutory social service provision in Sweden', *Social Policy and Administration*, vol 39, no 7, pp 740-63.

Deakin, N. and Wright, A. (1990) 'Introduction', in N. Deakin and A. Wright (eds) *Consuming Public Services*, London: Routledge, pp 1-16.

Drakeford, M. (2000) *Privatisation and Social Policy*, Harlow: Pearson.

Esping-Andersen, G. (1990) *The Three Worlds of Welfare Capitalism*, Cambridge: Polity Press.

Esping-Andersen, G. (1999) *Social Foundations of Postindustrial Economies*, Oxford: Oxford University Press.

Finlayson, G. (1994) *Citizen, State and Social Welfare in Britain 1830-1990*, Oxford: Clarendon Press.

Fraser, D. (2003) *The Evolution of the British Welfare State* (3rd edn), Basingstoke: Palgrave Macmillan.

Freedland, J. (1998) *Bring Home the Revolution*, London: Fourth Estate.

Gabriel, Y. and Lang, T. (2006) *The Unmangeable Consumer* (2nd edn), London: Sage Publications.

Giddens, A. (1994) *Beyond Left and Right*, Cambridge: Polity Press.

Giddens, A. (1998) *The Third Way*, Cambridge: Polity Press.

Harris, B. (2004) *The Origins of the British Welfare State*, Basingstoke: Palgrave Macmillan.

Hewitt, M. and Powell, M. (1998) 'A different "Back to Beveridge"? Welfare pluralism and the Beveridge welfare state', in E. Brunsdon, H. Dean and R. Woods (eds) *Social Policy Review 10*, London: Social Policy Association, pp 85-104.

Hills, J. (2004) *Inequality and the State*, Oxford: Oxford University Press.

Hirst, P. (1994) *Associative Democracy*, Cambridge: Polity Press.

Howard, C. (1997) *The Hidden Welfare State*, Princeton, NJ: Princeton University Press

IPPR (Institute for Public Policy Research) Commission on Public Private Partnerships (2001) *Building Better Partnerships*, London: IPPR.

Kemshall, H. (2002) *Risk, Social Policy and Welfare*, Buckingham: Open University Press.

Klein, R. and Millar, J. (1995) 'Do-it-yourself social policy: searching for a new paradigm?', *Social Policy and Administration*, vol 29, no 4, pp 303-16.

Knapp, M. (1989) 'Private and voluntary welfare', in M. McCarthy (ed) *The New Politics of Welfare*, Basingstoke: Macmillan, pp 225-52.

Le Grand, J. (1982) *The Strategy of Equality*, London: Allen and Unwin.

Le Grand, J. (2005) 'Inequality, choice and public services', in A. Giddens and P. Diamond (eds) *The New Egalitarianism*, Cambridge: Polity Press, pp 200-10.

Le Grand, J. and Robinson, R. (eds, 1994) *Privatisation and the Welfare State*, London: Allen and Unwin.

Leys, C. (2001) *Market-driven Politics*, London: Verso.

London Edinburgh Weekend Return Group (1980) *In and Against the State*, London: Pluto.

Marquand, D. (2004) *Decline of the Public*, Cambridge: Polity Press.

Mayo, M. (1994) *Communities and Caring. The Mixed Economy of Welfare*, Basingstoke: Macmillan.

Mishra, R. (1990) *The Welfare State in Capitalist Society*, Hemel Hempstead: Harvester Wheatsheaf.

Moran, M. (2003) *The British Regulatory State*, Oxford: Oxford University Press.

Morgan, P. (ed) (1995) *Privatization and the Welfare State*, Aldershot: Dartmouth.

Osborne, D. and Gaebler, T. (1992) *Reinventing Government*, Reading, MA: Addison-Wesley.

Papadakis, E. and Taylor-Gooby, P. (1987) *The Private Provision of Public Welfare*, Brighton: Wheatsheaf.

Pensions Commission (2004) *Pensions: Challenges and Choices: The First Report of the Pensions Commission*, London: The Stationery Office.

Peters, B. Guy (2005) 'I'm OK, you're (not) OK: the private welfare state in the United States', *Social Policy and Administration*, vol 39, no 2, pp 166-80.

Pollock, A. (2004) *NHS Plc: The Privatisation of our Health Care*, London: Verso.

Powell, M, (1995) 'The strategy of equality revisited', *Journal of Social Policy*, vol 24, no 2, pp 163-85.

Powell, M. and Glendinning, C. (2002) 'Introduction', in C. Glendinning, M. Powell and K. Rummery (eds) *Partnerships, New Labour and the Governance of Welfare*, Bristol: The Policy Press, pp 1-14.

Powell, M and Hewitt, M. (1998) 'The end of the welfare state?', *Social Policy and Administration*, vol 32, no 1, pp 1-13.

Powell, M. and Hewitt, M. (2002) *Welfare State and Welfare Change*, Buckingham: Open University Press.

Rhodes, R. (1997) *Understanding Governance*, Buckingham: Open University Press.

Rose, R. and Shiratori, R. (1986) 'Introduction', in R. Rose and R. Shiratori (eds) *The Welfare State East and West*, Oxford: Oxford University Press.

Shalev, M. (ed) (1996) *The Privatization of Social Policy? Occupational Welfare and the Welfare State in America, Scandinavia and Japan*, Basingstoke: Macmillan.

Sinfield, A. (1978) 'Analyses in the social division of welfare', *Journal of Social Policy*, vol 7, no 2, pp 129-56.

Smithies, R. (2005) *Public and Private Welfare Activity in the United Kingdom, 1979 to 1999*, CASEpaper 93, London: London School of Economics.

Taylor, A.J.P. (1970) *English History 1914-1945*, Harmondsworth: Penguin.

Titmuss, R. (1963) *Essays on the Welfare State* (2nd edn), London: Allen and Unwin.

Index

Page references for notes are followed by n

A

active citizenship 91
Active Communities Unit (ACU) 90, 92, 93
Afghanistan 209
Age Concern 86
Alcock, P. 2
Anttonen, A. 191-2, 193
Armingeon, K. 206-7
Ascoli, U. 143
Atkin, K. 119
Australia
  education 187
  healthcare 185, 186
  liberal welfare regime 179
  social security 182, 184
Austria
  education 187
  healthcare 185, 186
  social care 190, 191
  social security 182, 184

B

Bahle, T. 194
Balloch, S. 74
Bambra, C. 184-5, 186
Barnett, Correlli 32
Beck, U. 233
Belgium
  education 187, 188
  healthcare 185, 186
  social care 190, 191
  social security 182, 183, 184
Beresford, P. 9
Bettio, F. 191
Bevan, Aneurin 44, 224, 231
Beveridge, William 36-7, 88, 152, 228, 231
Beyeler, M. 206-7
Big Issue 86
Birmingham 75
Blair, Tony 44, 55, 66
  education 64
  local government 46
  voluntary and community sector 90
Boateng, Paul 91
Bolam, Angela 75-6
Bolivia 213
Bozeman, B. 14, 15
Brown, Gordon 90

Bryce, H.J. 48
Burchardt, T. 12, 225
Butler, J. 66

C

Cabinet Office 93
Canada
  education 187
  healthcare 185, 186
  social security 182, 184
carers 120-1, 227
  barriers to providing effective support 118-20
  comparative perspective 194
  effectiveness of New Labour policies 116-17
  financial support 115-16
  informal 109-10
  New Labour's policy response 112-15
  numbers and characteristics 110
Carers Allowance 109, 115-16
Carers and Disabled Children Act 2000 112, 114
Carers (Equal Opportunities) Act 2004 112, 114, 120
Carers (Recognition and Services) Act 1995 112, 116-17
Carers Special Grant 113, 121
catallaxy 55
central government 42-5
ChangeUp 92, 100
charitable sector see voluntary and community sector welfare
Child Benefit 133, 134
child poverty 43
Child Tax Credit 134-6
childcare 191-2
children 30
  tax credits 133-6
Chile 212, 213
China 213
choice 55, 77, 234, 235
  Foundation Hospitals 68-70
  three-dimensional accounts 12, 13
citizenship 24, 33, 232
civic renewal 90, 99, 101, 91.94
civil society 36, 84, 90, 226, 232, 235
Clarke, H. 118
classic welfare state 3, 24, 26-7, 223-4, 235

state provision 42, 45-6, 55, 225-6
welfare pluralism 5
collectivism 26-8
commodification 77, 229, 232
common good 42, 53-4, 77
communitarianism 51, 52, 84
community care 89, 109
    see also carers
community participation schemes 158, 160
community sector see voluntary and
    community sector welfare
Compact 90-1, 92, 94, 100
comparative perspective
    education 187-8
    healthcare 183-7
    mixed economy of welfare 178-81, 194-5
    purchase and provision 193-4
    social care 189-92
    social security 181-3, 184
concierge services 158, 160
Conservative Party
    ideology 51
    local government 47-8
    market welfare 32
    pensions 161, 162, 163
    privatisation 66
    residential care 73
    state welfare 28
    voluntary welfare 35
conservative/corporatist welfare regimes 6,
    7, 179, 180
    healthcare 183-4
    social care 189, 190
Constitution of Liberty, The (Hayek) 51
consumerism 227, 232
contracting out 162, 163
contracts 89, 98-9, 226
coordinated market economies 180-1
corporate welfare see occupational welfare
Croft, S. 9
Crosland, C.A.R. 12
Cross Cutting Review 91-2
Crossman, Richard 12
Czech Republic
    education 187
    healthcare 185
    social security 182, 184

D

Daly, M. 194
Deacon, B. 209
Deakin, N. 231
Deakin Commission 89-90

decision see choice
decommodification 6, 179, 224
defamilisation 224
defined benefit (DB) pension schemes 162,
    163, 164
defined contribution (DC) pension
    schemes 162, 163, 164
Delamonica, E. 212
delivery 235
Denmark
    education 187
    healthcare 185, 186
    social care 190, 191, 192
    social security 182, 183, 184
    welfare regime 181
dentists 230
devolution 27, 79n
    see also Scotland
Devon 75
direct payments 117, 192, 227, 230
disabled people's movement 118
Dixon, J. 209
Durham 75-6

E

education
    changes 230
    choice 55
    comparative perspective 187-8
    local government 45
    privatisation 64, 65, 67
    state provision 2, 27, 222, 223-4
education and training benefits 153, 155,
    159
El Salvador 213
elderly 29-30
    comparative perspective 190-2
    residential care 72-7, 230
employment 224
    and care-giving 119-20, 121
    see also occupational welfare
equality 77, 234
equity 234
Esping-Andersen, G. 4, 6-7, 179, 180, 181,
    183, 184, 189, 190, 191, 193, 194, 224
Etzioni, A. 90
European Social Forum 201
European Union (EU) 200, 210
    involvement in social policy 201, 202,
    203, 214
    pensions 212, 213
    surveillance and enforcement
    mechanisms 208, 225
exit 44, 45

F

fairness 143
Family Friends 98-9
family welfare 179-80
    comparative perspective 189-94
    in historical context 28-31, 36, 37
Farnsworth, K. 152
Ferrara, M. 189
Field, F. 9
finance 10-14
    comparative perspective 185-7, 193-4
    global and supra-national dimensions
        202, 203, 214
    see also state finance
Finch, J. 9, 108
Finland
    education 187
    healthcare 185, 186
    social care 190, 191, 192
    social security 182, 183, 184
Finlayson, A. 54
Finlayson, G. 5, 32, 33, 36
fiscal welfare (FW) see tax welfare
Foundation (Hospital) Trusts 13, 45, 68-70,
        79n, 226
France
    education 187
    healthcare 185, 186
    pensions 213
    social care 190, 191
    social security 182, 183, 184
    welfare regime 181
fringe benefits see occupational welfare
Fultz, E. 213
Futurebuilders 92, 100

G

G8 201
G24 201
Gabriel, Y. 231
Gaebler, T. 233
General Agreement on Trade in Services
        (GATS) 210-11
generalised reciprocity 108
Germany
    carers 112
    education 187, 188
    healthcare 185, 186
    pensions 213
    social care 190, 191, 192
    social security 182, 184
Giddens, A. 9, 232, 233
Gilbert, B. 6
Gilbert, N. 6

Glennerster, H. 11, 13, 35
global social policy 200-1, 214-15
    IGOs' prescriptions and impacts 209-14
    scale and scope of IOs' involvement
        201-3
    understanding influence of IOs 203-9
globalisation 54
Gorsky, M. 35
Gough, I. 178
governance 54, 230, 232-3
    neighbourhood 49
grants 89
Greece
    social care 191
    welfare regime 181
Green, D. 9
Griffiths Report 109
Groves, D. 9
Guthrie, Jonathan 74

H

Hacker, Jacob 140
Hall, P.A. 180-1
Harris, J. 5, 26, 27
Hayek, Friedrich von 51, 55, 63
Health, Work and Well-Being 168, 169
healthcare 2, 223-4
    changes 230
    comparative perspective 183-7, 188
    global and supra-national dimensions
        212
    local government 46
    occupational welfare 155, 159, 160-1,
        165-70, 228
    one-dimensional MEW 10
    privatisation 64, 68-72, 77
    regulation 12
    state welfare 44-5, 235
    three-dimensional MEW 14-15
    two-dimensional MEW 11
    voluntary welfare 34, 35
Hewitt, Patricia 72
Hills, J. 225
Hirschman, A.O. 45
Hirst, P. 9
Home Office 90, 91, 93, 99
Hood, C. 13
housing 224, 235
    local government 27, 45-6
    market welfare 3
    occupational welfare 158, 160
    privatisation 10, 64, 65
    state finance and voluntary provision
        48-9
    targets and performance indicators 52

housing benefit 47-8
Humphrey, J. 73
Hungary
  education 187
  healthcare 185
  social security 182, 184
Hutton, John 71

I

Independent Diagnostic and Treatment
  Centres (ISTCs) 70-2, 230
individualism 26
inequality
  choice and voice 235
  pensions 136-7, 138-9, 227
  tax welfare 142
inequity 234
informal welfare 3, 4, 9, 108-10, 120-1,
  222, 227
  barriers to providing effective support
    for carers 118-20
  effectiveness of New Labour policies for
    carers 116-17
  financial support for carers 115-16
  neighbourhood provision 49
  New Labour's policy response to carers
    112-15
  and voluntary welfare 96-7
  see also family welfare
informalisation 229-30
inspection 73
Institute for Public Policy Research
  (IPPR) Commission on Public Private
  Partnerships 11
International Classification of Non-profit
  Organisations (ICNPO) 87
international governmental organisations
  (IGOs) 201-3, 214-15
  social policy prescriptions and impacts
    209-14
International Labour Organization (ILO)
  201, 202, 203, 210, 225
  Conventions 207-9, 217n
  pensions 211-13, 225
International Monetary Fund (IMF) 200,
  210, 212, 213, 224-5
international non-governmental
  organisations (INGOs) 200, 201, 202
international organisations (IOs) 200-1,
  214-15, 224-5
  involvement in social policy 201-3
  understanding influence on social policy
    203-9

Invalid Care Allowance 109, 112, 115-16
Ireland
  education 187
  healthcare 185, 196
  pensions 213-14
  social care 191
  social security 182
Italy
  education 187
  healthcare 185, 186
  pensions 214
  social care 190, 191
  social security 182, 183, 184
  welfare regime 181

J

Japan
  education 187, 188
  healthcare 185, 186
  social care 191, 192
  social security 182, 184
  volunteering 180
  welfare regime 179
Johns Hopkins University 87
Johnson, N. 2, 8, 9
Johnstone, S. 73
Judge, K. 10

K

Kable 62
Kendall, J. 87-8
Klein, R. 6, 70, 235
Knapp, M. 2, 10-11, 13, 87, 229
Korea
  education 187, 188
  healthcare 185
  social security 182, 184

L

Labour Party
  classic welfare state 33, 223
  pensions 161-2
  see also New Labour
Laing and Buisson 72, 75
Land, H. 9
Lavalette, M. 2
Lawson, Nigel 139
Le Grand, J. 233, 234
Lebeaux, C. 6
Leibfried, S. 203
leisure benefits 158, 160

Lewis, J. 5, 24, 31, 35, 36, 88
liberal market economies 180
liberal welfare regimes 6, 7, 179, 189, 193
Liberals 26, 32, 33, 53
local government 226
  market provision 47-8
  state provision 45-7
  voluntary provision 48-9
localism 26
Lødemel, I. 181
London Edinburgh Weekend Return
  Group 231
Lowe, R. 34-5

M

Major, John 89
Malpass, P. 49
Mann, K. 7
market creation 64-5
market welfare 3, 8, 62-3, 179, 226
  comparative perspective 183, 184-5, 187-
  8, 189-94
  in historical context 31-3, 36-7, 222
  and state finance 47-8
  and voluntary welfare 97-8, 101
  see also privatisation
marketisation 62, 229
married couple's allowance 132
Mason, J. 108
Mayo, M. 222
Mehrotra, S. 212
mental health 74-5
Mercosur 201, 204
MEW see mixed economy of welfare
Mexico 213
Milburn, Alan 68, 71
Millar, J. 235
Miller, C. 12
Minns, R. 141-2
Mishra, R. 4, 234
mixed economy of welfare 2-4, 222, 235-6
  analysing 231-2
  comparative perspective 178-81, 194-5,
  224
  components 8-9
  dimensions 9-15, 229-31
  distributional impact 234-5
  global and supra-national dimensions
  200-1, 214-15, 224-5
  in historical context 24-5, 36-7, 222-4
  links to other debates 232-3
  New Labour 225-8
  and social policy 4-7

see also informal welfare; market welfare;
  state welfare; voluntary and community
  sector welfare
Mohan, J. 77
money purchase pension schemes 162, 163,
  164
Moran, M. 12
mortgage tax relief 7, 132, 142, 227
moving frontier 36, 222
Murlis, H. 151
mutuality 33, 84, 88
Myanmar 209

N

National Audit Office (NAO) 91, 93, 100
National Council for Voluntary
  Organisations (NCVO) 86, 87, 89, 94,
  100
National Health Service 11, 231
  Foundation (Hospital) Trusts 13-14,
  68-70, 79n, 226
  Independent Diagnostic and Treatment
  Centres 70-2
  market mechanisms 33
  mental health 75
  state welfare 27-8, 44-5, 186, 226
  and voluntary welfare 34
National Strategy for Carers 112, 113, 114,
  117, 120
nationalisation 10
Needham, C. 69
neighbourhood 49
Netherlands
  education 187, 188
  healthcare 186
  social care 190-1
  social security 182, 183, 184
  welfare regime 181
New Deal for Communities 49
New Labour
  carers 112-15, 116-17, 120-1
  children 30
  Foundation Hospitals 68-70
  housing 48-9
  Independent Diagnostic and Treatment
  Centres 71-2
  local government 45, 46-7
  market welfare 33
  MEW and SDW 225-8
  New Deal for Communities 49
  NHS 44-5
  occupational healthcare 168-70
  pensions 137-9, 163-5, 213
  PFI 50-1

privatisation 66–8, 77
residential care 72–3
social security 42–4
state welfare 28, 42, 51–5
tax credits 133–6
voluntary welfare 35, 100, 235
see also Labour Party
New Liberalism 53
New Public Management 89, 233
New Right
family welfare 31
market welfare 32
state welfare 28
New Zealand
education 187–8
healthcare 185, 186
liberal welfare regime 179
social security 182, 184
NHS see National Health Service
non-governmental organisations (NGOs)
204–5
see also international non-governmental
organisations (INGOs)
Nordic countries 179, 180, 188
Northern Ireland 27
Northumberland 75
Norway
education 187
healthcare 185, 186
social security 182, 184
nursery vouchers 65–6

O

obligations 52–3
occupational welfare (OW) 3, 7, 8, 130,
150–1, 170–1, 227–8, 235
comparative perspective 182–3
current forms 153–61
definitions 151–2
healthcare 165–70
pensions 161–5
and tax welfare 140
older people see elderly
one-dimensional mixed economy of
welfare 9–10, 229
Organisation for Economic Cooperation
and Development (OECD) 200, 201,
203, 212
and national policy reform 206–7, 208
social policy discourses 209, 210
Orwell, George 15
Osborne, D. 233
ownership 62, 64, 226, 230
healthcare 68–9
PFI 50–1

public service ethos 233
residential care 72–3, 75–6
Oxfam 201

P

Page, R. 2, 67
Papadakis, E. 229
Parker, G. 118
partnership 233
pay substitutions 153
pay supplements 153
Pedersen, S. 30
pensions
Beveridge 231
comparative perspective 183, 184, 224
global and supra-national dimensions
211–14, 225
market provision 47
occupational welfare 7, 8, 160, 161–5,
227–8
state welfare 42–3
tax welfare 7, 136–40, 141–2, 227
Pensions Commission 164–5, 227–8
personal responsibility 65
personal social services see social care
philanthropy 33, 84, 88
Pickard, L. 118, 119
Pierson, P. 203
Pitman, Henry 62
Plantenga, J. 191
Poland
education 187
healthcare 185
social security 182
Polanyi, K. 178
Poor Laws 26, 29, 31, 33, 192, 222
Portugal
education 187
healthcare 185
social care 191
social security 182, 184
welfare regime 181
Pratt, A. 2
pre-schools 96–7
Private Finance Initiative (PFI) 50–1, 226
private medical insurance (PMI) 7, 159
private welfare see market welfare
privatisation 10, 62–3, 77, 229, 231–2
ideology 63
Independent Diagnostic and Treatment
Centres 70–2
pensions 212–14
residential care 72–7
and social welfare 64–6

profit 69, 70, 71, 77
provision 10–14, 69, 230
  comparative perspective 185–7, 193–4
  global and supra-national dimensions
    203, 214
  see also state provision
public interest 53, 54–5
Public Private Partnerships (PPPs) 226
public service delivery 88–9, 91, 94, 100
public service ethos 68, 233
purchase see finance
Putnam, R. 90, 99

Q

quasi-markets 8, 10, 13, 44–5, 64

R

reciprocity 108, 227
redistribution 51
regulation 12–15, 79n, 230
  comparative perspective 180–1
  Foundation Trusts 70
  global and supra-national dimensions
    201, 202, 203–4, 207–9, 214–15, 225
  governance 232–3
  market welfare 226
  residential care 73–5
Reid, John 68, 69, 72
residential care 4, 10, 230
  privatisation 71–7
Revitalising Health and Safety Strategy
  168–9
Rhodes, R. 232
risk 233, 235
Rose, R. 4, 234
Ruck, M. 213

S

Sainsbury, D. 180
Salter, B. 11
Saltman, R.B. 186
Scandinavia 179, 180, 188
Schumpeter, Joseph 63
Scotland 27, 119, 120, 227
SDW see social division of welfare
Seldon, A. 5
self-help 33, 84, 88
self-regulation 14–15
Shiratori, R. 4, 234
Siaroff, A. 189
Silburn, B. 2
Silburn, R. 66

Sinfield, A. 7, 222
Small Potatoes 97–8
Smith, P. 73
Smithies, R. 225, 228
social capital 49, 84, 90, 99
social care 2, 224
  comparative perspective 189–92, 193–4
  informal welfare 108–21, 227
  occupational welfare 156–7, 159–60
  state welfare 27, 45–6
social democratic welfare regimes 6, 7, 179,
  183–4, 189, 193, 224
social division of welfare 2, 3, 7, 222, 235,
  236
  distributional impact 234–5
  global and supra-national dimensions
    200–1, 224–5
  New Labour 225–8
  see also occupational welfare; state
    welfare; tax welfare
social enterprises 97–8
social inclusion 52
social investment 51, 52, 54
social security
  comparative perspective 181–3, 184
  global and supra-national dimensions
    211
  occupational welfare 153, 154
  state welfare 42–4
  see also pensions
Somalia 209
Soskice, D. 180–1
South Korea see Korea
Spain
  education 187
  healthcare 185
  social care 190, 191
  social security 182, 183, 184
  welfare regime 181
Spicker, P. 7, 11, 12
state failure 8
state finance 4
  and informal neighbourhood provision
    49
  and market provision 47–8
  and state provision 42–7
  and voluntary provision 48–9
state provision 4, 55
  and market finance 50–1
  and state finance 42–7
state welfare 3, 4, 7, 8, 42, 235, 236
  comparative perspective 178–9, 181–2,
    183–8, 189–94
  distributional impact 234–5
  in historical context 26–8, 36–7, 222–4

ideologies 4–5
New Labour 51–5, 225–6
privatisation 231–2
and voluntary welfare 98–9, 101
see also state finance; state provision
Stoke-on-Trent 75
subterranean politics 140
supply diversity 53
supra-national organisations see
international organisations
Sweden
education 187
healthcare 185, 186
pensions 213
social care 190, 191, 192
social security 182
voluntary sector 180
Switzerland
education 187
healthcare 184, 185, 186
social security 182, 183, 184

T

targets 28, 43, 44, 54–5
tax allowances 130–1
tax credits 130, 131, 133–6, 141, 227
tax expenditures 47, 130, 131
tax reliefs 7, 8, 130, 131–2
pensions 162, 183
tax welfare 3, 7, 8, 130–3, 140–1, 227, 235
in comparative perspective 141–2
for retirement 136–40
tax credits 133–6
Taylor, A.J.P. 223
Taylor-Gooby, P. 229
Thane, P. 5, 26, 29–30
Thatcher, Margaret 28, 51
third sector see voluntary and community
sector welfare
Third Way 90, 100, 168, 232
three-dimensional mixed economy of
welfare 12–15, 225, 229–31
Timmins, N. 62
Titmuss, Richard
community care 9, 109
fiscal welfare 66, 130, 140
market welfare 32
occupational welfare 130, 151, 152, 227
pensions 139, 227
social division of welfare 7, 8
welfare models 6
total welfare 4, 234
transport benefits 158, 160

Treasury 43, 47, 91–2, 93, 135
Trickey, H. 181
Tumble Tots 96
Turkey 181
Twigg, J. 119
two-dimensional mixed economy of
welfare 10–12

U

Ungerson, C. 9, 194
United Nations (UN) 200, 201, 203
United States
education 187, 188
healthcare 183, 184, 185, 186
housing 3
ILO Conventions 209
liberal welfare regime 179
social care 191, 192
social security 182, 183, 184
subterranean politics 140
tax welfare 142
volunteering 180
welfare regime 6, 188
United States Agency for International
Development (USAID) 212, 213
upside-down benefits 130–1, 133, 136, 141,
142, 227

V

voice 45, 234, 235
voluntarisation 229–30
voluntary and community sector (VCS)
welfare 3, 9, 84–8, 108, 180, 226–7
comparative perspective 188
description 95–9
future prospects 99–100
in historical context 33–5, 36–7, 88–90,
222
policy context 90–4
and state finance 48–9
von Otter, C. 186

W

Wales 27
Walker, A. 11, 178
Webb, Beatrice 88
Webb, Sidney 88, 222, 223
welfare mix see mixed economy of welfare
welfare pluralism (WP) see mixed
economy of welfare
welfare regimes 6–7, 179–81, 194–5, 224

education 187-8
healthcare 183-7
purchase and provision 193-4
social care 189-92
social security 181-3
wellness services 166-8, 228
Wilensky, H. 6
Wistow, G. 193
Wolfenden Report 2
women
  charitable relief 33
  comparative perspective 194
  defamilisation 224
  informal care 9, 109, 110, 227
  life expectancy 29
  pensions 138
Wong, C.-K. 178
Wood, G. 178
work-life balance (WLB) services 156-7,
  159-60
Working Families Tax Credit (WFTC)
  133, 135
Working Tax Credit 134-6
workplace welfare see occupational welfare
World Bank 200, 201, 202, 204, 214, 224
  pensions 211-13, 225
  social policy discourses 209-10
  surveillance and enforcement
    mechanisms 207, 208
World Health Organization (WHO) 201,
  202, 203
World Social Forum 201
World Trade Organization (WTO) 201,
  204, 208, 210-11, 214, 224
Wright, A. 151-2, 231

Y

young carers 110, 111